the
serial killer
whisperer

How One Man's Tragedy Helped Unlock the Deadliest
Secrets of the World's Most Terrifying Killers

PETE EARLEY

A Touchstone Book
Published by Simon & Schuster
New York   London   Toronto   Sydney   New Delhi

Touchstone
A Division of Simon & Schuster, Inc.
1230 Avenue of the Americas
New York, NY 10020

First Touchstone hardcover edition January 2012

TOUCHSTONE and colophon are registered trademarks of Simon & Schuster, Inc.

For information about special discounts for bulk purchases, please contact Simon &
Schuster Special Sales at 1-866-506-1949 or business@simonandschuster.com.

The Simon & Schuster Speakers Bureau can bring authors to your live event.
For more information or to book an event contact the Simon & Schuster Speakers
Bureau at 1-866-248-3049 or visit our website at www.simonspeakers.com.

Designed by Akasha Archer

Manufactured in the United States of America

10   9   8   7   6   5   4   3   2   1

Earley, Pete.
    The serial killer whisperer : how one man's tragedy helped unlock the deadliest
secrets of the world's most terrifying killers / Pete Earley.
        p. cm.
Summary: "From *New York Times* bestselling author Pete Earley comes the true
story of a young man who suffers a traumatic brain injury that renders him incapable of judging or feeling repulsion, and subsequently becomes the most trusted
confidant of numerous imprisoned serial killers"—Provided by publisher.
"A Touchstone Book."
    1. Serial murderers—Correspondence. 2. Serial murderers—Psychology. 3. Se-
rial murders. 4. Ciaglia, Anthony—Correspondence. I. Ciaglia, Anthony. II. Title.
HV6515.E17 2012
364.152'32092—dc23
                                   2011025871
ISBN 978-1-4391-9902-2
ISBN 978-1-4391-9904-6 (ebook)

To my daughter
Traci Michele Luzi

Letters are among the most significant memorial a person can leave behind them.

—Johann Wolfgang von Goethe

I start every book with the idea that I want to explain how this seven or eight pounds of protoplasm went from his mommy's arms to become a serial rapist or serial killer. I think a crime book that doesn't do this is pure pornography.

—author Jack Olsen, quoted in the *New York Times*, 1993

contents

author's note

This is a true story.

When Anthony Ciaglia was a teenager, he suffered a traumatic brain injury, clinically died three times, and lapsed into a coma. When he awoke, he was a much different person. His brain injury had dramatically affected his personality. Afflicted by uncontrollable rages, he became bored and housebound. On a whim, he began writing to serial killers and soon was exchanging letters with more than thirty notorious murderers.

This book is not for the squeamish.

It contains uncensored passages lifted from more than three thousand pieces of mail exchanged between Ciaglia and unrepentant serial killers. These letters have been augmented by several hundred hours of telephone conversations that Ciaglia recorded, plus interviews that he conducted in maximum security penitentiaries.

The result is a chilling glimpse into the minds of psychopaths who discuss such aberrant acts as kidnapping, rape, torture, necrophilia, cannibalism, and murder as casually as most of us discuss the weather.

Much of what we know about serial killers comes from accounts written about their crimes and interrogations performed by homicide detectives or forensic psychiatrists. The letters printed here are unscripted, more reminiscent of chitchat between two buddies who've stopped at a bar after work. There are no pretenses, few niceties, and no preening for prosecutors or the public.

What follows is straight from a serial killer's mind to paper—and it is both terrifying and depraved.

Initially, Ciaglia wrote out of curiosity. *What makes a person become a serial killer?* But as he peered deeper into the prisoners' dark world, he began to question if he shared many of the same demons as them. Because of the uncontrollable bursts of anger brought on by his brain injury, Ciaglia wondered if he were destined to become a killer.

This book is a story about an average American family whose idyllic lifestyle is shattered by a terrible accident that pushes them to the brink of despair. It's also the story of a tormented man who eventually found purpose in the most unlikely way—by connecting with monsters.

Pete Earley

PROLOGUE

a typical saturday

Tony Ciaglia felt the familiar butterfly-rush in his stomach as he keyed open his private postbox at the UPS Store on Rainbow Avenue in Las Vegas. He called it his Murder Box. For the past four years it had been the absolute focus of his life. Some would even say it had saved him. There were seven new letters inside, each of them fresh installments of a true-crime drama that was playing exclusively in his own living room.

Shuffling the various letters like a deck of playing cards, he walked out into the 105-degree summer heat. He was six feet tall, weighing in at 225—a handsome dude with thick black hair gelled up into an Elvis Presley coif. His girlfriend, Crystal—a petite, exotic Filipino and Portuguese blend—was waiting outside in a BMW sedan. Tony welcomed the blast of air-conditioning that struck his unshaven face as he slipped into the passenger's seat. What he was hoping for was a letter from Joe Roy Metheny, inmate #270896, currently serving two life sentences in a Maryland prison without possibility of parole. Tony had been pressing Metheny to tell him about unsolved murders.

Metheny's mail was easy to spot because he always drew a cartoon on the outside of the envelope, just under the return address. The first time Metheny had written, Tony had been surprised that the prisoner's artwork had made it by prison censors and U.S. Postal Service inspectors. But after several years of uninterrupted correspondence, he'd concluded that no one really paid attention to Metheny's childish cartoons. His drawings always featured the antics of a round-faced baby with an oversized head and toothless grin. It was Metheny's trademark character—a serial killer's Mickey Mouse.

As Crystal maneuvered the BMW north onto Rainbow Avenue, Tony held up Metheny's envelope for her to see. "It's from Joe," he announced excitedly, a kid with a candy bar.

"Well, don't open it yet," Crystal chided, the mom telling him to wait for after the meal.

Tony had promised his parents, Chris and Al Ciaglia, that he wouldn't read any of the letters from serial killers unless one of them was present. Although Tony was thirty-two years old, he still lived with his parents, as he had his entire life.

Tony examined the envelope, searching the drawing for a clue. Metheny had used colored pencils to sketch his cartoon baby. A cone-shaped party hat was strapped to its cue-ball head and the infant was clutching a giant burned matchstick in his left hand and a cupcake in his right. A flame flickered from a single candle stuck into brownish pink icing. A birthday greeting!

"I see it!" he announced to Crystal, who was focusing on traffic. Metheny always hid some gruesome image cleverly inside his drawings, and now Tony saw it. Metheny's grinning baby was not clutching a birthday cupcake at all. What he was clutching was a woman's severed breast. The candle was rising from the graphically erect nipple. It was typical Metheny.

Inside Internet chat rooms and on serial killer websites, Metheny was known as the "cannibal killer"—a reference to how he had dismembered his female victims and served their ground-up body parts to unsuspecting diners at a roadside barbecue stand in Maryland. He prided himself on being the real Hannibal Lecter—life imitating art—and he had a small cult following on the Web among self-proclaimed devil worshippers and serial killer devotees.

"Do you know how much I could sell this for on the Internet?" Tony asked Crystal. Just as quickly he added, "I never will of course. Joe knows that. I would never do that."

Of all the serial killers that Tony corresponded with, Metheny was the most callous and graphic in describing his sexual debauchery. There was a cold-bloodedness about him that astounded Tony's family. When one of Crystal's friends died from cystic fibrosis, Tony wrote a short story about how angels had carried her to heaven. He'd sent copies to Metheny and his other serial killer pals.

Nearly all of them wrote back and told him that his story was touching. Except Metheny.

"Your story brought tears to my eyes," Metheny wrote sarcastically.

"C'mon Tony, you're going to have to do better than that if you want to make me to cry."

Tony had been up front with Crystal about his letter writing from the beginning of their now sixteen-month-old relationship. He'd warned her that if she became part of his life, he would share her with them. She'd agreed and he knew from the killers' written responses that Crystal was a hit. His killer pals especially enjoyed getting photographs of her because she was nineteen, slim, and sexy. Even his sex life with Crystal was not off-limits. Tony expected the killers to share their most intimate thoughts and he was willing to do the same.

"I'm their escape into the outside world," Tony had explained to Crystal. "These people depend on me. If I go on a trip and I tell them about it, it's like they went on that trip, too."

Tony and Crystal ignored the three barking white Labrador retrievers who greeted them when they entered the art deco–decorated foyer inside his parents' stucco and red-tile-roofed Spanish-style home.

Al was waiting. Fit and silver-haired, he was in his early sixties and a self-made man. He'd started out selling personal computers when they were first being introduced, then owned two pizza restaurants. Now he operated a Las Vegas mortgage business.

"Read Joe's first," Tony said, as the family gathered in the dining room.

The reading of letters had become a family ritual. Tony's parents, his younger brother, Joey, and Crystal would congregate around the glass-topped table. During the week, sometimes only Al and Chris would be available to review the six to ten letters that arrived daily. Joey and Crystal would catch up after they got off work. Everyone would discuss the correspondence before Tony would retreat to his bedroom and begin writing responses.

"If you start with Metheny," said Chris, a thin woman with no-nonsense short hair, "Crystal and I may have to leave."

"Let's see how gross he gets," Al replied, slipping on a pair of silver reading glasses.

Al began: "You are always asking me about my murders, well here is one that no one knows about. That's right, pal. I have never told anyone about this murder."

Al looked up and quipped, "He certainly knows how to get our attention."

Starting again, Al read,

*I never had to go far to find a victim for most all truck stops
across the U.S. had whores working in and around them. This is
a story of a young prostitute I killed in October, 1995. She was
working the 76 truck stop in Reno, Nevada. I was driving a blue
long nose Peterbuilt and I was hooked up to a freezer trailer.
That's a trailer with a freezer. I beat and raped that bitch in the
sleeper of the truck that night until I grew tired of her. Then I
put my hands on her neck and began squeezing. Her screams of
pain slowly dwindled down to mere rasps of agonizing grunts
and groans. The sounds she made slowly faded away, never to be
heard again. Sweet death had finally come down upon her. Now
her body was just a dead carcass, laying in wait for the decomposition to start the breaking down of cells.*°

Al checked Chris but she motioned him to continue. Crystal also
nodded. He continued reading.

*I layed there with my arms wrapped around her dead body
and slept for about three hours. I woke up to my alarm clock
going off at 5:30 a.m. I climbed over her and got dressed. I
throwed a blanket over her. Then I started the truck up. I got out
of the truck, locked the door and headed over to the coffee shop
to grab a bite and check the computer for loads heading East.
The closest thing I saw available to me that I was looking for was
a load of Ranch House salad dressing they wanted taken down
to Houston, Texas. The company was located over in Sharps,
Nevada, which is only about 25 miles north of the truck stop. I
decided to accept the job. I grabbed a coffee to go, and off to the
truck I went. I climbed up in the cab, checked everything out and
off I go. I got to the warehouse in Sharps that had the load. But
there was no one there because it was a Saturday morning. The
sign on the door said they opened up at 9 am and it was only 7:45
a.m. So I looked around and there wasn't a damn soul insight.
There wasn't nothing around this little ass business park so I*

---

* Spelling, grammar, and punctuation left uncorrected.

thought this would be the perfect place to ditch her stinking ass off. I dragged her dead ass out of the truck. I grabbed my little army shovel and off I went to around the back of that warehouse. I found a nice isolated area back there. I buried her in about 45 minutes. This industrial park wasn't very old, so the ground was pretty soft. And that's where she is to this day.

Al paused and then continued:

It was not for another two bodies later that I would realize what a waste of all that good meat was only ending up being nothing more than bug and worm food. . . .

Chris shot up from the table. She'd heard enough. "Okay," she said, exiting, but Crystal remained seated.

Al continued:

I have never shed a tear for those I have killed, nor will I down the road. Those sweet young drug addicted prostitutes that I killed back in my past were pretty much dead to the world long before I killed them. They were nothing more than walking Zombies looking for a few moments of pleasure from their sick, twisted daily lives of shame. I feel I have done those poor souls a favor. If I feel anything for them, I feel only some jealousy. For their pains are over. But, mine will continue on as I sit behind these bars till the day that I die.

Al said, "He signed it like he always does, Tony. It says, 'You take care, be safe out there, my best friend.'"

"Is his thumbprint there?" Tony asked.

"Yes," Al replied. Metheny always marked his letters with a thumbprint pressed into his own blood. "He's enclosed something in the envelope," Al added. Turning the envelope upside down, he gently shook it and a hard object hit the glass tabletop and bounced to a stop.

Tony snatched it. "It's a tooth! Roots and everything. A molar."

"Jesus!" Joey said softly, leaning forward to look at the object that his brother was holding. "Do you think he pulled it out himself?"

"Don't touch the blood," said Crystal.

Al read the final lines that Metheny had written along the margin of the letter.

I have enclosed my tooth for you. We never met but now you will always have a part of me with you. Ha! Ha!

"He sent me his own tooth," Tony said.

Al reminded everyone of the murdered woman. If Metheny had killed her as he had written, Tony would need to contact the police. But Metheny might be lying, too—getting his kicks by exaggerating his murder count. After several minutes, they'd formulated a plan. Metheny had not told them enough for Tony to substantiate the story, so notifying the police would be premature. Instead, Tony would try to flush more details from Metheny in future letters. He'd also try to verify the few clues that Metheny had given him. Was there a 76 Truck Stop within a twenty-five-mile radius of Sparks? Was there a warehouse that handled semitrailer truckloads of salad dressing? It wasn't much, but it was a puzzle worth pursuing. He wasn't about to dismiss the dead woman as Metheny had, simply as some "stinking ass." Metheny not only had murdered her, but had stripped away her humanity. If Tony could help locate her body, then he could return some of her worth, her dignity. She'd be someone again.

"That girl has parents somewhere," said Chris, who had returned to the room and heard enough to catch the drift of their conversation. "What he did to her—is unforgivable."

"He's bragged about others," Tony said. "I need to find more about them. He'll tell me, I know it. It will just take time."

For a moment, no one spoke, and then Tony said: "Dad, read the next one."

PART ONE

the accident

On the occasion of every accident that befalls you, remember to turn to yourself and inquire what power you have for turning it to use.

—Epictetus, a Greek philosopher

EXCERPTS FROM THE KILLERS' LETTERS

I was driving down Michigan Avenue. I guess it was around 11:00 p.m. I was searching for that perfect victim, a prostitute. Why did I choose hookers? The simple fact that they are a nobody.

I probably drove for at least two hours—up-and-down Michigan Avenue but I just couldn't find that right prey. I told myself that I will do one more lap and if I didn't find the right hooker, I would go home.

I had stopped at a red light, when I saw her. She had just gotten off a Detroit city bus. She was a black woman in a black leather shirt and jacket with high heels. I decided right then and there that I was going to kill her.

—serial killer John Eric Armstrong, who confessed to twelve murders

My cousin and I—before we were arrested—were in the process of getting money together to buy this house way out in the middle of nowhere. The house was set in a small clump of jungle-like woods, then all around that was prairie-like land. You could not see the house because it was set in the woods. But from the house, you could see for miles. We wanted to get it as our LAIR. It was the ideal place to enjoy the fruits of our labors and no one would ever know. . . .

—Florida serial killer David Gore, who hunted, tortured, and murdered women
with help from his cousin, Fred Waterfield

Family is so important and many don't take time to be with family like they should. Today's world has become too fast-paced and values are not practiced or taught like before when our grandparents were raising their children. . . . I believe I was born in the wrong era because I'm old fashioned when it comes to certain things. I wish life could be simple like it was on Little

House on the Prairie. It was about family, honesty, commitment, hard-work.

—Susan Smith, who was convicted of murdering her two sons—Michael, age three; and Alexander, age fourteen months—by sending her car into a South Carolina lake while the boys were still strapped in their car seats

Dear Anthony—Received your short missive asking what I'd like to be remembered for after I die. First, as a person who tried to help and be good to her roommates, friends and family, and as a good Catholic woman.

—serial killer Dorothea Helen Puente, who murdered elderly residents in a boardinghouse she operated in Sacramento, California. She buried seven of them in her front yard.

1

July 23, 1992

A half-dozen boys running barefoot down an embankment into a cove at Possum Kingdom Lake. It was shortly after four o'clock. The afternoon temperature had just peaked at 93.9 degrees. Unlike most man-made reservoirs in Texas, which were muddy, the water in this twenty-thousand-acre playground was clear blue. It was home to Camp Grady Spruce, a popular YMCA getaway about a hundred miles west of Dallas.

Tony Ciaglia, Andy Page, and Grant Cooper were among the first to reach the Yamaha WaveRunner jet-ski there. The boys had met three years ago when they were assigned to bunks in the same tent. They had been inseparable ever since. Best buds forever.

This was the first summer the camp had owned WaveRunners, and anything fast and exciting was a welcome respite at the conservative religious outpost, which traced its roots to 1992. Only in the last nine years had girls been permitted to attend the camp's two-week sessions. The boys formed a line behind the WaveRunner and with a twist of the throttle, the WaveRunner's powerful 650-cc engine roared to life. The first rider burst from the cove, sending a rooster spray rocketing from the tail of the red and white machine.

"Tony's counselor had the day off," Chris would later recall, "but it was hot and the boys wanted to take a WaveRunner out onto the lake, so they asked another counselor. He gave them the key and then disappeared, leaving them unsupervised."

WaveRunners were supposed to be ridden only as far as a red buoy bobbing about two hundred yards offshore. After reaching the buoy, the rider returned to shore to let someone else take a turn. Andy was next in line with Tony and Grant behind him. But as the WaveRunner was returning to the cove, Andy yelled to a younger camper named David standing on the dock close to them. He was waiting to go waterskiing. Andy asked David if he wanted to switch places.

David did. He jumped into the lake and got to the head of the line at about the same time as the returning WaveRunner. He climbed aboard the WaveRunner and took off.

As the others waited in the waist-deep water for their turn, Grant splashed Tony and asked, "Have you asked her yet?"

"When we get done here," Tony replied, smiling.

"You'd better hurry up."

Tony had a crush on Kelly Christiansen, a fellow fifteen-year-old from Dallas. Blond. Cute. He wanted to take her to the Friday night dance, the last social event before camp ended. Unfortunately, so did Andy. They'd been competing for her affections while Grant played the neutral friend, watching amused from the sidelines.

Tony had first noticed Kelly last summer, but she'd not shown any interest in him or any other boys. Tony had promised himself that this summer would be different. He'd searched for her as soon as his family pulled into the Southern Methodist University parking lot twelve days earlier. It was where campers boarded commercial buses hired to transport kids in Dallas to the camp. Seats in the buses were assigned alphabetically. Because "Ciaglia" followed "Christiansen," Tony had known Kelly would be sitting near him. He'd get an uninterrupted, two-hour head start over Andy.

Tony had been so eager to talk to Kelly that he'd scooped up his gear from the back of the family's Plymouth minivan and started running across the SMU parking lot without saying goodbye to his parents or Joey, his kid brother, three years younger. Joey also was going to camp—but at a different site.

Once inside the bus, Tony slipped into his assigned seat and immediately leaned forward to speak to Kelly. That's when he heard someone rapping on the bus window. Everyone did. It was Al, signaling Tony to come outside.

Tony trudged down the aisle, and when he got outside, his parents—both Al and Chris—hugged and kissed him. Tony was totally humiliated. He could feel all of the kids inside the bus watching him. He wanted to yell, "My dad's Italian, okay? That's what Italian families do! They kiss and hug whenever they say hello or goodbye." Just like in *The Godfather*.

He'd returned to his seat red-faced, without saying a word.

Despite that rocky start, this summer had been Tony's best. He, Andy, and Grant were CITs, counselors in training. The younger kids looked up to them. It was their year to be the cool, older kids who taught the newbies the camp's traditions.

Waiting for his turn on the WaveRunner, Tony appeared to be a teenager who had, as Texans liked to put it, "life by the horns." He'd won more gold medals that week than anyone else in a camp Olympics. Even better, he'd sat next to Kelly several nights during dinner.

Molly Ray, another camper swimming in the lake, noticed Tony and Grant waiting in line for the WaveRunner to return. She thought it was odd because campers were supposed to sign their names on a clipboard the night before if they wanted to ride a WaveRunner. She began swimming toward the boys to claim a turn.

Because Tony was facing Grant in the water, he had his back to the lake and didn't see the WaveRunner as it rounded the red buoy and began racing back toward the cove. But other kids did. The WaveRunner's young driver was not slowing down. David apparently planned to make a sharp turn at the last possible second and splash the older boys with the wake.

But the young driver had overestimated his skills. He couldn't accomplish the maneuver as planned.

Grant Cooper looked up from the water just as the WaveRunner smacked into the back of Tony's skull.

"It whacked him hard," Cooper said later. "He took the brunt of it. I tried to duck and turn, but it hit me on the side of my head and I went under."

Molly Ray would still remember the scene years later. "I saw this flash—this huge thing—suddenly shoot by me as I was swimming. The next thing I noticed was bright red in the water and, I thought, 'Oh my God! That's blood. That's blood in the water. Oh my God! That's from the WaveRunner and it almost hit me.'"

Grazed on the side of his head, Grant Cooper next remembered waking up on the shore. "I don't remember getting out of the water or how I got to the shoreline, but when I came to, I was walking around in circles and people were yelling at me because my head was bleeding. I had a gash on the side of my head and a concussion."

Grant looked for Tony. "He was floating facedown in the water where we'd been standing. People were rushing to drag him out. I remember thinking, 'Oh shit! Tony's not moving. I think he's dead!'"

2

By the time the tiger-striped CareFlight rescue helicopter landed at Possum Kingdom Lake, Tony had been dragged unconscious onto the shore and was surrounded by campers.

"The golden light in this kid's eyes is going out!" a park ranger yelled as two paramedics from the twin-engine chopper darted through the throng.

During the twenty-minute flight to Fort Worth, Tony's heart stopped beating three times.

Three times, he was clinically dead.

Each time, the CareFlight personnel brought him back to life.

Fort Worth trauma nurse Bonnie Sweitzer was waiting when the helicopter touched down at Harris Methodist Hospital, the closest trauma unit to the YMCA camp. She grimaced when she saw it was a teenage boy, still wearing his swimsuit. She hated it whenever a young person was flown to the trauma unit. At least with someone older, she could tell herself the victim had already enjoyed a bit of life.

Trained as a nurse-anesthesiologist, Sweitzer first had to decide if the trauma victim needed to be intubated or whether he could breathe on his own. The boy's eyes were not responding. He needed oxygen, and fast. Although he had only a small wound on the back of his head, he clearly had suffered a massive head injury. Seitzer had spent twenty years triaging patients. She took one look at Tony and gave him only a slim chance—a very slim chance—of surviving the next twelve hours.

Back at the YMCA camp, an official telephoned Al Ciaglia at his office inside a Pizzeria Uno restaurant, one of two eateries that Ciaglia owned in downtown Dallas.

"There's been an accident involving your son," the caller said.

"Which son?" Al asked, since Joey was at the YMCA's younger kids' camp across the lake from his brother.

"All I can tell you is there was an accident in the water at the Frontier Camp and your son is being CareFlighted to Harris Methodist Hospital in Fort Worth."

Al knew it was Tony. Frontier Camp was for older kids. The caller refused to say anything else about the accident even when Al got angry. There was no mention of the WaveRunner or the head injury. There was no indication that Tony was unconscious and in serious condition.

Chris was standing a few feet from Al listening to bits and pieces. By the time he put down the receiver, she was panicked. They had been planning on going to dinner with friends, which is why she was in his office. She worked for a medical company that hospitals paid to run their emergency rooms and as soon as she'd heard Al saying "CareFlight," she knew it was serious. The emergency helicopter responded only in critical cases.

Al checked his watch. It was a few minutes after five o'clock. Interstate 30, the main thoroughfare linking Dallas to Fort Worth, would be congested with Thursday evening rush hour traffic. The drive normally took about forty minutes, but it was going to take them longer.

Al used his car phone to call Harris Methodist Hospital's emergency room as he swerved in and out of traffic, passing some cars on the highway shoulder. Neither of them had heard of the hospital.

"Your son is here," a receptionist confirmed.

"Is he alive?"

"I can't tell you anything more over the phone."

"Please," Al pleaded. "Can't you at least tell me if he's alive?"

"All I can say is you need to get here as soon as you can."

Al and Chris left their car parked outside the emergency room entrance. They didn't care if it got ticketed or was towed. As soon as a nurse heard their name, they were taken into a private waiting room.

"Would you like a chaplain?" a woman asked.

Al exploded: "I want to see our son! Now! I don't want a chaplain. I want someone to tell me what the hell is going on!"

Trauma nurse Sweitzer was paged and told that the Ciaglias were in the hospital. She went to brief them.

"Your son has suffered a traumatic brain injury," she explained. "The skull is hard. It protects the brain, which is sort of like Jell-O. When your son got hit in the back of the head, his brain got knocked into the front interior of his skull and he suffered what we call the starburst effect."

"The what?" Chris asked.

"Starburst effect. Have you ever seen a baseball hit a windshield? There's the point of impact but then there are thousands of little cracks that spread out from that entry point like a starburst. We know there was a lot of damage at the impact point in the front lobe but we have no idea where those other cracks have gone inside your son's brain."

"Is he going to die?" Al asked.

"That's something you need to ask the doctor," she replied.

"Can we see him?"

"Of course," she said.

Tony was lying on a bed. He was unconscious, still dressed in his bathing suit. For Chris, the entire scene was surreal. A ventilator was attached to her son's face and the Darth Vader sound of air being sucked in and out of his body echoed inside the room. IV tubes were stuck into his tiny body, but she didn't see any broken bones; there were no bandages, no bloodstains, no black-and-blue bruises. In fact, Tony looked physically fit—and freshly tanned. He could have been taking a nap. The only mark that Al and Chris could see was a three-inch gash on the back of his skull.

"Will he wake up?" Al asked. He couldn't get over how normal Tony looked.

"You have to understand," Sweitzer said, "your son is in a coma. He's in critical condition."

Moments later, Sweitzer introduced them to Dr. George F. Cravens, the neurosurgeon on call that afternoon. He was one of Sweitzer's favorites. If she had a child who needed brain surgery, he's the surgeon she would have called.

But Chris wasn't so sure. She sneaked out of the room and telephoned her boss at the medical company to ask what he knew about Cravens. "He's one of the best in Texas," her boss assured her. "Don't move Tony to another hospital."

Cravens was professionally polite and concise. Tony had at least eight hematomas, blood leaking from vessel tears in his brain that was now pooling inside his skull. The largest pools were in the lower right and left frontal lobes, according to CT scans. Ideally, these pools of blood would be reabsorbed in the brain over time. If not, the blood would have to be drained and major tears in the blood vessels would need to be repaired—if they could be—during surgery.

Cravens explained that the large hematomas that were showing up on the CT scans were only the most obvious ruptures. Not only had Tony's brain been knocked forward into the hard interior of the skull, but the brain had then jerked backward after impact with the WaveRunner, causing further rupturing in the back of brain.

"The tissues in the brain have different densities," Cravens explained, not certain how much either Al or Chris could comprehend at a time like this. Still, he was obligated to explain. "What that means is that these different densities move at different rates of speed—it's just the physics of these things—so it's impossible for us to know how many shears and tears have happened inside your son's brain between the front and back portions due to this jarring. We just don't know where tiny shears have happened or how these shears are going to impact his brain."

It was a starburst effect, he said, exactly what Sweitzer had mentioned earlier.

Bleeding wasn't the only problem.

There was a more immediate threat.

Because his brain had been shaken so violently, it was swelling. The pressure was building inside his skull and there was no place for his brain to expand. In a healthy adult, the pressure in the brain was anywhere from 0 to 10 mmHg (units of pressure). Any pressure greater than 20 mmHg was abnormal. If the pressure went past 40 mmHg, there was a high risk of permanent brain damage. Cravens told them he was going to perform surgery to insert an inner cranial brain pressure monitor in Tony's skull.

"We have to do everything we can to control that pressure," Cravens said. "We can't let it get too high."

"How high is too high?" Al asked.

Cravens replied: "Anything above sixty mmHG will be fatal."

There were several ways to ease the pressure building inside Tony's brain. The first was with medication. The next was inserting a shunt or valve that would allow fluids to escape from the brain, easing the pressure. In the most extreme cases, a portion of the skull would be removed so that the brain could have room to expand.

"You might have to remove part of his skull?" Chris asked in disbelief.

"Let's get the monitor in first and see where we are here," Cravens said. "We're already giving him medication. What happens next will depend on the pressure readings."

Tony's blood pressure also posed a threat. Normally, the heart pumps blood at a rate of 120/80. Tony's was raging at 225/125, which put him at risk for a stroke, heart attack, or kidney failure.

As soon as Cravens left them alone, Al and Chris both began crying. How was this happening?

"He looks so great. Why can't he just wake up?" Al stammered.

Al telephoned his older sister, Carol Bulthuis, who lived an hour away, and told her about the accident. She began calling relatives and friends. Within a few hours, more than thirty family members and friends were huddled in the ICU waiting room.

Back at the YMCA camp, Joey Ciaglia was becoming suspicious. He'd seen his older brother earlier that morning when Tony and other CITs had visited the younger boys' camp. Tony had left for the opposite side of the lake at lunchtime.

Joey was suspicious because a counselor interrupted him while he was taking a shower just before dinner and asked him for his father's telephone number at the Pizzeria Uno. No one in the camp's main office could find an emergency contact number. When Joey asked why the camp needed to call his father, the counselor stalled and then offered a flimsy excuse.

Although Joey was only thirteen, he marched into the director's office and demanded to know what was happening. Within the hour, he was being driven to Fort Worth by a counselor to meet his parents at the hospital.

By 11 p.m., Cravens had inserted the pressure monitor through a hole that he'd drilled into Tony's skull. The ICU trauma team also began taking CT scans of Tony's brain several times an hour to track the pools of blood. Those scans showed the pools were getting larger.

"These next forty-eight to seventy-two hours are critical," Cravens told Al and Chris. "If he can get through them, there's a good chance he's going to survive. It will all depend on us getting the pressure in his skull and his blood pressure under control."

As soon as Tony was brought from the operating room to the ICU unit, Al, Chris, and Joey circled his bed. Chris counted eight tubes now connected to her son. Nurse Sweitzer showed them how to read the monitors tracking Tony's vital signs and measuring the pressure. Even though massive doses of drugs were being pumped into him, his heart continued to race. The only reason why Tony was still alive at this point was that he was young and healthy.

Chris held Tony's hand and began whispering to him. Immediately, the numbers on the monitors spiked—so dramatically that two ICU nurses rushed into the room. Even though Tony was unconscious, he was reacting to his mother's voice. The nurses told Chris that she needed to avoid talking to her son and not touch him; otherwise he might go into cardiac arrest and die.

Al, Chris, and Joey stood silently next to Tony's bedside, watching the green flashing lights on the pressure monitor, listening to the ventilator breathing in and out for Tony, and hearing the rapid beeping of a machine tracking his heart rate.

It was the worst experience in any of their lives.

A different neurosurgeon reported to duty later that night. After reading Tony's medical charts, he asked the Ciaglias to step into the ICU hallway so they could talk.

"I don't like to get people's hopes up," he declared. "If it doesn't look good, I'm the guy in the hospital who tells you the truth. I'm going to be truthful with you right now."

The doctor paused and then said, "I don't think your son is going to survive. His arteries are not going to be able to hold up. His blood pressure is too high and his brain swelling is incredible. Picture yourself on a bobsled at the Olympics, okay? You're going down a sheet of ice at a hundred and ten miles per hour and if you veer off an inch to the right or an inch to the left, then imagine what will happen. That's where your son is right now. He is on that speeding sheet of ice and what's probably going to happen is that his arteries are going to blow out and he is going to have a stroke and die."

Joey was furious. He wanted to punch the doctor. Al and Chris felt their knees were going to buckle. Both began to pray. They were desperate.

When they returned to Tony's ICU room, they stared at the monitor that was tracking the pressure inside his skull. The green numbers refreshed themselves every few seconds and they had gradually been moving upward. They were now in the mid-forties. Tony's heart rate also had increased. It was as if they were watching Tony inching closer and closer to death. And there was absolutely nothing they could do to prevent it.

Chris felt as if the air in the room were being sucked out. She began having trouble breathing. Al kept shaking his head in disbelief. *How could this be happening?* Joey wanted the doctors to do something, anything. This was his older brother. Why weren't they saving him?

When the pressure monitor reached 42 mmHg, Al whispered to Chris, "What did Dr. Cravens say the maximum was?"

"Permanent brain damage over forty."

"Do they need to open his skull?" Al asked impatiently.

Chris didn't know.

"They're monitoring him, right? I mean, they know the pressure is going up. They're giving him more meds. Do you think he needs more? Should we ask them?"

Chris didn't know.

"What kind of permanent brain damage?" Al asked.

Chris didn't know.

As they watched, the pressure went up to 43 and then 44.

"Oh my God," Al said. "The drugs aren't working. They've got to do something."

The monitor beeped and showed the pressure was now 46.

Al and Chris were so frightened neither could speak.

A few moments later, the numbers 47 and 48 appeared.

"Is he going to die?" Joey asked.

The next reading stayed at 48 mmHG.

And the next, and next, and next. All of the subsequent readings were 48 mmHG. The pressure had peaked and moments later, for the first time, the tiny numbers on the screen gradually began to decrease. The machine tracking his racing blood pressure also showed that it was now in fact slowing.

The next morning, Cravens told them Tony had survived the most critical stage.

"He's not going to die?" Al asked. He wanted to hear Cravens repeat it aloud.

"He's stabilizing," Cravens replied. "That's a good sign. He's going to survive."

Al, Chris, and Joey felt a sudden sense of joy. But their relief was short-lived.

Al kept visualizing a windshield that had been struck by a hardball. Where had those cracks gone inside his son's brain? What damage had they done?

3

Trauma nurse Sweitzer generally didn't check on patients once they went on to the ICU. But when she reported to work that weekend, the first thing she did was stop in the ICU to learn if the unconscious teen was still alive.

His face was discolored and his eyes were not responding to outside stimuli. Sweitzer didn't say anything negative to Al, Chris, or Joey, but when she saw a fellow trauma nurse later that day, she said, "I'm not sure we did this kid any big favors keeping him alive."

She'd seen scans of Tony's brain. If he ever did come out of his coma, she suspected he would be brain dead and require custodial care for the rest of his life. In layman's terms, he'd be a vegetable. What kind of life was that?

On Monday, three days after the accident, a nurse led Al, Chris, and Joey into a hospital office to watch a video about TBIs, traumatic brain injuries. He wanted to prepare them for what Tony might be like if their son regained consciousness.

The video showed TBI patients strapped into chairs, unable to walk, speak, or feed themselves. A doctor on the video explained that when the gray and white matter that makes up the brain is shaken violently, the membrane that separates it from rough patches of bone inside the skull is often torn. This, in turn, causes tearing and shredding of minute blood vessels. While brain imagining devices, such as CT scans, can detect where blood has leaked from these broken vessels, the scans are not sophisticated enough to detect "shearing of nerve fibers." Because of this, it was impossible for doctors to determine just how much damage a person has suffered and which parts of the brain have been impacted.

The doctor on the video mentioned the starburst effect. He said it was not uncommon for people who have suffered a TBI to lose cognitive abilities. The most obvious is loss of motor skills—the ability to use arms or legs. But TBIs often cause less noticeable damage as well. TBI victims frequently have a much more difficult time processing information, forming thoughts, and remembering things. They can be easily over-whelmed because their brains cannot handle a normal flow of sensory data.

It was at this point that the video doctor said something that com-pletely terrified both Al and Chris. Damage to the front lobes was es-pecially known for causing neuropsychological deficits, including major personality changes. "A TBI patient," the doctor said, "may awake from coma and have absolutely no idea who the people in the room around him are or who he is. He might have no memory of his past. A TBI patient may, in fact, be a completely different person from the one who existed before the injury, with a completely new personality that will be foreign to his family and to his friends.

"He might be a complete stranger," the doctor concluded, "even to his own parents."

Chris had cried every day—nearly every hour—since the accident and by the end of the video she was sobbing again. Could it be possible that Tony wouldn't even know who she was? Had her son become a completely different person? Could Tony be a TBI survivor who was "a complete stranger," even to his own parents?

Mixed with their grief was anger. Why had the hospital shown the video to Joey? How was a thirteen-year-old supposed to deal with that kind of information, especially when his own parents were struggling to comprehend it? They returned to Tony's bedside depressed and terrified.

Even though Tony was unconscious, a physical therapist exercised his legs and arms every day. Tony began losing weight. He no longer looked like the healthy, tanned teen who had won gold medals in every event at the camp Olympics.

Dr. Cravens warned them that there was a limited amount of time that Tony could be intubated on a ventilator without causing harm to his vocal cords. If Tony didn't begin showing signs soon that he was coming out of his coma, a tracheotomy would have to be done to insert a tube into his throat to help him breathe. The neurosurgeon suggested that Al and Chris find a motel or apartment in Forth Worth rather than continuing to sleep in the hospital. "You need to get some rest," he said, "because you are starting down a very long road here."

It was becoming clear that Tony was not simply going to wake up and be discharged. If Al and Chris needed more evidence, they got it when a well-meaning nurse took Chris aside and explained that she had been praying for Tony.

Chris had thanked the nurse for her prayers and then the nurse had corrected her. "Oh, I'm not praying for him to wake up," she said. "I'm praying for God to take him. I've seen what happens when people with brain injuries this severe survive. You don't want that."

Another nurse told Al that playing music to people in comas helped stimulate the brain. The hospital was piping country-and-western songs into his room. Al ducked outside and looked in the glove box of his car. He grabbed a tape of Elvis Presley hits. Al thought listening to the King's music would be soothing. He also hoped it might jar Tony's memories of a family vacation that they'd taken years earlier to Graceland in Memphis. Al put a cassette player near Tony's bed and hit the play button. The comforting voice of Elvis echoed inside the chamber.

Ten days after the WaveRunner accident, Al and Chris got a piece of hopeful news. Tony was "tracking"—following a light with his eyes. But he remained unconscious and otherwise unresponsive. Two days later, he began resisting when physical therapists moved him out of bed and strapped him into a wheelchair. On the morning of the seventeenth day in the hospital, Tony woke up.

Al and Chris had been warned that having a family member come out of a coma was nothing like what they had seen on television soap operas. Many were angry, some violent. They frequently were disoriented and groggy, and could go through several different stages before they became fully conscious. Becoming fully conscious could take days, even weeks.

Tony's head was covered with bandages where the brain pressure monitor had been inserted and then removed. The nurses had just strapped him into a wheelchair when Al and Chris were allowed to see him. He looked up when he heard them enter the room.

"Tony, honey," Chris said.

He stared at his mother and then at Al.

"Hi Mom. Hi Dad," he said.

Al and Chris burst into tears.

Even though Tony had recognized them, he couldn't respond when they asked him questions. He couldn't form a sentence. All he wanted to do was sleep.

Joey arrived later that day carrying a Chicago Bulls baseball cap. His parents were natives of the Windy City and Al had made certain his boys were avid Chicago sports fans. Joey offered the hat to his brother, but Tony couldn't take it because his right side was paralyzed.

In a halting motion, Tony reached for the hat with his left hand and placed it on top of the bandages on his head.

Chris's hands began to tremble. Grabbing Al's arm, she whispered: "He put it on his head! He knows it goes on his head!"

4

Not long after he awoke from his coma, Tony was taken by ambulance to the Dallas Rehabilitation Center to recover. Chris was afraid to leave Tony alone because he was so young. Still on medical leave from her job, she moved into Tony's room at the center.

His room filled with cards. A steady stream of friends stopped to see him. His neighborhood friend, William "Buddy" O'Connell, brought him a baseball that had been popped into the stands during a recent Dodgers game in Los Angeles.

"I couldn't believe I got it," Buddy said, "and the first thing I thought was: 'I'm giving this to Tony.'"

Tony's high school basketball coach promised a reserved spot on the tenth-grade squad, even if he needed extra time to get into shape. A church in the Ciaglias' neighborhood held a prayer vigil for Tony's speedy recovery.

Rehabilitation at the center was done in the mornings because those hours were the most productive for people who'd suffered TBIs. From the moment he arrived, Tony pushed himself. It was painful, difficult, tedious work. At first it took all of his energy to make simple movements—ones that he used to do without a thought. He had to relearn how to walk, talk, eat, swallow, and perform other rudimentary functions.

But Tony was determined to get better. He worked hard and his fortitude slowly began to pay off. The paralysis on his right side started to dissipate. As soon as he could, he insisted on standing. He was not going to be bedridden. It wasn't easy. Often he was in pain. But he soon began walking. Baby steps, at first, while clutching the shoulders of a person directly in front of him to keep his balance.

Chris was sleeping in a bed next to his and at night she ran a piece of string from her wrist to Tony's in case he tried to get up and then fell.

From shuffling, he moved to bigger steps while pushing an empty wheelchair. Other patients took the afternoon to rest, but Tony insisted on pacing up and down the hallways under the careful watch of his mother. He kept going, challenging his body, until he was able to walk the length of the hallway without the wheelchair to steady him. But even that wasn't enough. He began picking up his pace. He was going to run.

He was so dedicated to getting better that his therapists began calling him the "the *Cliffs Notes* for TBI recovery." If people wanted to see the power of sheer determination and relentless work, they needed to watch Tony.

His mental rehabilitation wasn't progressing nearly as fast—or as well. A series of brain scans showed that much of his right temporal lobe and left frontal lobe had been destroyed.

At first, Tony could answer questions only with a yes or no. He couldn't initiate a conversation. He slowly began improving, but even after a month of therapy, his words came out in bursts and were out of sequence. He sounded like a confused Yoda from *Star Wars*. Al and Chris dubbed Tony's jumbled syntax "Brain Injury Dictionary."

In addition to having trouble forming thoughts, Tony could not do consecutive tasks. During therapy one day, he was asked to decide what he would need to pack in a suitcase for an overnight trip. He couldn't. In another exercise, he successfully followed written directions and mixed together the ingredients to make cookies, but forgot to turn on the oven.

Chris taped a list on the bathroom mirror enumerating the steps that Tony needed to take each morning—take shower, dry off, apply deodorant, put toothpaste on toothbrush, brush teeth, comb hair, get dressed. His little brother, Joey, worked with him in the afternoons, writing words on a white erasable board in Tony's room. One day, he wrote: *plate, spoon, fork, knife,* and *car,* and asked his older brother which item didn't belong. Tony couldn't tell him.

Bits and pieces of information Tony had learned growing up had been wiped from his memory. He had no idea where the state of Texas was located on a U.S. map. Even reading children's books proved difficult. One of his therapists took him to a shopping mall one day to teach him how to step on and off an escalator.

Tony also was having trouble with basic etiquette. He gobbled his food so quickly he would gag. He began packing on pounds because he didn't appear to know when to stop eating.

He remembered nothing about the WaveRunner accident.

Chris played checkers and brought in other board games, but they were difficult for Tony. He was impatient, easily frustrated, and miserable.

By the end of his eight grueling weeks in rehab, Tony began begging his parents to take him home. He missed his friends from the neighborhood—Buddy, Tim, and Colby. Before the WaveRunner accident at summer camp, the four of them had spent the summer golfing, riding skateboards in the Ciaglias' cul-de-sac, playing street hockey, and sleeping over at one another's houses. Late at night, they would sneak out and "spitball cars" by soaking an entire roll of toilet tissue in water and then throwing it at an unsuspecting motorist driving by. The paper wad would explode on impact, covering the vehicle with wet globs of shrapnel while the boys hid behind bushes.

Tony was beginning to look healthy again. Al and Chris decided to sneak him out of the center. Al drove the family car to a side door while Chris hustled Tony down a hallway. Joey stood watch. The family rode to Keller's, a drive-in restaurant in Dallas famous among locals for its hamburgers. Tony gorged himself. They sneaked him back to his room afterward. After that late night escape, Al and Chris decided it was time to bring Tony home. It had been nearly three months since the WaveRunner accident.

In late September 1992, they told Tony's treatment team that they wanted Tony discharged. His therapists argued against it, claiming it was much too early. Parts of his brain were still waking up. It could take years and years for the brain to fully recover. Many patients never did recover fully. Oftentimes, the most that could be hoped for was that survivors would regain about 70 percent of their cognitive abilities. The effects of Tony's brain injury were still emerging. Al and Chris agreed to two more weeks, but said that would be enough. Their son was discharged in late October but continued as an outpatient receiving ongoing therapy for another year at the center.

Al would later remember that his family was tired of hospitals and rehab therapy. "Tony wanted his old life back," Al said. "All of us did and we felt it was time to go home and get our lives back to normal."

While Al's two restaurants were located in downtown Dallas, the Ciaglia family lived in the upper-middle-class suburb of Plano, some eighteen miles north of the city. In January 1993, Chris called the principal at Shepton High School and told him that her son was ready to enroll. Ninth- and tenth-grade students attended Shepton before completing eleventh and twelfth grades at a separate senior high school.

Schoolwork had always come easily to Tony, so Chris and Al were optimistic. It might take him a bit longer to complete a math problem or write an essay, but both of them believed Tony's overall intelligence had not declined since the accident. The wiring in his brain had been short-circuited, but not his IQ. Or so it seemed to them.

Shepton High School's mascot was a stallion, the western symbol of power and unbridled freedom. On the morning when Chris and Tony entered the school's lobby, they were greeted by a large paper sign the students had made.

THERE'S A STALLION IN THE HOUSE!
WELCOME BACK TONY CIAGLIA,
SHEPTON'S ITALIAN STALLION!

It seemed like every one of the school's twelve hundred students knew about the WaveRunner accident. Tony had always been popular. He was outgoing, gregarious, and a natural athlete. Because Tony was a "jock," he was part of the school's elite crowd. Within a few weeks, Tony made his first appearance in a Shepton basketball game. He warmed the bench until late in the fourth quarter, when his coach sent him in. As soon as Tony walked onto the court, the entire gymnasium erupted with applause and cheers. Seconds later, he was fouled while shooting a basket. A hush fell over the gym as he moved to the foul line.

Tony concentrated intently for several seconds and then launched his first shot. The ball arced high in the air, hit the rim, and tumbled down through the net. His second free throw swished through without even touching the hoop.

His classmates screamed and rocked the gym with chants of "Tony! Tony! Tony!"

From their seats in the wooden bleachers, Al and Chris were overcome with emotion. Tears welled. For them, this moment seemed to be the perfect Hollywood ending to an incredible story about a loving son who had died three times aboard a CareFlight helicopter, been revived, survived a massive TBI injury, returned to his school, and rightfully reclaimed his life, as a hero.

There was only one problem.

Tony's most difficult struggles were just about to start.

5

Al returned to managing his pizza restaurants. Chris returned to her medical job and Tony and Joey left for school each morning. Life in the household seemed to be returning to normal.

But it was a facade.

Within days after Tony's awe-inspiring debut on the Shepton basketball court, he announced at dinner that he was quitting the squad.

"Why?" Al asked. "You love the game and did great the other night."

"I can't remember the plays."

Neither Al nor Chris was alarmed. They figured he'd return to the team when he was ready.

As a precaution, Tony had been put on medication in the hospital to prevent epileptic-like seizures. During a follow-up examination with a hospital neurologist, Tony and his parents were told that he no longer needed to continue taking drugs. Almost immediately, Tony began having what his parents thought were anxiety attacks. He became nervous and sad, and was easily upset.

One Friday night, Chris drove Tony to the house of Tom, a friend, for a party. She hoped going out with his pals would cheer him up. When they got to the house, she turned in her car seat to ask Tony when she should pick him up. What she saw stunned her. Tony's eyes were glassy and his entire body was trembling. She had never seen him so furious.

He threw open the car door. "I'm going to kill Tom," he said, bolting from the vehicle.

Chris literally tackled her son as they were racing across the front lawn, and she refused to get off him until he promised to return home with her. By the time they got there, Tony was sobbing and went right to bed.

On Monday, Tony refused to get out of the car when Chris drove him to school. "I never want to go in that building again," he told her. He began crying. She drove him home and called Al.

Tony told his parents that none of his old friends at school was speaking to him.

"One girl asked me, 'When'd ya get so stupid—in your coma?'" he said. Other kids at school were calling him a "retarded stallion."

Whenever he tried to join in conversations at school, students would circle closer to prevent him from being part of their group. Even teachers mocked him. When he made a mistake in one class, the teacher began telling the other students, "Be careful, you don't want to do a 'Tony,' do you?"

"I hate my life," he told his parents.

Of all his teenage friends, Tony had been the closest with Buddy O'Connell. Nearly two decades later, O'Connell would become emotional when he recalled during an interview for this book how he and other students had treated Tony in high school after the accident.

"At first, everyone at school was very excited to have Tony back and it was really a big deal," O'Connell said. "The whole school welcomed him home, but as soon as that novelty wore off, everyone forgot that he needed special attention and none of us who were his best friends really knew how to handle it."

Like all high schools, Shepton had its social cliques. "Everyone wanted to be cool and when you had a friend who was off, someone like Tony, well . . . he wasn't cool and you didn't want to be seen with him or have him around," O'Connell recalled.

O'Connell's voice broke with emotion as he continued: "I have a sister who is mentally handicapped and I've always been aware of how cruel kids can be, but I was going through puberty and trying to find my own identity in ninth grade and scared at being rejected. What happened was that Tony went from being one of the most popular kids to being someone no one wanted to associate with. Kids are cruel. The mentality was, 'Well, if you can't keep up with us, too bad for you.' Tony simply couldn't keep up after his accident. He sort of just disappeared as a person."

Al and Chris urged their son to make new friends and invite them to their house on weekends. Al was a drummer and the family had a keyboard and other musical instruments the kids could use. They also had a swimming pool and a pool table. Al and Chris promised the refrigerator would always be stocked with soft drinks and finger foods. Tony made calls, but no one was interested in coming over. He was heartbroken.

One afternoon, Chris heard Tony humming a song. She asked him if he knew what it was. He wasn't sure but the tune seemed stuck in his mind.

"It's Elvis Presley," she said. "When you were in your coma, the doctor and nurses told us it was important to stimulate your brain but your dad couldn't stand the country-western that was being piped into your room so he played an Elvis tape to you."

Chris bought Tony several books about Elvis and got all of the movies that Elvis had appeared in. To help pass the time at home, Tony began singing. He'd always enjoyed it. Chris got copies of the lyrics to every song that Elvis recorded. Al bought his son a karaoke machine. Tony began using it as he copied the King's voice. He studied Elvis's mannerisms and dancing. The same single-minded determination that Tony had shown while in rehab he now showed in his quest to perform like Elvis. He spent hours practicing. Al and Chris were thrilled because it gave him something to do. Both of them also were surprised at just how good Tony was becoming at transforming himself into the singing legend.

One night when Chris asked Tony to carry his dirty clothes to the laundry room, he punched his fist into the door, screamed obscenities, and ran off outside. Chris telephoned Al at work and began searching the neighborhood. She and Joey drove through the neighborhood searching for Tony. They found him in a nearby elementary playground, sitting on top of the monkey bars.

"Tony, you're not a monkey!" she said softly, trying to coax him down. He'd always loved monkeys and she thought her comment might make him laugh. He came down, but he was not laughing.

During the ride home, Chris told him, "Tony, these outbursts can't keep happening. I don't know what I'm going to do with you."

"I know, Mom. I'm sorry. I'm not trying to hurt you."

Not long after that, Joey came home from school one afternoon and found Tony in their parents' bathroom, an entire bottle of aspirin dumped into his palm.

"I want to die," Tony told his little brother.

Al and Chris took Tony to see Andrew W. Bulino, a well-known family therapist in Plano who specialized in helping difficult-to-treat adolescents. As Bulino listened to them describe the WaveRunner accident and Tony's recent emotional outbursts, the therapist quietly wondered if he really wanted to take on Tony as a patient. This teenager was different from other adolescents whom Bulino counseled, because his problems didn't stem from a personality disorder or a mental illness. He had a traumatic brain injury. How could Bulino help someone who had lost the ability to use parts of his brain? The last thing Bulino needed was for a teenager to commit suicide while he was under his care. Plano was a close community. Word would spread quickly. On the other hand, Al and Chris were clearly desperate. Tony seemed to be a sincere kid.

During their first session together, Tony announced, "I'm going to kill myself. As soon as we leave your office. You can't stop me. No one can."

Bulino believed him.

"Look, your life has been fucked over," Bulino said bluntly, "and your life is still fucked. You've experienced a huge tragedy and things are never going to be the same again for you. You will never get your old life back. But if you are willing to work at it, I think we can do something together to make your life better. But we have to get to work on it—and right now. We can't do that, if you kill yourself—can we?"

"No," Tony said quietly.

"Will you give me a chance to help you? Will you promise not to kill yourself?"

Tony nodded.

Stepping outside his office, Bulino was direct with Al and Chris.

"Your son is actively suicidal. Our first priority must be keeping him alive and the easiest way to do that is to admit him in a hospital right now. It may not help him therapeutically, but it will, at least, keep him safe."

"Isn't there another way?" Al asked. "Tony's had enough of hospitals."

Bulino said, "Yes, but it's not going to be easy. If we don't put him in a hospital, then one of you is going to have to be with him every moment of the day and night—and I mean *every* moment. You can never let him out of your eyesight—not even for a second. Because he is suicidal. Are you willing to do that?"

Al and Chris both said yes without even discussing it.

Bulino telephoned Dr. Jeffrey Glass, a local psychiatrist, and told him about Tony and his parents. Bulino suspected that Tony's recent rages were actually petit mal seizures, a classic sign that something is wrong inside a child's brain. Glass agreed to examine Tony at a clinic and start him on neurological medications to calm the storms raging in his head.

Bulino theorized that the WaveRunner accident had not destroyed the nerves in the back of Tony's frontal lobe, because they controlled movement. Tony clearly had full use of his motor skills.

But Tony's brain had been damaged in the prefrontal cortex, which governs the higher cognitive functions and the determination of personality. Planning, organizing, problem solving, and the ability to focus are all based in the area of Tony's brain that had been damaged. Even more worrisome, some of the worst damage had happened where emotions are regulated and behavior is controlled.

"Your son," Bulino told Al and Chris, "has a very limited ability to control his own emotions. Coupled with that, he has a total lack of inhibition. Tony is going to have difficulty discerning what is and isn't acceptable social behavior, especially when it comes to sexuality."

Tony's age also was working against him. "Normal adolescents are prone to mood fluctuations, especially during puberty," Bulino said. "Tony is going to have a much worse time with mood swings because the stabilizing parts of his brain are just not functioning." In some ways, Tony could remain much like a fifteen-year-old boy throughout his life.

Because of Tony's brain damage, he might go from feelings of "overwhelming joy" to becoming "actively suicidal" within seconds, the therapist warned. "You might never know what set him off. A sideways look from a stranger in an elevator might be enough to cause him to explode.

"You need to prepare yourselves for another difficulty. Brain injuries are not clearly visible. If Tony had bandages on his head and he acted oddly, people would understand something was wrong. But your son looks fine and people are not going to realize his brain is not working properly when he acts out. This will make matters even more dangerous."

Bulino recommended that Al and Chris remove Tony from school. Their son was being rejected there and that rejection could cause him to explode in anger. The therapist didn't want Tony getting into a fistfight and possibly suffering even more brain trauma.

"Our first goal is to keep your son *alive*," Bulino warned. "Everything else is secondary."

Tony needed to stay in a safe and supportive environment.

Bulino suggested a two-pronged approach. He would use cognitive behavioral therapy to teach Tony how to recognize when he was about to lose control and how to put brakes on his emotions. Psychiatrist Glass, meanwhile, would search for the right cocktail of antipsychotic and mood-stabilizing medications to level Tony's brain.

Bulino said he wanted to see Tony a minimum of three times a week. He had never seen a patient so often, but Tony was so fragile that Bulino didn't want to risk not seeing him every other day. The therapist also wrote down his private phone number for Al and Chris to call at any hour if there were an emergency.

From that moment on, Tony slept at the foot of his parents' bed in a sleeping bag. Meanwhile, Chris and Al pulled Tony out of school. Although Al owned two restaurants, he turned over the day-to-day operations to a subordinate. The entire focus in life became taking care of his son. He went with him to every one of his psychiatric appointments and therapy sessions. Oftentimes, Al served as Tony's memory.

During a therapy session, Al would say, "Tony, you need to tell Drew Bulino about what happened on Monday."

"What happened Monday, Dad?" Tony would ask.

Al would nudge him with reminders.

Tony began keeping a journal about how he felt.

"The sun is shining bright and it is warm outside. Too bad it is such a beautiful day and I feel like a piece of garbage," he wrote in his first entry. "I felt great for about an hour before my mind finally woke up and began to start thinking because when I start to think, everything gets very depressing. My great confusion is growing worse day by day. Also, I get bad thoughts about other people and I hate kids with a very deep passion who once were my friends. My anger toward the world is growing stronger and stronger every day, and I feel as if my whole world is caving in." Continuing, he explained that he did not want to be someone who was out of control and angry all of the time.

The following day, he wrote: "This is the worst day I have had since my accident but I am getting kind of used to having bad days. Thoughts of suicide are growing stronger and I cannot handle them. They got so bad today, I think I might have to be hospitalized. When I was sitting in my dad's office I broke out in tears. I was crying hysterically and didn't know why. Why is this happening to me?"

At home, Al and Chris discovered they could not parent Tony the way that they had before the accident or as they were parenting Joey.

"I don't know how to handle Tony," Al told Bulino. "He makes me so mad. I lose my temper, especially when he swears at me. I tell him, 'You can't talk to me like that! I'm your father.' And I try to reprimand him like any father normally would but it doesn't work. He runs away."

Bulino said, "Al, remember, I told you that one of the problems with Tony is he looks so darn good, he looks fine, but he's not. Imagine you have a broken arm and it's in a sling and someone walks up to you and punches you in that arm. That would hurt you. Well, Tony has a broken arm, too—an injury—but it's in his head and when you get mad at him and yell at him, you are causing him severe pain and he can't handle that. You've got to learn how to talk him down, calmly. How to reassure him."

Tony's memories of his life before the accident were both a curse and a blessing. Tony would talk during every therapy session about how much he hated his former friends because they had abandoned him. During those sessions, Bulino would remind Tony that he had been happy once and assure him that he could be happy again once he learned how to control his emotions.

"I just want things to go back as they were," Tony said during an intense session, breaking into tears.

"Tony, I am nearsighted," Bulino responded, "and no matter how much I want twenty-twenty vision, if I drive home without my glasses, well, we are all going to be in trouble. You can't wish your brain injury away, but you can move forward and have a good life."

Al and Chris began avoiding public places where Tony might cause a scene. But they didn't want him to become a hermit who was afraid to leave home. They were caught, fearing to let him go out by himself, yet not wanting to isolate him at home and deny him the freedoms that other teenagers received. They had Joey to look after and both of them felt they were ignoring their younger son. Plus, they treated Tony differently. They tolerated profane and inappropriate outbursts from him because of his TBI—outbursts that they never would have allowed from Joey.

Tony spent six months sleeping at the foot of his parents' bed and was never allowed to be alone. He spent his waking hours being driven to psychiatry appointments and therapy sessions, or sitting next to his dad in the Pizzeria Uno manager's office. He was lonely and miserable. Al and Chris felt overwhelmed. What kind of life was this for their teenage son?

Because of the medications that he had to take, his weight ballooned.

Once an active teen and athlete, Tony was lethargic, went to bed at 8 p.m., and took naps. Different combinations and dosages often sent him into an emotional tailspin.

Chris hated that her son had become a "pincushion." Every day seemed to be an experiment. The carefree boy she'd once known, the one who would have walked across the street to avoid an argument, now became confrontational for no reason. The "old" Tony had been gregarious, a wisecracker, a loving son always eager to please his parents. The "new" Tony was distant, forgetful, painfully withdrawn at times. And angry—always angry.

It was his rage that frightened Al and Chris the most. They couldn't tell if it was a result of his brain injury or the constantly changing cocktail of medications. By the time Tony turned sixteen years old he was taking sixteen pills a day, many of them powerful antipsychotics.

Even on the days when Tony did well, Chris felt an abiding sadness. Al was physically drained. There was no relief. At night, when they heard a sound, Al would jump up and check to see if Tony was still sleeping at the foot of their bed. Every day, Al and Chris wondered if Tony might become depressed and kill himself. They were trapped inside an ongoing nightmare.

About a year after Tony had left school and started being kept home, Tony's psychiatrist and therapist decided that he was no longer "actively suicidal" and could move out of his parents' bedroom. He was no longer talking about killing himself, but he still was emotionally unstable. Al and Chris were frightened about having him go anywhere by himself. In a role reversal, Joey became his older brother's shadow.

Whenever Tony left the house, Joey was with him. Joey's friends became Tony's. Even when it meant Joey would miss a high school party or Friday night football game, he refused to go without his brother.

Al and Chris noticed that Tony had become more and more religious after his coma. He prayed obsessively during the day, as many as twenty times. Whenever he passed a church, he crossed himself. Given what he had been through, his parents assumed it was a natural reaction.

Chris decided to enroll Tony in a youth choir at their neighborhood Roman Catholic church. It seemed a safe place for Tony to go and he loved to sing. The first practice went well, but within minutes after Chris dropped him off at the second practice, the church's secretary called her.

"You need to come get your son," Chris was told. Tony was being booted off the choir. He was sitting on the sidewalk outside the church when she arrived.

"It wasn't my fault," Tony said. "I was standing on the risers and I started falling so I reached out and put my hands on this girl in front of me and she started this big yahoo."

"Why did she get mad?" Chris asked.

"I hit her butt by accident but she accused me of grabbing her and she told the choir director." That was it for the church choir.

Tony tried roller hockey but got into an argument with another player. That escalated into a shouting match with the boy's father. Al had to step in to prevent punches from being thrown. An attempt in a church-run basketball league ended up much the same—Tony hanging on a rim, spewing obscenities, and taunting officials. At a local rink, Tony got into a profanity-peppered pushing match with another kid ice-skating.

Even Joey became leery of taking his brother out in public. Tony would always cause a ruckus and Joey would have to step in. One night Joey broke down and told his dad, "I'll never be happy because my whole life is going to be like sitting on a powder keg because of my brother."

Joey was only fourteen, but the experience had aged him beyond his years. He knew what he had to do. "It's okay. I'll be there because he's my brother, but it's not easy."

Joey was a goalie on one of the Dallas area's premier traveling ice hockey teams and Al and Tony went with him and the team to a tournament in Las Vegas. Inside the arena, Al led Tony into the nosebleed seats to keep his son away from other fans. But the game drew a large crowd and they were soon surrounded by other parents. When an older woman and her two adult sons sat in a row above them and began cheering for the opposing team, Al began feeling uneasy. The game was physical from the start and filled with penalties, but Tony kept calm during the first period. Early into the second, a member of the opposing team slammed into Joey in front of the goal and Tony flew from his seat and screamed a profanity at the player.

Looking down from her seat above Tony, the older woman said, "You need to watch your mouth!"

Tony turned, called her an obscene name, and then, without warning, doused her with a huge cup of Coca-Cola and ice. Her two adult sons shot from their seats with clenched fists.

Al jumped in front of Tony and yelled: "He didn't mean it! He's got a brain injury."

But that didn't stop the woman's furious sons. Al raised his arms palms up and continued pleading with them to stop.

"He didn't mean it."

The woman's two sons hesitated. That was long enough for two security officers to race up into the stands. The altercation caused such a commotion that the players on the ice stopped to watch. Tony's anger had turned into embarrassment. He apologized over and over. But it was too late. Al and Tony were escorted out of the rink.

Al and Chris spent hours reading everything they could about traumatic brain injuries. There wasn't much, but what had been written was frightening. Tony fitted the symptoms listed in a medical textbook perfectly.

Damage to frontal lobes can cause: impulsivity, emotional and/or social withdrawal, aggression, outbursts of rage and violent behavior, disorganization, impaired social judgment, uncharacteristic lewdness, inability to appreciate the effects of one's own behavior or remarks on others, loss of social graces, boisterousness, impaired communication 'skills, such as an impaired capacity to understand conversational inferences.

Al kept repeating to himself: "It's the brain injury, not my son. It's the injury."

A pattern developed. After each outburst, Tony was embarrassed, depressed, and would apologize. But even with medication and thrice-a-week therapy, he seemed incapable of controlling his emotions.

He was miserable and suffering. So was everyone else. And no one knew how to change things.

6

Al made it a practice each night to sit at the kitchen table with Tony after dinner and talk to him about his day. Al used it as a teaching moment. They would talk about what Tony had done that was good and what had led him to get into trouble.

"There's something I need to tell you, Dad," Tony announced one evening. "It's about something that happened, but I've been afraid to mention it."

Al braced himself and said, "Tony, we can talk about anything. You should never be afraid to tell me stuff."

"I'm afraid you won't believe me because I'm not even sure I believe it myself. It might have all been a dream. I don't know, but it has to do with the WaveRunner accident."

"I didn't think you remembered anything about the accident."

"I don't, nothing about that afternoon," Tony said. "But what I'm talking about, it happened—when I was dead." He looked at his dad wide-eyed. "I think I had an out-of-body experience."

Al nodded.

"I left my body. I was just this spirit. I was traveling, moving upward. It's hard to describe. It was beautiful. I felt warm and very peaceful," Tony said. "I was in this shaft, like a tunnel but the bottom and top were open, and the walls of it were made of white light, but not a color of white that we know. It was more like Mom's crystal glasses. I was a bit scared at first. But I felt very warm, warmer than I've ever felt anywhere. I was all alone and with nobody, but I wasn't alone."

"What do you mean, Tony?"

"I don't know. I felt this strange feeling of being welcomed. Embraced. I just felt I belonged there and that everything was going to be okay. I wasn't sure where I was but I knew one thing—I felt no pain. I was so at peace with myself."

Tony continued: "I kept moving through this crystal shaft of white light. It seemed to go on and on. Then I stopped. There was this giant, grayish white mass. It was just incredible!"

Al wasn't sure what to say.

"I didn't know what it was," Tony said, "but I knew this mass that was right in front of me was something holy. It was something powerful. I felt it was an honor for me to be seeing it and as I watched, this mass of energy began to take shape. It became a man, but he didn't have a face."

"It had a man's head?" Al asked, trying to imagine a picture.

"It had a man's head and it had a face," Tony said, "but it didn't have a face. There was a shape, but no features, not like a mouth or eyes. It's hard to describe but I think, Dad"—Tony paused—"I think it was Jesus Christ."

"I've read about out-of-body experiences," Al said reassuringly. "Some people have talked about seeing bright lights, just like you did."

"I'm sure it was Jesus. He called me by my name. He actually talked to me. He said, 'Anthony Albert Ciaglia, do you know where you are?'

"And I said, 'No, I'm not sure. I'm confused.'

"He said to me—and I remember it like it just happened—'Have no fear for you are with your Father in heaven.'"

"That's incredible, Tony," Al said.

"Jesus told me He was giving me a choice. He said, 'You can stay here and live in peace and happiness and join up with your family when it's their time to be here, or, the other choice is for you to go back.'"

"Jesus said you could come back to us?"

Tony said yes. Al studied his son. Tony had never been a liar, nor was he given to exaggerating stories. From the look on Tony's face, Al could tell that his son believed what he was describing. Whether it had been a dream or a delusion, or had actually happened—Tony clearly was convinced that he had met Jesus.

Tony said, "Jesus told me He would grant me a second chance at life. But Jesus also said, 'You will lose everything if you go back. You will have to work harder to do everything you once did so easily. You will have to relearn for yourself how to do everything you once took for granted. Nothing will be made easy for you or simple. You will lose your friends and your life as you know it. But you will be given a new purpose for your life.'

"Then Jesus asked me what I wanted to do," Tony continued. "I looked at the light. I told him: 'I can't leave my family. I don't want my parents to tell my brother that I'm dead—that he'll never have a big brother again. I can't do that to him. I don't want to leave any of them. I don't want that for my mom and dad. I want to go back.'"

Now it was Tony who was examining his father's face, looking for some shred of either acceptance or disbelief.

Continuing, Tony said: "The next thing, I was waking up out of my coma. That's why I thought it was just a dream. I thought I had imagined it, and it didn't really happen. I figured it was just something that happens when you are in a coma. Now I know it actually happened."

Al asked softly, "How do you know, Tony?"

"Because everything Jesus told me is coming true. I came back and I lost my old life just like Jesus said I would. Look at me now. I'm like a completely different person. My old life is gone."

Overcome with emotion, Tony started to cry. Al left his kitchen chair to comfort him.

"I'm glad you chose to come back, Tony," Al said. "Your mom and Joey are, too. We're all glad you didn't die."

"Do you believe me—that this happened? Am I going crazy?"

"Of course I believe you, Tony. Other people have had out-of-body experiences." Now Al's eyes were filling with tears, too. "I'm just glad you didn't die."

Tony covered his face with his hands.

"Dad," he whispered through his fingers.

"What?"

"I'm not sure I made the right choice coming back here."

EXCERPTS FROM THE KILLERS' LETTERS

Bittaker tape recorded his "experiences" with our last victim while I drove the van, smoking joint after joint, trying to drown out the horror. Then he tapped me on the shoulder and said, "I'm done with her, it's your turn." There was just no way I could do it. Everything was wrong! He looked a bit crazed also and had the 38 snub nose stuffed into his waistband. I felt empty inside as I figured he wanted me to end her life. He had done the others himself. Now it would be my turn. So he drove for a short time.

He'd been with her a good forty-five minutes to an hour—her screaming most of the time. I feared if I didn't make her scream too—he'd freak. So I tapped her right elbow with a hammer and pleaded quietly, "Please scream." And she did—for some time. Enough I felt to quell any doubts he may have had. And as I feared, he did say out loud, "You do her. I've done all the others." My heart sank . . . I did it and turned away . . . Killing her, killed part of me too. It's what keeps me from looking directly into any other woman's eyes. I feel great shame and loss. I deserve death. And I have tried it a few times The closest I have come was in the county jail after confessing in court and showing detectives and the DA where we dumped the others in the mountains. I figured I'd given prosecutors all they needed to condemn Larry cause I didn't want to face anyone ever again. I hung myself in my cell and as I was blacking out—I smiled.

Sadly, I woke up, strapped down on a bed. The DA coined the phrase—"the Screamer Tape" when they played the tape in court of what we did to that girl. I give the DA credit for being dead accurate about that tape. I was forced to listen to it beginning to end, once and I swore to myself never again. It's a perfect example of the worst that man can do to another human being. It's also why I'll never ask for forgiveness from God! I don't deserve it. I curse the day I was conceived.

Tomorrow, I would've have gone to my first parole board hearing, but I waived my right to it and that decision cost me an additional TEN YEARS until my next opportunity . . . I waived the hearing so I would not have to listen to that "tape-recording."

—Serial killer Roy L. Norris, whose accomplice, Lawrence Sigmund Bittaker, tortured sixteen-year-old Lynette Ledform with pliers in the back of a van while driving around. They tape-recorded the entire incident before Norris murdered her. Together they kidnapped, raped, tortured, and murdered five young girls chosen at random.

You ask me about Bill Bonin. Sexual things????? PULEASZE. That's a laugh. First, there is no chance of any sexual thing going on here in prison on death row. Second, even if there were, he and I were not compatible in that way. He liked boys, ya know, 12–13 at the oldest, and he wasn't my type either—mentally or physically, but he was okay as far as being on the same exercise yard. I don't think we would have been friends on the street, but here I saw him nearly every day on the yard from my first day January 1990 until he left to be executed. . . . You asked how I felt when they executed him. No, I wasn't hurt. We all knew it was coming for quite awhile . . . and no one was really close to him. No one here is close, really. He said goodbye to whomever he wanted the last day on our yard but there was no group hug, in fact, some were probably happy to see him go. He certainly wasn't particularly strong or brave physically . . . How do I feel about being on death row—waiting to die? We all die . . . I'm sending you the book titled, "Tuesdays with Morrie." It has some good insights on living and dying. . . .

—serial killer Randy Steven Kraft, convicted of murdering sixteen men, but suspected of killing at least fifty others. Tony had asked in a letter if Kraft had engaged in sex in prison with another serial killer, William Bonin, who was convicted of fourteen murders but suspected of fifteen more. Both Kraft and Bonin kidnapped, raped, tortured, and dumped their male victims along California highways, but the killers didn't meet until they were put on death row in San Quentin. In 1996, Bonin became the first prisoner executed by lethal injection in California, and although he expressed no remorse for his crimes, he gave the warden a note that said, "I feel the death penalty is not an answer to the problems at hand. I feel it sends the wrong message to the people of this country. . . ."

On my first day of school, it didn't go well. The kid behind me kept making fun of my shoes and clothes because they were hand-me downs. He kept it up and got the whole class laughing so I turned around and stuck my pencil right through his hand. He screamed, the teacher screamed louder, and I stood up and threw my chair at him. They called my mom and she just looked at them and said, "You're all liars. You're just out to get my son." Of course they called child services, but I never seen them cause a couple days later . . . I ran away from home. Even though my parents knew where I was, they never came looking for me. One less mouth to feed was fine with them. . . .

—serial killer Glen Rogers, aka the Cross-Country Killer, who was convicted of four murders, but once bragged that he'd murdered up to seventy women while traveling aimlessly across the United States

7

Al and Chris enrolled Tony in a private school, but he ended up getting into a fight with another student and had to withdraw. In a frightening incident, he exchanged angry profanities with a teenager and then knocked her down while they were arguing inside a shopping mall. Tony escaped just in time to avoid the mall's security guards.

Determined that Tony would graduate from high school but worried how Tony would interact with his classmates, Chris arranged for a teacher to homeschool him. Nancy Smith began coming to the Ciaglias' house three times a week. She had been instructing kids at home for more than fifteen years, but she had never had a student with a severe brain injury. Most of the students that she taught were homebound for only six to eight weeks while they recovered from a persistent illness or from injuries such as broken bones. With Tony, she spent two years.

Smith believed that most of her students could concentrate for only about twenty minutes before they needed a break. These breaks were a good time for her to switch from one subject, such as math, to a different one. During her first session with Tony, she checked her watch and told him after twenty minutes that he could leave the dining room table where they were working. She suggested that he use the bathroom or get a snack.

Tony stepped from the room, but returned a minute later toting a worn karaoke machine.

"Do you like Elvis?" he asked her.

"Not really," Smith replied.

Undeterred, Tony plugged in the machine and began to sing one of Elvis's songs. When he finished, Smith gushed, "That was amazing!" From that morning on, Tony sang to her nearly every time she came to their house; and sometimes, for fun, he would answer her questions in his "Elvis" voice when they were studying.

Therapist Bulino was aware of Tony's fascination with Elvis and thought the accolades Tony received were good for his badly battered self-esteem.

From the start, Smith was struck by how eager Tony was to please her and the amount of time that Al and Chris were willing to spend helping him with his studies. When Smith finished teaching Tony his lessons, Al or Chris would ask her what homework Tony needed to complete and if there were subjects that Smith wanted them to focus on. She decided that Al and Chris would do anything for their son no matter how much time or money it required.

Tony's brain injury had caused him to forget information, but much like grooves on a record, the information was there. It's just that Tony couldn't access it. Smith discovered that Tony could no longer remember the Pledge of Allegiance, but once she told it to him and he repeated it to her, he knew it.

With Nancy Smith's help, Tony graduated from high school with the same diploma that his classmates at Shepton High School received. But he didn't attend graduation. He wasn't interested in running into any of his old classmates. Instead, his parents had a party for him in their home and he borrowed a cap and gown from a neighbor.

Al heard that Minyard Food Stores, a Texas grocery-store chain, was hosting a contest in Dallas for Elvis performers, so he submitted a photo of Tony with his hair combed like Elvis's, and a tape recording of him singing. The judges invited Tony to compete.

On morning of the show, however, Al and Chris became worried. They had thought the contest would be an amateur event, but there were more than a thousand spectators in the Dallas convention center when the Ciaglias arrived. The other contestants were dressed in white jumpsuits studded with rhinestones. Tony wore a blazer and slacks.

"You don't have to do this," Al told his son as they walked backstage.

"I'll be okay," Tony answered. "I can do this."

Al and Chris waited nervously in the audience—afraid that the stress of being onstage would send Tony into one of his violent and profane outbursts.

"This is nothing at all like what I'd expected," Al said. Chris agreed.

When his name was called, Tony strolled onto the stage, took the microphone, and began singing. Even Chris was surprised at how good her son sounded. No one could tell from watching him that he had a brain injury. Tony ended up in a tie for first place with Johnny Lovett, a well-known Dallas-based Elvis impersonator, so the judges asked both singers to do another song and let the audience decide by applause who would be the champion. The prize was a leather jacket that had been worn by band members during Elvis's final tour, and a year's supply of jelly doughnuts.

Tony won.

Tony enjoyed singing Elvis songs so much that he volunteered to perform at an educational center for Down syndrome children and at the Dallas Special Olympics. He appeared at area nursing homes.

Having won in Dallas, Tony could now compete in the nation's oldest and largest national Elvis competition, called Images of Elvis, in Memphis. It attracted more than 250 participants and more than 1,000 spectators. He wore a gold lamé custom suit like Elvis wore in 1957. This was the only time he ever dressed as Elvis. He did not want to copy everyone else. He was not an impersonator. He was a tribute artist who performed as the King would have if he were alive today. Tony's singing was good enough to earn him a spot in the final ten, and when it came his time to perform, he began by telling the audience how he had been hit by a WaveRunner, died three times, lapsed into a coma, and then had to relearn how to speak. He talked about how his friends had deserted him and how his brain injury had radically changed his life. He talked about how blessed he was to be alive and performing.

"I never dreamed I would be on a stage today singing to you," he said, "which is why I chose this song."

With that, Tony began singing "If I Can Dream." When he finished, he fell to his knees, made the symbol of the cross on his chest, and pointed upward to heaven.

He did not win, but he received a standing ovation and there was not a dry eye in the place.

Dallas often was referred to as the "buckle of the Bible Belt." It wasn't uncommon for born-again Christians to ask strangers if they had been saved. So Al and Chris were not surprised when Crystal Blackman, a seamstress who had done some tailoring for the family, telephoned one day and announced that she'd had a revelation from God about Tony.

"I need to tell Tony about a dream I had," she told Al, who'd answered the phone. He put Tony on the line but listened in. "Oh, Tony," she gushed, "I have been praying and praying for you and last night God gave me the best news. God's healed your brain. He's healed you, Tony. You don't have to take medication anymore—ever."

Tony was elated. She had sounded so convincing that even Al thought a miracle might have happened. Tony was scheduled to see his therapist that afternoon and Blackman's claim was the first thing Tony mentioned.

"Tony, I believe in miracles," Drew Bulino said, "but I am certainly not in favor of you stopping your medication."

That's wasn't what Tony wanted to hear—or believe. As Bulino listened to Tony talk, he realized that one reason Tony and his parents thought God might have healed Tony's injury was that everyone had told them Tony was a modern-day miracle. His out-of-body experience had added to the miraculous aura. Bulino knew Tony absolutely believed God had spared and chosen him for a special purpose.

Bulino gently argued with Tony, but the young patient was obsessed with the seamstress's prophecy. In the end, Bulino gave in. He didn't think for a moment that Tony was going to be able to survive without his multiple medications, but Bulino also suspected that Tony would eventually try going off his pills. If not now, later. It was inevitable. Nearly every patient tried it at some point. Bulino reasoned that having Tony stop now, when his parents could watch him, was safer than sometime later, when Al and Chris might not be around to catch him when he fell.

And he would fall.

"I really do believe God has healed me," Tony steadfastly declared. "I can feel it."

Tony stopped taking his medication and he felt fine, at first.

It took a week before he crashed. Without his pills, his emotions spun out of control. He would be happy and then sad and then angry. He would fall on the floor, kicking and screaming—as if he were a child throwing a tantrum. He would break into tears. It was as if his own brain were torturing him.

"This is not your fault," Al said, trying to soothe him. "It's the brain injury. You got to start taking your medications again."

Tony did, but the medications needed time to kick in.

One afternoon, he ran out the front door. No one knew where he'd gone.

Al called Tony's cell phone, but he didn't answer. Al kept dialing. An hour later, Tony picked up. He was on his way to Oklahoma, driving north on Interstate 35 at a hundred miles per hour.

"I'm going to kill myself," he said. "I'm going to drive into a bridge. If a cop stops me, I'm going to attack him so he'll kill me."

Al spoke quietly and calmly, just like he'd been told to do whenever Tony became upset. He tried to reason with his son. Chris got on the line, too.

"I just wish that for one day, you could be me," Tony said. "Then you would know why I don't want to live anymore."

He felt betrayed. God hadn't healed him. Why had God sent him back to earth? He hated the constant ups and downs.

Tony hung up on his parents.

Unsure what to do, Al telephoned Drew Bulino. Then Al took off in his car, driving north toward Oklahoma, to find his son before he killed himself.

Tony was surprised when he answered his phone and heard Bulino's voice. His therapist called him *Anthony*. Bulino had noticed during their sessions together that Tony reacted differently when he was called by his full name. For some unexplained reason, it made him focus.

Bulino reminded Tony of their agreement. "You promised me, Anthony, that you would not end your own life. That we'd work things out together. Do you remember that?"

"Yes," Tony said.

In a sad voice, Tony said he was tired of being sick, tired of taking medication, tired of getting angry at his parents and brother. He wanted to end it.

Bulino said new medications were being developed. Perhaps his psychiatrist could find a better cocktail of drugs for him. While there might never be a cure, because no one could fix his brain, Tony could live a meaningful life.

"Tony, you're upset, but you don't want to do this, do you? You want to get better. Think of all the work that we've done. You'll be happy. You can get better."

He asked Tony where he was on Interstate 35. Tony wasn't sure. Bulino asked him to read the next road sign that he came to and Tony said: "Someplace called Thackerville." It was a few miles across the Oklahoma line.

"Is there a bridge that goes over the interstate?" Bulino asked. There was. "I want you to take the Thackerville exit and turn left and go over that bridge and then get back on the interstate and head home," Bulino said. "Your dad is already driving north and he will meet you. Will you do this for us, Tony?"

There was a pause and then Tony said, "Okay, I'll come home."

8

Al was done with Dallas.

Five years after the WaveRunner accident, he could not think of a single reason why his family should continue living in Texas, but he could name many reasons why they should move.

Tony no longer talked about how much he hated the teenage friends who had abandoned him. But he would occasionally spot one of them at a shopping mall and come home angry. There were too many bad memories for him in Dallas.

Al was weary of managing two restaurants while taking care of his son. He was burned out and ready to try something new as a midlife career. Joey had completed high school and enrolled in Lake Forest College, outside Chicago; he was no longer around to shadow Tony.

The entire family needed a fresh start and Al knew just the place: Las Vegas. It was a city, as Joey once joked, "where Tony can walk down the street in a chicken suit and nobody will notice."

Before Al and Chris were married, Al had worked briefly in Las Vegas as a casino craps dealer. Over the years, he and Chris had frequently vacationed on the Strip. He counted several pit bosses and casino hosts as his friends.

Al and Tony moved first into an apartment in Las Vegas while Chris remained in Dallas to sell their house. One night, Al and Tony went to the Brown Derby inside the MGM Grand casino on the Strip to see Bobby Barrett, a Frank Sinatra impressionist. Barrett noticed that Tony resembled Elvis and invited him to sing a few songs. The audience loved him, so Barrett suggested that Tony sing during the two nights that Barrett was off. He was that good.

The Brown Derby hired him to perform four times a night, singing as many as fifty-two songs. Even though he had a brain injury he was able to remember the lyrics, and the exercise was good for his memory. Stars such as Tom Jones, Wayne Newton, Tony Curtis, Bill Medley,

Rodney Dangerfield, Floyd Mayweather, and Charles Barkley stopped in to see him.

After nearly a year in the Betty Boop lounge, Tony was called into the entertainment director's office and told that his act was "too successful." The lounge was in the massive MGM casino and when Tony began singing, customers were being drawn away from the endless rows of flashing slot machines into the lounge to listen. All of the MGM slot machines were monitored by a computer, and it showed that Tony's act was actually costing MGM money because of decreased slot play during his performances. The drinks that customers bought didn't make up for the quarters that were not being dropped into the machines. The casino decided to stop offering live entertainment in its lounge.

Much to his parents' surprise, Tony wasn't that upset. When Al offered to help him find a different venue on the Strip to perform in, his son shrugged.

"Dad, I really like being Elvis and I plan to sing every day, but I've achieved everything I wanted with him," Tony explained.

As it happened, Dr. Raymond Moody, the nation's most famous expert on out-of-body experiences, was at the University of Las Vegas as the chair of consciousness studies. Al and Tony enrolled in one of his classes. Dr. Moody was famous for coining the term "near-death experience" (NDE), which first appeared in his book *Life After Life*, a huge best seller. He'd interviewed more than twelve hundred people who claimed to have had NDEs.

Al and Tony met privately with Dr. Moody after class and he listened to Tony's story. He told them that it was similar to others he'd recorded. Most out-of-body experiences included feelings of peace and painlessness, a sensation of rising up and entering a tunnel at an extremely high speed, and encountering people made of bright light. Moody told Tony and Al that oftentimes NDE survivors reported talking to Jesus or God, and that this holy presence often gave them a choice about staying with Him or returning to earth. Those who returned said they did so because they didn't want their loved ones to suffer.

"That's exactly what happened to me!" Tony exclaimed. "Everything you described—it's what I saw and felt."

There was only one unusual aspect to Tony's NDE. While survivors often questioned why their lives had been spared and showed more appreciation for life after they returned, few felt they'd been sent back to serve some higher purpose that God wanted accomplished.

Tony did. But he had no clue what it was. Neither did Dr. Moody.

"If it's going to happen, it will," Al assured his son.

He just had to keep looking.

9

"You need a hobby," Nick Ponzo told Tony. "You can't feel good about yourself if you are sitting around all day with nothing to do."

Ponzo was Tony's new therapist in Las Vegas. During their twice-a-week sessions, he'd noticed his client becoming more and more restless. Ponzo wasn't surprised. Everyone in Tony's family was moving forward in life, except for him.

Chris was decorating the new house and Al had launched a company called AJ Capital Mortgage. Tony was its chairman and financier. It was an impressive title and he even had an office, but his brain injury kept him from doing any actual work. Al was the company's CEO and Joey had moved home to run daily operations. At the time, the Las Vegas real estate market was booming and AJ Capital was able to offer mortgages at lower rates than local banks. As the company's chief salesman, Joey was phenomenal. He was so persuasive that several professors at the University of Las Vegas, where he was earning a finance degree, remortgaged their houses through him. Al shepherded the deals through the loan process. Launching the company had been Al's idea. He thought it would be a great way to ensure that Tony always would have a job. Every day, Tony went to work with his father and brother. That way they could keep an eye on him. At night, they went home together.

During his therapy session with Ponzo, Tony mentioned that he enjoyed writing.

"What sort?" Ponzo asked.

"About my life—and short stories, too."

"Then start writing," Ponzo said.

Al and Chris saw Tony's interest in writing as a milestone. After the WaveRunner accident, he'd struggled to relearn grammar and composition. Taking Ponzo's advice, Tony started writing stories at the mortgage office. His descriptions of what he was feeling as a traumatic brain injury survivor were powerful. They also were the most difficult for his parents to hear.

I spend every day in a tunnel of darkness. . . . When we lived in Dallas, I used to go out in my backyard and stand there, right in the middle of a thunderstorm, just wanting and waiting for a lightning bolt to come down and take me. It seemed that the only time I would communicate with my family was when I was verbally insulting them. I don't know what it was or why I was acting like such an ungrateful animal at this time, but for some reason I loved to make my mother cry. . . .

In a story titled "Emotions," Tony wrote:

I sit here in a dither. I sweat. I scream. I want to cry. I want to rip my hair out strand-by-strand. Can I punch the wall? No, that would be stupid. I'd just break my hand. Who cares! Just do it, Anthony, it doesn't matter. It's not like you aren't already in enough pain. Ya, that's right, I am in a whole lot of pain. . . . I don't know if I can go on much longer like this. I feel it has to break sometime. I'm scared. I want to run, but as I run—it is like one giant circle. It leaves, but always comes back sooner or later. Will it End? Can't somebody just come and take it away. Why can't I buy a new brain? I'm always going to be brain injured. If you read this, can you tell me where you can buy a new brain? I will give every penny I've got for it. I'm stuck at the bottom of a well and it is filling up with water very rapidly.

Al and Chris urged Tony to share his personal writing with Ponzo. The therapist told Tony that it wasn't uncommon for people with brain injuries to be chronically depressed. It had nothing to do with how their lives were going. They could be successful or they could be failures, and it wouldn't change anything because the damage to their brain was causing them to feel sad and worthless.

Obviously, having Tony write about his feelings gave him something to do. But his writings were so bleak that Ponzo urged Tony to consider another pastime. He suggested collecting stamps or coins—some other hobby that would occupy his days.

One night while Tony was surfing the Internet in his bedroom, he stumbled upon a website that billed itself as the largest seller in the world of "murderabilia"—"true-crime" collectables.

"We do NOT glorify anyone," the website's anonymous owner declared in a long-winded statement.

We are not forcing anyone to view or purchase anything offered here. Collecting criminal artifacts is a perfectly legitimate and knowledgeable interest which for some becomes a hobby. There are collectors who seek items from such individuals as Hitler, Hussein, Osama Bin Laden, Kadafi, Arafat, Castro and other leaders who are responsible for the suppression, depravation of human rights and murders of hundreds of thousands. . . .

The owner explained that most criminals were not barred from selling their artwork or autographs despite the so-called Son of Sam laws, which prohibit criminals from financially benefiting because of their crimes. For some, the website claimed, sales of autographs were the only way for convicted murderers to afford basic toiletries.

Under the rubric "What do you have to say to the victim's families?" the website's owner wrote: "Without the media, we would have never heard of most of these infamous historical cases. We have never sought out victims' families as others would do. . . . We do not advertise this website and quite honestly if you don't like what you see, leave!"

Tony was spellbound. The website featured more than 150 items just about Charles Manson, the mastermind behind the Tate/LaBianca murders. For $2,499, you could buy ten strands of Manson's hair. A handwritten note by serial killer Ted Bundy, who confessed to thirty murders, was for sale at $1,750; a Valentine's card signed "Love Jeff," by Jeffrey Dahmer, who murdered seventeen men and boys and ate some of their body parts, was listed at $3,999. Five original oil paintings by John Wayne Gacy, who raped and killed thirty-three boys, could be bought for $2,000 to $3,000 each.

Tony searched for other similar websites. At another, you could buy serial killer playing cards; a letter by David Berkowitz, the "Son of Sam" killer; or a lithograph by James Earl Ray, convicted of assassinating civil rights leader Martin Luther King, Jr.

As Tony sat in his bedroom jumping from one "murderabilia" website to another, his interest peaked. He decided to buy a letter that Ted Bundy had reportedly written while awaiting his execution on Florida's death row. Within minutes after Tony's credit card payment was accepted, his phone rang. It was the website owner calling—despite the late hour. Was there anything else Tony was interested in buying?

The owner said that serial killers were willing to do paintings upon request, including fetishes—if Tony had any.

"You buy this stuff directly from serial killers?" Tony asked.

Dodging the question, the website owner asked if Tony wanted to buy locks of Manson's hair, one of the priciest items for sale. Tony said no.

When Tony told his parents the next morning about his purchase and the call, Chris got upset. Why had he wasted his money buying a letter written by a murderer?

"I know serial killers hurt people," Tony said, "but this letter—imagine, it was in Ted Bundy's hands. He touched it. He wrote it, just like I write my stories. Having it connects me to him."

"You shouldn't reward serial killers for murdering people," Chris lectured.

That night, however, Tony was on the Internet, searching for more information, and the more he learned, the more suspicious he became.

How could a buyer know Ted Bundy had written a document, even one that contained his signature? Bundy could have signed a blank sheet of paper, only to have someone else type a letter and claim the killer had written it.

The next morning, Tony announced: "I'm going to write to serial killers."

His mother had told him that she didn't like him paying criminals—so he was simply going to write to them. Although Chris didn't know much about serial killers, she knew a lot about Tony, especially how susceptible and obsessive he was. Chris was worried for another reason, too. She'd read an article that suggested there could be a link between some traumatic brain injuries and murders of passion caused by uncontrollable rage. Some TBI survivors had lost their ability to empathize; others couldn't control their anger. If a serial killer claimed that a TBI had turned him into a monster—well, Chris wasn't certain how her impressionable son might react. "I don't think writing to them is a good idea," Chris said. "This isn't safe. I don't want you doing it."

But Tony was adamant, and Al took his side. Al had always been curious about the criminal mind. He was tired of seeing his son getting more and more morose, going to the mortgage business every day with nothing to do, returning home with nothing to do. Besides, Al thought, what were the chances that a serial killer was actually going to reply? It would be something to keep Tony busy.

They reached a compromise. Tony could begin writing to serial kill-ers, but only if he let his parents read the letters that he sent to them and any responses that he got.

Tony knew his parents didn't think he was serious. He immediately set out to prove he was. He spent the next several days collecting names, finding mailing addresses, and studying cases. After more than a week, he'd compiled a list of twenty-nine serial killers to write to. For a TBI survivor, who didn't even have the ability to think far enough in advance to pack his own suitcase, Tony had done a remarkable job.

Despite the subject matter, Chris and Al were impressed.

"I'm not going to ask them right off about their murders," Tony an-nounced, "because that's what everyone who writes them does. I'm going to write to them and tell them that I am a very interesting guy who has been through a lot of very interesting things in my short lifetime. I'm going to tell them that I live in Las Vegas and if they want a pen pal who wants to become their friend and not someone who just wants to get their autograph or hear details about their murders, then I'm that person because I really want to get to know them as people, not serial killers, but as people."

In his painstakingly crafted introductory letter, Tony told his story about the accident and his uncontrollable rages. He described his out-of-body experience and how God had spared his life, allowing him to return to earth to be with his family. He was writing to serial killers be-cause he was an outcast from society—just as they were. He didn't fit in. He wasn't your normal, boring guy who went to work each day.

"I will never judge you," he wrote. "I'm looking for a friend and I think you could be that person, not because you are a serial killer, but because you are an interesting person."

That afternoon Tony mailed twenty-nine letters.

Chris was nervous. "If this makes Tony happy and gives him some-thing to do, good," Al said. "But there's not much chance it's going any-where."

EXCERPTS FROM THE KILLERS' LETTERS

Dear tony,
        . . . my first kill, it was in the early 1970s, in the state of Ohio,

town of Hamilton. my dad was a drunk and his job was to clean the united way building on 3rd street, but it was us kids who did the work. he would leave us to sweep, mop and dust, while he walked a half block to a corner bar. on many nights he would drink until 11 p.m. and bring a woman back to the building. i would be sitting there while he and her went into the bacement . . .

it was a Friday and my mom called a dozen times but i always lied and said he was outside working. well, this night, a woman named marry with blondish hair came up from the Bacement to use the Bathroom . . . i was sitting in a big room playing with a deck of cards as she walked through. she was drunk and mean, and when i didn't speak to her, she called me a Bastard and more, she walked over and just look at me. i said my mom would Kick your ass, she smacked me on the head and laughed, and headed Back to the Bacement.

from where i was sitting she walk away down a long hallway . . . at the end of it was the Bacement door, it was a long stairway down, i watched as she walked to that door, my face turned hot, my emotions were Blowing up in my mind, my hole body was shacking. i Jumped up and ran at her and yelled Bitch, she turned around Just as she got to the Basement door i ran into her hard and Knocked her down the steps. she went down them on her head. i heard my dad yell, he looked up the steps at me and said what's the hell's wrong with you, you no good for nothing son of a Bitch. I didn't say anything i ran into another room and hid. my dad always controlled us with fear, and never talked to us, so i was scared to death.

a wile later he called my name, after of course yelling out all seven Kids names, he never could get our names right. i want to the stairway and looked down, she was still laying there, i could only see her feet. dad looked up and said get down here Boy. i walked down the old wooden steps. he said Boy, you make a mess anywhere you go, and handed me a Roofing hook Kneif, and said you got to Kill her now no one can no anything about tonight. i looked down she wasn't awake, she mite have already been dead i don't know. he said stab her here and pointed at her chest. i knew better than not to do what he said, i was scared. I didnt do anything for a minute, then he yelled now real loud. i closed my eyes and stabbed her. But the knife didn't go in far, he said, again again again, again untill I felt warm Blood on my hands and the smell of Blood like nothing I ever smelled befor. a drop got in my mouth i could taste the Blood. it dried on my face and the smell stayed for days.

my dad want to the corner of the Basement got a Big Tent Bag, the united way used for there Big outside tents they set up. he made me help him put her in the Bag and tie it tight and drag the Bag up the stairs and out to the car, a 88 oldsmobile, green, we put her in the trunk. . . .

i never talked to dad about that night. a few years later in 1978 dad was found at the Bottom of those same Basement steps. he had a heart attack and was in a coma for over a year . . . he never remember anyone . . .

as far as i no, the woman still remains off old highway 25 in Kentucky in a Big united way tent Bag. I was only ten or so when this happened But it was beginning of a long horror filled teenage life. For 25 years, after it effected every aspect of my life . . .

NOT 2 months after this event, i was arrested for atempted murder, placed in OYC, this repeated its self over and over after 7 institutions and over 200 felony charges as a Juvinile. That's all a hole other storie.

This is a true storie written by glen Rogers on 2/13/09

—serial killer Glen Rogers, aka the Cross-Country Killer

PART TWO

the serial killers

We serial killers are your sons, we are your husbands, we are everywhere. And there will be more of your children dead tomorrow.

—serial killer Ted Bundy

Since the psychopath has no real emotions, they develop their own personality throughout their life by mimicking those around them.

—Charles Montaldo, private detective, writer

10

Tony's traumatic brain injury caused him to become easily obsessed, and the world of the serial killers put an endless buffet before him. Having mailed his letters, he began doing research and was immediately overwhelmed.

Where to begin? Most historians looked to ancient Rome and Caligula, the self-absorbed Roman emperor from 37 to 41, in their search to find the first serial killer. While overseeing games, Caligula ordered his guards to throw an entire section of the crowd into the arena during intermission to be eaten by animals because there were no criminals available and he was bored.

The Middle Ages produced Gilles de Rais, a French nobleman who lured children, mainly young boys, to his residences, where he raped, tortured, and mutilated them. Dozens of his victims—and there were thought to be between eighty and two hundred of them—had their severed heads stuck on poles so that de Rais could judge which was the most fair. Vlad the Impaler, the inspiration for Dracula, surfaced during the same era.

However, Jack the Ripper, who cut the throats of at least five London prostitutes in 1888 before removing abdominal organs in three of them, typically is viewed as the world's first serial killer.

In America, the honor goes to Herman Webster Mudgett, better known under the alias of Dr. Henry Howard Holmes. He committed his murders inside the "Castle," a hotel that he built in Chicago ten miles from the site of the 1893 World's Fair. Holmes designed the three-story, block-long building to deceive guests into believing they were entering guest rooms. What they actually encountered was a maze with over one hundred windowless rooms, doorways opening to brick walls, oddly angled hallways, stairways to nowhere, and a secret chute that enabled him to drop his victims' bodies into the basement. There, he placed the corpses in lime pits or used acid to strip them clean so that he could sell the skeletons to medical schools. He was convicted of murdering twenty-seven, but authorities speculated that Holmes actually could have killed as many as two hundred. The true number remains unknown because he was known to have lured dozens of unsuspecting strangers from the fair to his hotel never to be seen again.

The Roaring Twenties produced Carl Panzram, who admitted killing twenty-two victims, nearly all men. He raped them, not because he was a homosexual, he told detectives, but because he wanted to humiliate and dominate his victims. During the Depression, it was the cannibalistic pedophile Albert Fish who shocked the nation. Convicted of three murders and suspected of two others, Fish bragged that he had molested one hundred children. In addition to torturing his victims, Fish told the police that he cut off a boy's ears, nose, and other body parts and added them to a stew.

William Heirens became notorious in 1946 when he left a plea scrawled in lipstick on the bedroom wall of one of his three victims: "For heavens sake catch me before I kill more. I cannot control myself."

The end of World War II saw an increase in serial murders, including one of the most infamous cases. What was ironic about the serial killer Ed Gein was that he technically was not one. Gein was convicted in the 1950s of a single murder and was suspected of only one more. He also was insane. But after authorities learned that he had exhumed corpses from local graveyards and fashioned trophies and keepsakes from their bones and skins, he became Hollywood's serial killer stereotype. It was Gein who inspired Norman Bates in *Psycho,* Leatherface in *The Texas Chainsaw Massacre,* and Buffalo Bill in *The Silence of the Lambs.*

In the 1960s and 1970s, so many serial killers surfaced that the FBI decided to recognize them as a separate criminal category. Albert De-Salvo, aka the Boston Strangler, nurse-killing Richard Speck, cult leader Charles Manson, and the never identified "Zodiac" made headlines. The 1970s ushered in Berkowitz, Bundy, and Gacy—so well-known that they could be identified by only their last names.

There were so many murderers committing horrific acts that the FBI began to differentiate between them. FBI criminologist and former army criminal investigator Colonel Robert K. Ressler coined the term "serial killer" to separate them from "spree killers" and "mass murderers." As defined by the FBI, a serial killer murders two or more victims at separate times.

Between 1906 and 1959, the nation averaged 1.7 serial killer cases every year. That number jumped to 5 per year in the 1960s, and by the 1980s it had risen to 15. By 1990, there were 36 new serial killers identified each year, an average of three a month.

Among them was Jeffrey Dahmer, whose actions seemed to combine the worst horrors of his predecessors—rape, torture, dismemberment, cannibalism, and necrophilia. Before the start of the new century, the police arrested Aileen Wuornos, who was incorrectly portrayed in the national media as the nation's first female serial killer. She was convicted of killing six men in Florida—men who she claimed had either raped or tried to assault her while she was working as a prostitute. It was an ironic twist since prostitutes had been the serial killers' primary prey for decades.

The most recent figures from law enforcement estimate there are at least 50 serial killers on the prowl at any given time in the United States. Some claim the number could be as high as 200. The FBI has estimated that serial murders could claim an average of 11 lives a day in the United States during the twenty-first century.

Eleven lives per day.

A landmark 1993 study found there is an 88 percent chance that a serial killer will be a male, an 85 percent chance that he will be Caucasian, and a 71 percent chance that he will operate in a specific area and not travel across the country. The average age when they first kill is 28.5 years. Their victims are mostly complete strangers (62 percent). Most serial murderers are thought to follow a pattern when they murder, at least initially, such as targeting only prostitutes or young girls. Some develop particular rituals. Many collect souvenirs to remind them of their crimes.

While serial killers have been routinely portrayed as being insane, few actually meet the diagnostic criteria used by psychiatrists to diagnose someone with schizophrenia or bipolar disorder, the most common mental disorders. Most are calculating and do not show signs of disorganized thinking.

For years, serial killers were referred to as psychopaths or sociopaths, but those terms were ruled too vague. Now serial killers carry a diagnosis of "antisocial personality disorder." The *Diagnostic and Statistical Manual of Mental Disorders* (DSM), the bible of the psychiatric profession, defines antisocial personality disorder as "a pervasive pattern of disregard for, and violation of, the rights of others that begins in child-hood or early adolescence and continues into adulthood."

Its symptoms include:

a failure to conform to social norms with respect to lawful behavior; deceitfulness, as indicated by repeatedly lying, especially for personal profit or pleasure; impulsivity, or failure to consider consequences; irrita-bility or aggressiveness, as shown for repeated physical fights or assaults; reckless disregard for safety or self or others; consistent irresponsibility; a lack of remorse, as indicated by being indifferent to or rationalizing having harmed, mistreated, or stolen from someone else.

Serial killers show no feelings for their victims. They show no re-morse. They are typically extremely manipulative, superficially charm-ing, and completely narcissistic. Many are sexual deviants.

Studies have found only three childhood commonalities in serial kill-ers, and these apply to only a slight number of them. They include a his-tory of bedwetting beyond what is generally accepted as normal, animal mutilation during childhood, and a fascination with starting fires.

So what does the serial killer as a trope say about American society?

Each year "normal people" buy artwork, hair and nail samples, bones, and all manner of murderabilia. As a society, we are obsessed with shows like *Forensic Files, CSI, Dominic Dunne's Power, Privilege and Justice*, and *48 Hours Mystery*. The Internet Movie Database listed 3,403 movies and television episodes that featured such killers. It included Alfred Hitch-cock's classic *Psycho* and Showtime's antihero *Dexter*—the list and differ-ent personas seemed endless: *Se7en, American Psycho, Zodiac, Perfume: The Story of a Murderer, The Silence of the Lambs*. Serial killers were the butt of jokes in *Scary Movie. Family Guy* satirized them. True-crime writers memorialized them. They horrified and repulsed us, yet like a car accident that you pass by while driving, it is impossible to look away.

Some sociologists argue that suburban sprawl and a lack of interper-sonal community connectiveness coincide with the rise in serial mur-ders. But Robert Simon, a nationally known forensic psychiatrist who has studied criminal behavior for decades, believes it is the "Dr. Jekyll and Mr. Hyde" nature of serial murderers that fascinates us.

"Most serial killers appear outwardly quite ordinary, like your neighbor or mine, living normal, everyday lives in which, just as we do, they fill the car with gasoline, hold down a job, and pay taxes," Simon explained in a professional article. "From behind this veneer of ordinariness their Mr. Hyde personality, representative of the darkest aspect of humanity, jumps out to torture and kill victims—and to transfix us."

Continuing, Simon asked, "How is it possible for someone who appears to be the guy next door to commit multiple horrific murders? People have always been gripped by the dark side of human behavior, especially when it is cloaked in the light of normalcy. Serial killers are at the far end of the spectrum for human cruelty. Our minds follow an inescapable syllogism: 'I am human. Serial killers are human. Am I, like them, capable of monstrous deeds?' Most people, having posed this question to themselves, conclude that the answer is 'No, I am not even capable of thinking about such evil.'"

Tony Ciaglia had no preconceived thoughts about what made serial killers modern-day monsters. He was simply a naive young man struggling with a traumatic brain injury who was bored, lonely, curious, and looking for a friend.

Nor did he sense, when he mailed his first batch of letters, that he was about to begin a journey that would eventually cause him to question his own sanity and to ask himself the very question that Simon had posed: "Am I, like them, capable of monstrous deeds?"

11

Tony checked the Murder Box at the Mail Boxes Etc. store on Rainbow Avenue every day, eagerly anticipating a reply to his mass mailing. The day that he found a single letter waiting, he rushed home and exclaimed: "I got one!"

Al and Chris gathered in the dining room as Tony carefully sliced open the envelope with a kitchen knife, making certain he did minimal damage.

> *Dear Anthony,*
>
> *Let's not get so formal. Just call me ART or ARTHUR if you will. Mr. ARTHUR SHAWCROSS was my father. I read your story and I have to say that you did well on a comeback. . . .*

Al instantly recognized the letter writer. "That's the Genesee River Killer! Arthur Shawcross! He's one of the most notorious serial killers alive."

With a huge grin, Tony continued.

> *Anthony, I had a fucked-up childhood! INCEST IN THE FAMILY! Between myself and my mom. Started at age four that I can recall. Then at age 7 & 9. Oral sex. At age 14, she took my youth! I was hooked. I did it with my sisters, cousins and all the girls within three miles of our place . . . Plus back when I was nine I did it with a woman I called Aunt Tina. But she turned out to be my mom's best friend. I never knew.*

Tony was elated. Shawcross was already sharing intimate details of his life. The murderer wrote that his mother's relatives had come to America from Greece. His father's were from England.

What's that make me? A Good Cook! Ha. Ha. But somewhere in my genes is a bad seed.

Tony had described his traumatic brain injury in his initial letter and asked the serial killers if they had moments of uncontrollable rage—as he did.

Anthony, rage did not enter into the picture. My murders were calculated. . . . I was killing for a purpose.

Tony knew Shawcross had confessed to murdering eleven women in Rochester, New York. He'd killed them because he was trying to rid the city of a hooker who had HIV—the AIDS virus—and was deliberately spreading it. At least that is what he claimed to the police. They'd called his explanation a laughable attempt at justification. But their skepticism hadn't kept Shawcross from peddling the same yarn to Tony.

If I'd found her and finished her first, the murders would have stopped.

Shawcross jumped from one thought to another in his four-page note: "I am cooking chicken and rice soup tonight, Anthony. Good Flavor. I put the rice, gravy, and chicken patty together and then, I . . ." After describing his recipe, Shawcross asked: "What happened to the boy who drove that WaveRunner that hit you?" Then he changed thoughts again: "I'll be 62 on June 6th. Wish a few women would come visit me dressed to kill. Ha Ha. . . . Yeah, pussy is great, but pussy killed me! Many men say they've licked pussy, but I'm the only one who has actually eaten it!" That last line was a reference to cannibalism, which Shawcross had claimed to have done to several victims, eating pieces of their vaginas. "You can ask me anything, Anthony. I'm happy to tell you what I did."

In the letter's final paragraph, Shawcross offered Tony a business proposition. The murderer explained that he received letters nearly every day from people wanting his autograph. One writer had even sent him a dollar bill to sign.

I came across one of David Berkowitz's order forms [in the prison commissary] and it contains his signature. Did you know

the "Son of Sam" now calls himself, "the Son of Hope." Yah, sure.
But his signature is an item you can sell. Not many have his ac-
tual signature and we could split some good money for it if you
put it on the Internet.

Al was happy that Shawcross had written, but he didn't like the idea
of having Tony sell murderabilia on the Internet. "I warned you these
guys would try to use you," he told Tony.

"Don't worry," Tony answered. "I just got to show him that I want to
be his friend and I'm not interested in selling stuff."

Tony disappeared into his bedroom to draft a reply.

> Dear Arthur,
>   . . . I will never sell anything you write to me or anything you send
> me . . . I'm so sorry Arthur about your childhood. I couldn't even imag-
> ine what affects incest would have on a youth. Do you talk to your sisters
> or for that matter does anyone in your family come and visit you? Be-
> cause I want to be your friend and I could come visit you . . .
>   Arthur, when you look back on what transpired in your life, do you
> have any feelings or thoughts about those girls in anyway whatsoever?
> The reason I ask is because I know a lot about serial killers, but it's only
> through the books and research I've done. The books say your feel-
> ings aren't there and that you don't choose not to feel anything—you
> just can't feel anything. No guilt, no remorse, just nothing because you
> can't . . . Are you empty like these books say?

Tony was so hyped up that night that he couldn't sleep, so he pored
over stories about Shawcross, eager to learn everything he could. There
was plenty to read.

While in his twenties, Shawcross killed two children in his hometown of
Watertown, an upstate New York city by the eastern end of Lake Ontario.
Ten-year-old Jack Blake disappeared in May 1972 and four months later
the nude body of eight-year-old Karen Ann Hill was found. She had been
raped and strangled. The evidence against Shawcross was circumstantial.
No one had seen him commit the actual crimes and no one knew where
Blake's body was hidden. The local prosecutor offered Shawcross a plea

deal. If he led police to Blake's body, he would be charged only with manslaughter in the Karen Ann Hill murder and there would be no criminal charges filed against him for killing Blake. Shawcross agreed and led the police to the boy's corpse. It was too decayed to tell if the youth had been sexually molested, but police speculated that Blake had been raped, because he was found naked. Like Karen Hill, Blake had been strangled.

A judge gave Shawcross an indeterminate sentence, which was common at the time in New York. Shawcross could be kept behind bars for up to twenty-five years but officials also could have freed him in as little as ten months. Watertown residents were so furious about the plea bargain that the local prosecutor did not seek reelection. Shawcross spent fourteen years and six months in prison. He was forty-one years old when he was paroled in April 1987. He was released under strict supervision to live in Binghamton, about 150 miles south of Watertown.

His stay in Binghamton, however, didn't last. Someone tipped off a local television station and the pedophile and double murderer was forced to flee on the same night that his mug shot was broadcast. State parole officials next hid him in a smaller town, but he was discovered and driven from there, too. In late June 1987, Shawcross silently slipped into New York's third-largest city, Rochester. Parole officers figured he could disappear into its population, which was then 250,000.

Shawcross arrived with a companion. In prison, he'd divorced his third wife and developed a pen pal love affair with a nurse named Rose Marie Walley. She moved with him into an apartment house two blocks from one of the city's busiest thoroughfares. Within a month, Shawcross had taken on another lover, Clara Neal, the mother of ten grown children, who lived nearby.

Less than one year after Shawcross was released from prison, Dorothy "Dotsie" Blackburn, a Rochester prostitute with a cocaine addiction, disappeared. The mother of three had last been seen on a Lyell Avenue corner, where prostitutes hawked their wares. Nine days later, on March 24, 1988, a deer hunter spotted what he thought was a discarded store mannequin floating in Salmon Creek. It was Blackburn.

Salmon Creek flowed into the Genesee River Gorge, a twenty-two-mile scenic waterway that often was touted as the "Grand Canyon of the East." It would become Shawcross's favorite dumping ground.

Because Blackburn was a known drug abuser, her death didn't cause much concern. But a year later, other corpses started surfacing along the river. Shawcross became the chief suspect after a police surveillance helicopter spotted him standing near a bridge close to where the body of a twelfth victim had been dumped. Investigators suspected he'd come to watch the police recover the body.

After his arrest, Shawcross confessed to committing eleven murders during a twenty-two-month spree. Police suspected that he'd killed a twelfth time, but they didn't have enough to charge him. He was sentenced to life in prison without the possibility of release.

Tony had landed a very big fish, but he was not the first pen pal to approach Arthur Shawcross. Tony read on the Internet that Shawcross was the "most studied serial killer in American history." More than thirty forensic psychiatrists had interviewed him. Yet none of these experts had been able to agree about what made Shawcross kill.

Could Tony?

The idea was so exhilarating that Tony didn't sleep a wink that night. The private mailbox he rented would have the next day's letters posted by 2 p.m.

Tony couldn't wait to see who would be next to respond.

EXCERPTS FROM LETTERS BETWEEN ARTHUR SHAWCROSS AND TONY

Dear Anthony,

Oh, I do have feelings and emotions. Watching TV, I shed a tear on tragic spots of personal loss of someone. If not feelings, what is it? . . . I may have felt no guilt or remorse at the murders, but this was because I am a different personality from most. Strange feelings I had Anthony, but feelings. How to describe them? I only know they are there . . .

You asked about my family . . . I've not spoken to my sisters or brother since 1972. I am dead to them all! Mom is dead and so is Dad . . . my only friend is a woman who lives in Rochester who has stuck with me for more than twenty years. Blonde on top, shaved on bottom! I watched her do it! Ha. Ha . . .

Dear Arthur,

What is prison like? People always joke around saying if you go to prison don't drop the soap . . .

Dear Anthony,

I have never been anyone's bitch. I've had fights in here. Five of them and did not lose a one. One black man hit me with a wooden stool from behind. I turned around and he was looking at what was left of that stool. I snatched him by the neck with my left hand and lifted him and held him there as he kicked his life away. It took a guard to place his baton across my throat and whisper in my left ear "Let him down Art." I had blood all down my back from the head. That black dude could not talk for a few days. The guy was given a new charge by the state, but I refused to testify. Back at my cell, I had guys come and give me coffee and I took it. Even prison has its moments. Guards anywhere will try to get under your skin. With me, it's Mr. Shawcross. Respect and Fear. . . . Some guys look at me with fright in their eyes. It's good to keep those around you on edge. Without respect in prison, you are nothing. . . .

Check this out Anthony. Ever fuck a girl and she asked you to throttle her in the process? Strangle her? I did that to one and she flooded. I had to use CPR to bring her back four times in one session. After a while, I think she got off that way—until I didn't bring her back. Ha. Ha. Can you send me a photo of a showgirl, blonde maybe?

Dear Arthur,

One thing I like about you Arthur is you'd be the first to admit you're evil and you could be my best friend or my worst enemy . . .

Dear Anthony,

During my trial, I had three blondes in that courtroom flirting with me. They sat three rows back and I knew they wanted me to fuck each of them and I would have. I had sixteen letters to write today. I got a request for some of my hair from a woman. She wanted groin hair and she got it too, but none with any follicles. That way no witch can set me up with DNA. I may be dumb but not that way. This one girl who writes, man, is she something. She wrote and told me what she wanted me to do to her—and with her. If only I could. Want to laugh? Her boyfriend watches her get fucked by other men. Crazy as that may sound, she also

watches him fuck other women and joins in . . . and now she
wants a serial killer to fuck her! That's sick.

I have to be careful, Anthony. Sometimes I get a letter from
some bitch and it turns out to be some asshole just trying to get
me to write a letter so he can sell it on the Internet. That's why
I don't sign them. Only my letters to you get signed. I type them
and don't sign them to all others. When I first came in, a guy sent
me cards to sign, then he typed notes on them and sold them like
those were my words. It was fraud. . . .

You have to be careful always. When someone in here comes
up to me and starts talking about my case, I just tell them, "Tell
me your story and then I will speak of mine and not before."
When they start lying to me, I just tell them to fuck off. . . . One
thing nobody should do in prison is brag about who or whom he
or she has killed. That just leads to a lot of bullshit with people
around you. I get asked: "How many people did you actually
kill?" I say, "All of them" and let it go at that.

Dear Arthur,

It's cool being from a family who sits down at the dinner table and
discusses letters that a serial murderer has sent me in the mail. You'd
like my family, Art. They are wonderful people . . .

Dear Anthony,

You and your family should discuss me at breakfast when you
eat your cereal—being that I have a stigma of being a serial killer.
Ha. Ha. If you are curious, I do eat an assortment of cereals . . .

Dear Arthur,

. . . Why did you kill two children? That doesn't seem to be your
thing. . . .

Dear Anthony,

Don't ever ask me about those kids again . . . I will never talk to
you about them. . . .

Dear Arthur,

I seemed to have touched a nerve . . . You can't get upset at me because how am I supposed to know what will offend you and what won't if I don't ask? Also, in one of your early letters to me, you told me that I could ask you anything and you wouldn't get upset . . .

It's not like here on the outside everyday you run into a cold-blooded killer and can talk freely with him about this kind of stuff . . . Who would have thought you could offend a serial killer?

Dear Anthony,

I was a wee bit upset with you. It's just certain subjects are very hard to speak of and on. I will answer your questions Anthony, even when it touches a nerve. Just bear with me . . .

When it comes to murder, a conscience can be blocked, Anthony. I can do something and place that something upon a shelf and close the door for a later look-see. I started doing this back when I was a small child! Compartmentalization.

I would be willing to bet that you have rubbed shoulders with someone who has killed before. Can you honestly say that you will never kill someone no matter what they ever did to you personally? Something to really think about Anthony.

My violent past history is exactly that. Tell me, Anthony, are you the same person you were twenty years ago? Think before answering that . . . But why cry about something someone did? It does no good except run a person to get medication because he can't sleep. Anthony, I see men do just that, get on meds to be able to sleep. Guilt kills them. I have seen other guys always washing their hands and that is a sign of washing the blood off. Ha. Ha.

Shit, I just drink it.

I agree, Anthony, I am one evil SOB and I am YOUR best friend.

Dear Arthur,

I have read about this one girl you took down named June Cicero. The article quoted a Rochester cop and he said he went up to a prostitute that everyone knew and who also looked out for all the other girls, he said, "June, don't you know why the heat is so heavy on the streets? You should go home tonight because it's just not safe out here right now." June answered back to the cop that she understood that someone was killing prostitutes, but she'd rather stay on the street. Not thirty minutes later, she hoped in the car with the wrong guy—you—and that ended up being the last car she ever would get into alive . . . Tell me about her, please.

Dear Anthony,

The prostitute by the name of June Cicero or something like that was about thirty years of age and blond. Blond on top that is and brown down yonder. She was reputed to be the toughest broad on the street and the smartest too . . . but to me, she was the easiest one of all . . .

I remember every one of them, Anthony. And yes, I know every detail also with each one. Why did I use my bare hands? To feel life slipping away and then release your grip and bring them back. Ah, that is a feeling, Anthony, that is a feeling. So powerful, so real.

I will say this Anthony, staring at someone who is about to die is amazing because everything around you becomes calm and peaceful.

You have chosen to call me a serial killer who murdered for sexual thrills and I might be a sociopath. I was always a loner and that counts for most of the serial killers or so I am informed. I did not hang out in bars and socialize with booze of any kind. That made me stand out in society. So be it. I accept that I am different.

But I am more than a mere sociopath. The FBI informed me I am 47XYY human male. That means I have an extra Y chromosome. Some doctors believe that men like me with extra Y chromosomes have extraordinary strength and are genetically born to be killers. . . . A 47XYY is considered a predominate, super male, Anthony. Does that mean I am part of our past or our future? Does that mean God made me to murder? Think about that Anthony. Did God create me to murder?

Anthony, I have a reporter from the New York Post who asked if he could write an article about me looking for a new woman in my life. It was his idea but he wants to make it look like I am advertising. What a liar. But it's okay. I told him I prefer blondes, redheads and platinum blondes, but will answer all letters from whomever sends them. I get requests from the media every week in here and they all say the same thing—the reporters want to talk to me. They want to make me famous. Ha. I am already. Why else would they speak to me? I ask them to help my daughter by sending her a few bucks because if they pay me directly, the state takes it. Son of Sam. If they refuse to pay, I say fuck'em. Unless it's a woman and then I ask for a photograph and I may speak to her depending on her looks.

A Canadian reporter corresponded with me and I knew she liked me. When she was doing an interview, she had to use the bathroom and I told her to bring me back a sample on her fingers to smell. She just smiled. I have always had a way with women. It is the 47XYY. They are attracted to the super male. It is nature at its rawest.

Dear Anthony,

. . . Here is the clipping that asshole wrote about me in the New York Post. . . . Of course this reporter made up most of this, but that is how the media does. I just hope I get lots of letters . . . All publicity is good publicity—right?

CANNIBAL SEEKING WOMEN
By Jamie Schram

New York's real-life Hannibal Lecter is hungry for love, actively looking for a sweetheart who will meet his smorgasbord of requirements, the Post has learned. Cannibal killer Arthur Shawcross—who was sentenced in 1991 to life in prison for strangling 11 Rochester-area prostitutes and eating some of their body parts—says he wants a new bride. . . .

"I do prefer blonds, redheads and platinum women over the rest, but will accept someone from any race who might be smart, have a good job and is not destitute," Shawcross, 61, told the Post during an interview . . .

Shawcross said his "lady love" should be between 24 and 100 years old, live within 150 miles of the prison, and own a car so she can visit. "I want hugs and kisses, touchy-feely," says Shawcross, who expects his flame to embrace conjugal visits in a trailer at the prison.

12

Tony hadn't been as happy as he was now since before the WaveRunner accident. Of the twenty-nine letters that he initially mailed, he'd received responses from twenty serial killers. Al and Chris were shocked. Nearly all of the killers mentioned how they had been touched by Tony's story about his brain injury. Since sending out his first batch of letters, he'd written to another dozen serial killers. Within days, ten of them responded. Within a few months, he was corresponding regularly with a virtual who's who of murderers. He kept an alphabetized list on his computer. It included:

John Eric Armstrong, aka the Psycho Sailor, believed to be the most-traveled serial killer in recent times. A former U.S. Navy sailor, Armstrong was so mild-mannered that he was nicknamed "Opie" by his shipmates. Yet he confessed to slaughtering at least twelve hookers between 1993 and 1998 in foreign ports. He was convicted of killing four Detroit prostitutes.

Kenneth Bianchi, and with his cousin, **Angelo Buono,** were known as the Hillside Stranglers. During a two-month spree in 1977, the two men kidnapped, raped, tortured, and killed eleven women in California. From there, Bianchi moved to Bellingham, Washington, where he murdered twice more before being arrested. In return for testifying against Buono, Bianchi was spared the death penalty.

Ian Brady, aka the Moors Murderer, an English killer who, with help from his girlfriend, sexually abused and murdered young children.

Harvey Carignan, the subject of a best-selling book by true-crime writer Ann Rule, was suspected of being a prolific serial killer although he admitted only two murders.

Richard Norbert Clarey was convicted of three murders in Michigan but confessed to as many as a hundred killings dating back to when he was only fifteen years old and lived in Germany.

Douglas Daniel Clark was accused of murdering five women with his partner **Carol Bundy.** They were dubbed the Sunset Strip Killers.

Hadden Clark admitted two murders in Maryland, including the killing of a six-year-old girl.

Cynthia Coffman, along with **James Gregory Marlow,** was accused of murdering two women during a 1986 cross-country rampage. She was the first woman to get a death sentence in California after that penalty was reinstated.

Richard Allen Davis was convicted of kidnapping, molesting, and killing Polly Klaas, a twelve-year-old girl abducted from her Petaluma, California, home. Californians were so outraged by the contempt that Davis showed his victims' family during his trial that voters passed a "three strikes law" intended to lock up repeat offenders for life.

Harrison Graham, a mentally retarded drug abuser, was convicted of killing seven women and sexually abusing their corpses in Philadelphia. Police found several body parts scattered around his house.

Waldo Grant admitted murdering four men between 1973 and 1976 in Manhattan, including one victim whose body was sawed into three pieces, wrapped in plastic bags, and left in a shopping basket in Central Park.

Elmer Wayne Henley was an accomplice in the Houston Candy Man Murders, one of the most horrific cases in Texas history. Beginning at age fourteen, Henley took young boys to a house owned by Dean Arnold Corll, a sexual sadist, where they were raped, mutilated, and murdered. From 1970 to 1973, Corll killed twenty-seven boys, ages thirteen to twenty. He was fatally shot by Henley after the serial killer tried to victimize him.

Patrick Wayne Kearney, aka the Trash Bag Killer, admitted thirty-five murders in California, mostly of young men.

Randy Kraft, aka the Scorecard Killer, was convicted of fifteen murders but suspected of being responsible for as many as fifty-two more. He picked up boys and young men in the 1970s who were hitchhiking or frequented gay bars. Kraft kept a coded list of sixty-one cryptic references to sixty-five of his victims, most of whom were rendered helpless with drugs before he tortured, sexually abused, and murdered them.

Gregory Miley was an accomplice of California serial killer William Bonin, aka the Freeway Killer. He admitted helping kill two boys. Bonin was convicted of sexually molesting, torturing, and murdering fourteen and was suspected of killing as many as twenty more.

Roy L. Norris was convicted of kidnapping, torturing, raping, and murdering five teenage girls during a five-month period with Lawrence Bittaker. Together they hunted for women on the Pacific Coast Highway and in Los Angeles neighborhoods in a 1977 GMC van nicknamed "Murder Mack" because it had no side windows.

Clifford Olson, a Canadian serial killer, murdered two children and nine teens.

Dorothea Puente stole Social Security checks from boarders in an old-age home that she ran in Sacramento, California, in the

THE SERIAL KILLER WHISPERER

1980s. Those who complained about their missing checks were killed. Police charged her with nine homicides, including seven whose corpses were found buried in her front yard.

Richard Ramirez, aka the Night Stalker, was convicted of thirteen murders, five attempted murders, eleven assaults, and numerous burglaries in Los Angeles.

Glen Rogers, aka the Casanova Killer or the Cross-Country Killer, murdered four women in four different states. Using his good looks, he approached women in bars, had sex with them in their apartments, and then strangled them or beat them to death. After he was captured, he bragged to detectives that he'd killed seventy women.

Jim Ruzicka, a sexual deviant, raped and killed two teenage girls after abducting them from their homes at night. One victim was found hanging from a tree. He was arrested after he raped a thirteen-year-old girl. "I asked her if she wanted to ball and she didn't say 'no,' so I figured she wouldn't mind," he told police.

Pamela Smart was a twenty-three-year-old schoolteacher's aide in New Hampshire in 1990 when she recruited her lover, fifteen-year-old student William Flynn, and three of his friends to kill her twenty-four-year-old husband. Although she was not a serial killer, Tony found her interesting.

Susan Smith was convicted in July 1995 of a double murder after she strapped her three-year-old-son, Michael, and his fourteen-month-old brother, Alexander, into their car seats and then drove the car into a South Carolina lake, where they drowned. Like Pamela Smart, Smith was not technically a serial killer.

Bill L. Suff, aka the Riverside Prostitute Killer, strangled twenty-two prostitutes during a sex-murder rampage that began when he was paroled in 1984 in Texas, where he'd served ten years for beating his baby daughter to death.

Tony wrote each killer personalized letters and he always included stories in them about his family and how he spent his days. If a killer showed an interest in sports, Tony talked football. If a murderer was interested in Las Vegas nightlife, Tony described the Strip. He thoroughly researched each killer's crimes and trials so that he could discuss the smallest details with them. In some cases, he contacted their families, including their parents and children.

Within a few months after he'd mailed off his first batch of letters, Tony's entire life revolved around serial killers.

And he was beginning to refer to several of them as "best friends."

13

It was important for Tony to keep a daily routine. On an average day, he would sleep until mid-morning and then troll the Internet for news about serial killers, scouting for new murderers to write to. He'd go to lunch and then hurry to his private mailbox to retrieve that day's letters. When he got home, he would take a nap and then wait for Al to get off work. Usually, Al would read the letters aloud and then Tony would retreat to his bedroom to formulate his responses. Sometimes he would go to bed again and wake up later that same night. He would work into the morning painstakingly drafting his replies.

Because he didn't do well with change, Tony went to the Yassou Greek Grill and ordered exactly the same gyro for lunch each day. His dad joked that Tony was like Elvis Presley because the King used to be obsessed with fried peanut butter and banana sandwiches.

The Greek grill's owners, Peter Papas and his son, Christian, were neighbors of the Ciaglias and Christian was the same age as Tony. They became friends. One afternoon, Tony spotted a new face working behind the counter. She was a knockout with smooth olive skin, long black hair, and a pretty smile.

"You've got the most beautiful brown eyes I've ever seen," Tony told her.

Nineteen-year-old Crystal Torres didn't enjoy being the center of attention, nor did she like having men, especially someone nine years older, flirting with her. She was shy. She'd also been warned about Tony. When the senior Papas hired her to work part-time at the grill between her classes at a community college, the younger Papas had cautioned her about Tony.

"A friend of mine comes in here nearly every day," Christian said. "He's a great guy but you shouldn't get too friendly with him."

When she asked why, Christian said that Tony was handsome and outgoing, but also volatile. It wasn't hard for him to meet girls. But he never was able to keep one. If Crystal got involved with Tony, he'd break her heart.

With that warning fresh in her mind, Crystal was prepared when Tony approached the counter and complimented her. She thanked him but cut the conversation short. She'd grown up in Southern California in a home she described as dysfunctional. For the most part, she'd been on her own since age fifteen and could handle herself. She wasn't afraid of Tony. But she'd just separated from a boyfriend and didn't need the hassle of another one.

Tony refused to give up. He spoke to her every day. One afternoon, Crystal ducked into the back storage room to avoid Tony when she spotted his car arrive outside the grill. It didn't do any good. Tony brazenly followed her and offered to help her with her chores. He brought his parents and brother in for lunch and insisted that she meet and sit with them. When the senior Papas said it was okay, she had no choice. Finally, after several days of nonstop flirting, she lied and told him that she already had a boyfriend. It only seemed to make Tony more persistent.

"I'm working here," she snapped one afternoon.

"I'll help you," he cheerfully announced.

"Okay, you can clean the bathroom." She hated mopping it and thought he'd leave. Much to her shock, Tony grabbed a mop and began swirling water across the tile.

Not long after that, Crystal saw Tony bring a homeless man into the grill and buy him lunch. The derelict had been panhandling outside and Tony had refused to give him cash but had invited him into the grill, where they had sat down and eaten together. She thought Tony was sweet.

At about that same time, one of Crystal's coworkers mentioned that Tony had been asking other employees what he needed to do to get Crystal to go out to dinner with him. Crystal mentioned that Tony wasn't her type. He always wore flashy shirts and dress slacks.

"If he toned it down and wore a T-shirt for a change, that would help," Crystal replied.

The next day, Tony arrived wearing a T-shirt.

When she took her lunch break, he asked if he could join her, and by the time they finished, she'd agreed to go out on a date.

He took her to Pasta Mia, an Italian restaurant on Flamingo Road, and as the hostess was showing them their seats, Crystal noticed Al and Chris sitting at a nearby table.

"We didn't know you were coming here, honest," a clearly embarrassed Al said.

"You should have," Tony replied. "This is where I take all of my first dates."

Crystal had never bumped into parents on a date; nor did she like knowing that she was just another in a line of women being brought to the same restaurant. She thought about leaving.

But she didn't and when Tony began telling her about the Wave-Runner accident and TBI, the pieces—how he always came to the grill at exactly the same time and always ordered exactly the same sand-wich—began fitting together. After dinner, he drove her to her apart-ment and asked if she would go out on a second date. She surprised herself by agreeing. She'd had a good time.

The next night, he took her to the horror movie *The Hills Have Eyes.* They spent their third date with his family watching a DVD. When she mentioned she was looking for a better-paying job, Tony talked to Al, who offered to hire her as a receptionist at the family business, AJ Capi-tal. Al assured her that it wouldn't be a problem even if she and Tony eventually broke up. During her first week at work, Tony called so many times that she worried other employees would resent her, especially when he began taking her to lunch each day. But Al said he liked having Crystal spending time with Tony.

By this point, Tony had told Crystal about his pen pals. She'd been wor-ried at first. But Al, Chris, and Joey assured her that they didn't believe it was dangerous. After all, nearly all of the serial killers were on death row in prison. She had to admit that she found the letters fascinating.

The longer they dated, the more Crystal felt at ease. She'd decided they were a well-matched couple. He was outgoing, even flamboyant. She was reserved. He treated her well, always fussed over her. But it wasn't only Tony whom she was drawn to. Crystal's parents had divorced when she was nine, ending a tumultuous and, in her eyes, an emotion-ally and physically abusive relationship. Alcohol had been involved. For the first time in her life, Crystal felt she was part of a grounded, safe, and loving family whenever she was with Tony, his parents, and his brother—and that was both new and important to her. The Ciaglias came as a package: a traditional, close Italian family, right down to the big family meals on Sundays.

Everything was going great until one night, about six months into their relationship, when Crystal and Tony were watching television in his bedroom. Tony began complaining about one of her girlfriends. Crystal knew Tony had been feeling out of sorts. He hadn't wanted to go out to dinner or to nightclubs on the Strip. He just wanted to rest in bed all day. Even getting letters from the killers didn't seem to pep him up. His parents were worried that some of his medications had stopped working. That had happened before. Sometimes they simply were no longer effective and no one could explain why.

Crystal didn't react to his grumbling because she didn't want to get into an argument, but when he kept bad-mouthing her girlfriend, she finally said, "If you can't say anything nice about her, then maybe you shouldn't say anything at all."

Tony bolted upright and began screaming. He snatched a glass from beside his bed and threw it against the wall, shattering it. Al and Chris rushed into the room and Al escorted Tony out into the living room. Crystal had never seen Tony lose control.

It reminded her of when her own parents would fight, and she didn't want to go through anything like that. She had begun collecting her things to go to her apartment when Al returned to the bedroom.

"Crystal," he said softly, "this is what can happen when someone has a traumatic brain injury. The part of their brain that controls emotions is broken and sometimes, something will set Tony off and he really can't control it. What you have to understand is that it is not him—it is the brain injury that is causing him to become violent."

Al told her that Tony was mortified that he had yelled at her. Now he was afraid she was going to leave and never come back.

"No one is going to be angry if you don't want to talk to Tony tonight," Al assured her. "Even if you decide to end your relationship with him, we will understand. Actually, it would be better if you did leave now if you don't think you can handle this sort of thing because if you keep seeing Tony and then leave him later, it's just going to be tougher for him to handle."

Al paused, then went on: "But you've got to understand this is not who Tony is as a person. It is his brain injury. He doesn't want you to leave without letting him apologize to you. He owes you that."

Crystal hesitated. Her first impulse was to run as far away from Tony as possible. But she genuinely cared about him and his family. She told Al that Tony could come back into the bedroom.

As soon as Tony appeared, he began to cry. "I'm sorry," he kept repeating. "I'm so, so sorry."

Several years later, when she recalled that night, Crystal would explain her actions. "I couldn't just walk away. I could have because I was young and what happened was scary—so how could anyone hold that against me? But I thought, 'Okay, let's chill out here and see if this is going to be a regular thing or after I get to know him better if there are ways to prevent something like this from happening.' I was falling in love with him.

"After that night," she explained, "whenever Tony felt bad and felt a rage might be coming on, he would tell me and I would go be with him and just lie down next to him and not say anything but just be there beside him to help him get through it and just by having me lying down next to him, he would begin to feel better and that made me happy. It wasn't long after that night, that we decided to see only each other and I was glad, because when you are in love with someone, you accept them for who they are."

14

Of all the serial killers, Tony felt the most drawn to Arthur Shawcross. A prolific pen pal, Shawcross wrote Tony an average of six letters a month. Single-spaced, often as long as five pages, the letters were methodically typed without corrections or rubouts. Shawcross wrote about the weather and prison life. He described fixing equipment as a prison maintenance handyman. He offered Tony recipes and inserted into his envelopes four-leaf clovers that he had picked in the prison yard.

There was a common thread in every letter. Everything he wrote was about himself—his thoughts, his wants, his needs, his desires, his complaints. And, on the basis of his letters, a reader would have believed that Arthur Shawcross was superhuman in his physical strength, stamina, and intelligence. It soon became a running joke inside the Ciaglia household. Anytime anyone in the family ran into a tough situation, they would chuckle and say, "Well, if Art were here, he'd take care of it."

Shawcross peppered his letters with gossip from inside the Sullivan Correctional Facility, a New York state maximum security prison since 1980. He clearly saw himself as a celebrity and he reveled in that role.

> *Big doings here, Anthony. Three men hung themselves in segregation . . . plus another man was taken and placed in a strip cell holding tank with nothing but his underwear, but somehow he managed to stab himself to death with an ink pen. Where'd that come from?*
>
> *. . . One of our female guards was fired! Why? For sucking a black cock—an inmate's. They were caught in the basement by one of our super cops but word is the cop let them finish before interrupting. . . .*
>
> *. . . You and your family missed a good fight. While out in the yard two guys were throwing a softball. One man kept throwing over the tables where we were all sitting. The man next to me told him if the ball hits him, he is going to beat the shit out of the one*

who threw it. Sure enough, while we were talking, he gets hit in the back of the head. He was cut too from something on the ball. He ran to the man who threw it and went to slugging him . . . the cops ran over there to break it up and one of them got punched and hit the ground. That is when an alarm went off and the yard door opened and out came a wall of blue. Cops everywhere. . . .

Sullivan held just under six hundred male inmates in four secure pods that were located in the middle of a unique, circular compound. Nearly all of the convicts were violent felons and 60 percent were serving life sentences. The prison's website identified Shawcross as one of its most infamous inmates, along with David Berkowitz—an Internet coupling that enraged Shawcross. He wrote openly about how he despised the Son of Sam.

If you are going to take someone's life, you should do it by looking them right in the eyes and putting your hands around their necks and squeezing and watching the light go out. Not shooting them. They deserve that and you do too . . . The so-called Son of Sam is a coward . . .

. . . I have had men ask me what is the best way and fastest way to stick someone. I tell them to go to the commissary and buy a dozen pencils and a plastic cup with a cover. Sharpen the pencils and shit and piss in the cup and place the cover on it. Then shove the pencils point down into that goo and leave it for a few months under the bed. Then take out one of the pencils and "give" it to someone as a "gift" in the chest. He will be very thankful. Ha. Ha. . . .

Shawcross considered himself to be a self-trained gourmet chef. He filled his letters to Tony with recipes that he'd invented. He urged Tony to offer them to his mom so she could fix the meals for the entire family. He called his recipes the "Shawcross way." When Tony mentioned that his mother had made a spaghetti sauce that Shawcross had suggested, the serial killer demanded to know how much the family had enjoyed his recipe.

Al and Chris installed a separate phone line in Tony's room. They called it the "murder line" because Tony gave the number to his prison pen pals to call. Shawcross began telephoning once a week. He often asked to speak to Chris, who was frightened to speak to him at first, but soon began looking forward to his calls, The murderer would ask her what meals she was planning on serving her family.

In addition to fancying himself as a skilled cook, Shawcross believed he was a talented artist. He spent hours doing intricate ink drawings and paintings. Many of them featured a grim reaper and naked women. He sent several to Tony. When Chris complained about a chronic pain in her neck, Shawcross drew a female figure and identified different pressure points that he claimed could be massaged and pressed for pain relief. He also began mailing Tony pages of poetry, often giving them dramatic titles, such as "The Butcher" and "Misery." One of Tony's favorites was called "Serials."

Serials

Why is there a commonality to people like us:
Can it be our independency and
Self-sufficiency that keeps our subsequent
Bizarre behavior of the rush

What with the severity of violence
In the frenzy to execute anyone
Without remorse, without a conscious thought,
Leaves one with memories in the silence

The force we feel that no one finds
Or the unshakable belief and cumulative pitfalls,
Or the depression in combinations
Or severe pain of our kind.

I for one enunciate that I
Am Much Much More then stated by the People,
The Press, or the Worlds Eye.

If you see in me agitation, insanity, furor,
Excitability, delirium, violence or just plain evil,
Then I suggest that you all look into the Mirror.

While Shawcross complained about the *New York Post* article about him wanting a new wife, he wrote that the prison had been inundated with letters.

> *Sunday I responded to sixteen letters and got caught up, but then Monday five more came in. . . .*
>
> *I got me a sweetheart card from a girl who says she has dropped 300 pounds in weight and is down to 240 now just for me, hahahahah But I would need a board across my ass on her to keep from falling in. So I told her I wasn't her type . . . Imagine being rejected by a serial killer! Ha.*
>
> *. . . I have a letter here from a woman who signed off: I love you. Grrrrr. She sent a large photo also. Very nice looking woman at that. Must be my magic touch. Ha. Ha. She said that she loved me—but from a distance. Hahahahaha. I do understand.*

Shawcross began forwarding Tony letters written by reporters and others who wanted to interview him. All of them flattered him and played to his already inflated ego. A freelance writer in England wanted to know "the political beliefs of famous inmates." But when the writer noted that he didn't have sufficient stamps to send for Shawcross's reply, the serial killer bristled. "Does this fool think I can afford stamps?"

When a research assistant for a professor at Tri-State University in Angola, Indiana, wrote asking Shawcross to mail her one of his drawings for display in a criminology class, Shawcross scowled: "Are these people nuts! If she gave up some pussy, I might place a black dot on a canvas for her . . . but I don't give away my artwork. I'm famous!"

When a well-known London television company offered to give Shawcross a chance to "explain himself" but warned that it didn't pay for interviews, Shawcross scribbled on the letter: "I decline. Cheap bastards. Claim they have a tight budget. They can make millions off me."

One of the most brazen interview requests came from a Denver-based freelance television producer and author who wrote that he was in contact with "some of the biggest television networks and their hosts—names such as Oprah Winfrey, Larry King, *Dateline, 60 Minutes. . . .*" The producer asked Shawcross to sign over his exclusive television rights, explaining: "If I market your story right, I think we could bring in anywhere from $50,000 to $200,000, and you would get forty percent. Not only can you make money, but you could also use this opportunity to work for you in other ways. For instance, you could use it to tell your side of the story, proclaim your innocence, discuss problems with jail/court system or show some remorse and win sympathy. . . ."

Shawcross declined.

A self-described "writer, author, national speaker and anti-violence advocate" named Phil Chalmers from Aurora, Ohio, sent along snapshots that showed him standing beside TV talk show host Montel Williams and celebrity Jessica Simpson. Another photo showed Chalmers arm in arm with David Berkowitz, which promptly killed all chances of Shawcross ever agreeing to speak to him.

The most bizarre request Shawcross sent Tony wasn't from the media, but was written by a fellow serial killer. In a letter dated June 28, 2008, Shawcross wrote that he had been contacted by Keith Hunter Jesperson, who had been convicted of killing eight women in Oregon, California, and Wyoming between January 1990 and March 1995. Jesperson was nicknamed the *Happy Face Killer* by a newspaper reporter because he drew a smiley face on the wall of a toilet stall where he left an anonymous confession to his first murder. When that didn't elicit a response, he began taunting the police in letters signed with his smiley face moniker that he mailed to newspapers. After he was captured, Jesperson confessed to dozens of murders, but most of them had happened when he had a conclusive alibi. Detectives concluded that the six-foot, six-inch-tall, 240-pound murderer, dubbed "Baby Huey" because of his appearance, was exaggerating for attention.

In his letter to Shawcross, Jesperson explained that he wanted to exchange "helpful" information that would be beneficial to them both. Jesperson asked which Internet dealers in serial killer collectibles were paying Shawcross the best prices for his autographs and drawings. What percentage was Shawcross collecting for his autograph?

He bragged about how many people wanted his autograph, explaining that he was the most infamous serial killer in the Northwest.

Jesperson then asked Shawcross why he had refused to take responsibility for killing Kimberly Logan, a black prostitute whose body was found in Rochester during the same time period when Shawcross had been murdering hookers. The police had long suspected him of murdering Logan, but Shawcross had refused to admit it.

Jesperson wrote:

. . . Arthur, why would you deny killing Kimberly Logan? Because she is black? My cellie is a card-carrying member of the KKK and he has fucked them. He just has a policy to never marry them or date them openly or have children with them. But come late night TV and he is up playing with himself looking at the black videos. Let's face it, they do have great bodies. Once I was in Tampa, Florida and this cute petite black woman dressed in spandex got into my truck. We were in the sleeper and she asked me "You're not a serial killer are you?" I just about fell off of my bed laughing. "Of course not girl" I told her and paid her what she wanted. After an hour or so, I let her go. No intention of killing her. That's isn't what I'm about . . .

Continuing, Jesperson explained that an English true-crime writer named Christopher Berry-Dee was "100 percent accurate in his books" and Jesperson urged Shawcross to contact Berry-Dee so he could write Shawcross's life story. "Tell it like it is . . . just to clear the air. The truth sells."

In closing, Jesperson wrote:

. . . Over the years I have gotten lots of letters from people. I write several killers in the USA to sort of get a line on who is good and who is bad in working with when they write. Would you like to be included in this arena? I must tell you, however, that I feel you killed and had sex with Kimberley Logan and if this relationship [between us] is going to work, I must know the truth about her. If I'm right, just write out the words in the opening sentence of your response: "I did her" and I'll know you will not lie to me when we exchange information as pen pals. I really hate wasting my time with people who feel a need to try to get over on me . . . I feel we don't have to prove to each other how bad we can be— which puts us so far head of the rest of them. Send me a letter. I have some real funny stories on what can be done on those who fuck with us. . . .

Shawcross was enraged after he read Jesperson's letter.

> *Dear Anthony, I swear to you and our friendship that I know*
> *nothing about the murder of Kimberly Logan. This fool is looking*
> *to make a name for himself. I told him that if he was in this man's*
> *prison, he would be my bitch for life and would do everything I*
> *told him to do!!! As big as he is, he would make one hell of a fag!*

A month later, Shawcross wrote to Tony again about Jesperson.

> *. . . I now have a problem with an asshole across the ocean—*
> *this writer named Christopher Berry-Dee. He and Keith H. Jes-*
> *person are as thick as thieves! Jesperson sent my response to him*
> *to this fucker and now Christopher Berry-Dee is telling the world*
> *that I killed a woman by the name of Kimberly Logan—an un-*
> *solved case still in Rochester, New York. This man better be very*
> *careful of what he says about me when he comes to the States be-*
> *cause I can sue him for slander! I only need to find a lawyer to do*
> *the deed Pro Bono. That fucking Jesperson is Berry-Dee's bitch in*
> *the joint and tried to get me to confess . . . Tony, you can't trust*
> *these serial killers.*

Shawcross explained that he was so weary of writers and TV produc-
ers miscasting his story and misquoting him that he'd decided it was
time to set the record straight—and he wanted Tony's help.

By this point, Shawcross already had been the subject of three non-
fiction books, the best being *The Misbegotten Son: A Serial Killer and
His Victims,* by veteran crime writer Jack Olsen. What set Olsen's book
apart, according to a flattering review published in the *New York Times
Book Review* in March 1993, was its author's "uncanny ability to obtain
first-person accounts from virtually every major player in the killer's
blood-splattered script; wives, girlfriends, co-workers, police officers,
therapists and even the only prostitute known to have survived an encounter with the killer—by playing dead to help him achieve a necro-
philic orgasm." The reviewer noted that there would be only one way for
any future authors to improve on what Olsen had written—and that was
by getting Shawcross himself to open up.

Since the release of Olsen's book, Shawcross had granted a handful
of interviews, but he told Tony that he had never told anyone "the truth"
about his life. None of the psychiatrists or the police detectives who had

spent time with him had been able to penetrate the "real Arthur Shaw-cross."

I will admit Anthony that you have become my best male friend in this life and I want you to be the first to know the real Arthur Shawcross. I am already 25 pages into writing the truth about myself and my crimes. When you read it, you and you alone, will know exactly what happened and why I did what I did . . .

15

Tony couldn't wait to begin reading Arthur Shawcross's autobiography when a large manila envelope appeared in his private mailbox. He carefully put each page into a plastic sheet in a binder to preserve it.

The forty-two pages of single-spaced narrative covered events from Shawcross's birth in October 1944 until his honorable discharge from the army in the spring of 1969. The serial killer titled this section "Growing Up in the House of Sin." He had dedicated his autobiography to "My best friend, Tony Ciaglia."

It was a wordy, poorly written, rambling document that began with Shawcross explaining that his parents, Arthur Roy Shawcross, then age twenty-one, and Bessie Yerakes Shawcross, age eighteen, were forced by Bessie's father to get married because she was pregnant. What no one in the family ever admitted, Shawcross wrote, was that his actual father was not Arthur Roy Shawcross but another man. Shawcross told Tony that this historical tidbit had never been made public. He had never revealed to anyone that he was a bastard child and he had never known his actual father's identity. This caused him to wonder if his father's "seed" had been "bad," dooming him from the start to become a murderer. What sort of man, Shawcross asked, impregnated his mother and then never bothered to contact his child?

"I was unloved from birth," he wrote. Meanwhile, his parents showered affection on his two younger sisters and brother. The only way Shawcross could get attention was by acting out. His father responded with his belt, beating him with it and his fists and verbally abusing him.

Shawcross wrote that forensic psychiatrists had interviewed his family members and reported in their evaluations that he had been a bedwetter. He denied that to Tony, writing that it was his brother, James, who actually had wet the bed that they shared as children. "Jimmy was always wetting the bed, but who gets blamed—me." When Arthur finally told his parents, Jimmy got a beating. "Man oh man, did Jimmy ever get a whipping and for some odd reason, I felt good inside that he got spanked but good. It made me happy watching him get that belt."

At age nine, Shawcross fell into a lake at a family picnic and was rescued by his father. He was paralyzed from the waist down but doctors were unable to determine what caused the paralysis even after a spinal tap was done. They theorized it might have been encephalomyelitis, an inflammation of the brain, but his brothers and sisters accused him of faking the injury to get attention. His mother helped him with physical therapy by rubbing and moving his legs. In his narrative for Tony, Shawcross claimed that this is when his mother first began sexually molesting him.

> *Mom started doing a thing to me—to my penis—that at first made me cry. Then she would spank me with a leather strap and tell me not to tell anyone! So I did everything she asked of me. Oral sex she did to me and then I to her! I did not like it either. More so when we had fish for supper; I would get sick instantly and go to my bed. Mom knew why and said nothing.*

Shawcross wondered if oral sex with his mother, pain from the whippings that she gave him for resisting her sexual advances, and having fish for dinner somehow became confusingly linked in his mind. "I did end up loving to fish and I did eat pussy," he joked.

His sexual encounters with his mother continued for months, whenever his father left the house.

> . . . At age fourteen, mom came at me with something in mind that I did not want any part of. Intercourse. After the first time, I ran away. I wrote a note and laid it on my pillow and it said I am going to Syracuse and not coming back.

Public records later showed that Shawcross had, indeed, run away from home at age fourteen, fleeing to Canada, where he planned to live in the woods, using snares to catch rabbits and surviving on fish from streams. But he was intercepted by border guards who called his parents. His father beat him so badly that when he returned to school, a nurse noticed and Shawcross was taken away from his parents and put in foster care—facts also later confirmed by public records. Still, Shawcross wrote that he never told authorities that he had been having sex with his mother.

At age fifteen, Shawcross had another sexual encounter, this time with a woman who he believed was his aunt Tina but who actually was his mother's best friend.

> *Mom drove to Watertown to get groceries and I stayed home with a cold. Tina walked around the house in her underpants and bra. I watched her too. She knew I was watching and when she finished washing that morning's dishes, she came over and started kissing me here and there and down below. Then she had me do the same with her that I'd done to mom. That made me sicker then with mom. I threw-up on her. She slapped me in the face. I went out the back door and got some rain water to wash my face off. . . . I went in and locked myself in the bedroom . . . That night at supper time . . . I saw fish on the platter. I slid out of my chair and went outside to puke. Mom came out and asked what was the matter. Then she got close and smelled something on me and started slapping me and I was fighting back. Then mom went back in the house and started right in on Tina . . . Mom can swear in three languages: English, Italian and Greek. Dad had to take Tina to the bus station in Watertown and she was never heard from again. I ran off that night.*

In his account, Shawcross wrote a dozen pages about his exploits hunting and fishing in the Watertown woods. Being alone stalking animals and fishing was when he was happiest. He wrote nothing to Tony, however, about the crimes that he committed as a youth. According to criminal records released later to his biographers, Shawcross was arrested as a teen for shoplifting, burglarizing houses, and arson. He had a reputation for being a liar and a bully.

At age nineteen, Shawcross married Sarah Louise Chatterton, age twenty, a fellow clerk in a local store, and a year later she gave birth to a baby boy. But Shawcross didn't mention his son in his biography for Tony. Much like his own biological father, he had nothing to do with his own child. Nor did Shawcross comment in his autobiography on a statement that he'd made to a psychiatrist, one of the many who had interviewed him after he was accused of being a serial killer. When asked about his first marriage, Shawcross had said that he had lost interest in Sarah almost from their wedding night because she'd refused to have oral sex with him. "I was obsessed with it and sex," he told the psychiatrist. "I'd pick up girls near where we lived near Sandy Creek, N.Y. We'd have sex. I couldn't stop. It was all I wanted to do."

There was no mention in Shawcross's typed account for Tony of his previously documented obsession with masturbation, either, often to the point that his penis was covered with blisters from rubbing.

Shawcross told Tony that Sarah filed for a divorce after he was drafted in April 1967 into the army because she had fallen in love with another man.

The next thirty pages of Shawcross's autobiography described in tedious detail his alleged exploits in Vietnam as an army soldier. He provided Tony with technical descriptions of weapons and vivid, often horrifying accounts, of battles that he claimed he'd fought in.

> Now we headed to the Stone Quarry. A small village on the Cambodian Border. A few gray houses and huts. There were several American soldiers there and two tanks plus 25 Rock Vietnamese—like our Special Forces in Green Berets. Here is where everyone heard one hell of a scream and a Sergeant Major came out of a building with his pants at his ankles and blood squirting all over the front of him! He reaches down to his .45 and puts it to his head and fires. He drops down three steps to the ground. His prick was sliced in half! That ticked off the Vietnamese and they went into that building and brought out everyone in there. Lined them up by size and started to check the woman. The first woman found with a rubber cup in her pussy with double edged razor blades in the middle of it was taken and tied down and two saplings were brought down and hooked to each leg. Then the woman was cut from her asshole to the naval with a machete about a half inch deep. Then the trees were cut lose. She split almost in half. Guts hanging between the trees. The next woman to have a razor was staked to the ground and one of those old fashion pumpers that fire departments used to use, the hose was shoved into the cunt and the pumper was hit. That woman exploded gore all over the place. The next one was an old woman. She was beheaded! All the other people in that building were shot. Then picked up and tossed back inside and then set fire to it. Men, women and children . . .

Such stories made Tony and his parents begin to question Shawcross's truthfulness. Strapping a woman to two bent poles that ripped her torso in half when sprung was a common torture in old black-and-white

Tarzan movies. But Tony could find no mention of such barbaric acts in Vietnam. When he checked the Internet, he found several references to *"vagina dentate"*—Latin for "toothed vagina"—and stories almost identical to Shawcross's about Vietnam prostitutes who supposedly inserted razor blades into their vaginas. But all of those stories had been exposed as urban legends.

"If he is lying," Al said, "then you have to ask yourself why? And remember, Tony, you can still learn a lot about people—from their lies. Maybe he is describing a fantasy or he is reinventing history, making it the way he wanted it to be in Vietnam. If that's what he is doing, then he is telling you something about himself and how his mind works."

In his autobiography, Shawcross wrote that he'd killed for the first time in Vietnam as a soldier.

> I cried like a fool that first time, but after about six you tend to lose the squeamish sensation inside. Another time while up at Dak To [a major battle] there was a firefight . . . People were charging the bunker line . . . I shot into several and they did not fall. Scary for sure, but then I shot one in the head and the body dropped so I called out "Shoot them in the head!" They had a Beetlenut leaf and opium base paste in their mouths and they never felt the bullets hit them. That's how they kept charging us. But shooting them in the head did the trick.

Just as he had done in his letters, Shawcross always made himself a hero.

He described innumerable secret missions, claiming that he often went out on his own into the jungle to hunt and kill the enemy. One day, he came upon an older woman carrying AK-47 assault rifles. She was hiding the weapons, so Shawcross stopped her and "cut her head off with a machete."

> I cut a sapling and sharpen both ends and shoved one end in the soft earth about thirty feet from where she was hiding the Ak-47s. I put her head on that stick staring at where she'd hid the weapons. Those people are highly superstitious and I knew they would never go near that spot if they thought the woman's spirit was there . . .

Continuing, Shawcross wrote that he followed a footpath the woman had been using until he reached several huts, where he found more weapons. A young girl was in one of the huts and when she refused to answer his questions, he dragged her to the spot where he had decapitated the older woman and tied the girl to a tree. As she watched, he dismembered the woman's corpse, started a fire, and roasted a piece of flesh over the flame.

I sprinkled water and powdered rock salt on the flesh as it cooked. When it was roasted well done, I went over to the woman and asked her several questions. She said nothing. I went over and picked up the meat and bit into it and ripped off a chunk. That woman pissed herself and fainted in fear. It was the first time I had tasted human flesh and I spit out the meat and rinsed out my mouth. Tossed it up on an ant hill and carried the unconscious young girl down to a stream and stripped her naked. Gagged her and dropped her in that cold water. She woke up fast. I screwed the living shit out of her and then washed her off and myself too. Carried her back up to the tree and retied her. She told me everything I wanted to know in broken English. Then I stood to the side of her and spoke low. I went and looked North and whispered that someone was coming and when she turned to look, I used my machete to take her head off . . . I took the head and placed it on a pole facing all of the huts. . . .

Shawcross wrote that he had felt a rush of adrenaline and satisfaction during those two killings that was unlike any emotion that he'd ever felt, even though he'd killed before as a soldier. He ended his autobiography by recounting how he had returned to the U.S. a completely obsessed man.

I was forever hooked from that point forward on killing.

He promised that he would write about the second half of his life as a serial killer in his next installment to Tony.

Tony had done extensive research about Shawcross's crimes, trial, and life, and in Jack Olsen's definitive book, *Misbegotten Son*, he'd read that Shawcross had given his defense attorney handwritten accounts about two murders that he'd committed in Vietnam. The accounts in Olsen's book were nearly identical to what Shawcross had told Tony—with one exception. There was no mention in them about cannibalism. Olsen also reported that prosecutors also had claimed during the trial that Shawcross had *never* engaged in combat while in Vietnam.

At Shawcross's trial, defense attorneys had called psychiatrist Dorothy Otnow Lewis, a Yale University professor who specialized in studying serial killers, to testify about the accused serial killer's mental state. She'd spent three weeks on the witness stand. Lewis said that Shawcross's war experiences had caused him to suffer post-traumatic stress disorder. She said he suffered from multiple personality disorder, most likely caused by childhood beatings and sexual abuse.

The prosecution countered with its own expert witness, forensic psychiatrist and criminologist Park Elliott Dietz, a favorite of prosecutors. (He later would testify in cases involving John Hinckley, Jr., Jeffrey Dahmer, Andrea Yates, Susan Smith, Richard Davis, the Menendez brothers, the Unabomber, and the D.C. snipers and claim all were sane when they committed murder.) Dietz insisted that Shawcross was a malingerer, a faker, and said there was no evidence that the murderer had a mental disease or defect.

At one point, the defense sent brain scans of Shawcross to experts for interpretation. Those scans showed that he had scars on the frontal lobes—possibly caused by childhood beatings—that could have influenced his ability to make proper decisions. The defense was not allowed to introduce the scans into evidence. However, the judge did permit their expert to tell jurors that a cyst was found on Shawcross's temporal lobe that could have interfered with his ability to control his emotions. That cyst could have mimicked a traumatic brain injury.

The debate whether Shawcross had engaged in combat in Vietnam could have been easily answered if the defense or prosecution had tracked down his fellow soldiers. But because Shawcross was on trial for killing prostitutes, not two women during an unpopular war, no one bothered.

Military records obtained by a local newspaper confirmed that Shawcross had served in Vietnam with the Fourth Supply and Transport Company of the Fourth Infantry Division. But the newspaper reported that there was nothing in the records that indicated Shawcross had fought enemy troops.

"This is frustrating," Tony told his father. "Is he lying to me?"

"A lot of terrible things happened in Vietnam," Al said in Shawcross's defense. "There was a lot of confusion over there. I'm also not sure the U.S. Army would want to admit that it had a serial killer running around cutting people's heads off."

When it came down to it, Al said, "Tony, you're going to have to decide for yourself how much of what Art has told you is true and how much isn't. You aren't a psychiatrist. You aren't a neurosurgeon. You're not an FBI profiler. You're not a reporter or a prosecutor or a researcher. But you are something that none of these others are. You're his friend."

A SERIAL KILLER'S DREAM: ARTHUR SHAWCROSS

Dear Anthony,

. . . I have had the strangest dream Anthony. I woke up and my prison cell door was open and it was near dawn and everything was quiet. I looked out and all the cell doors were open. The guard was dead . . . The man in the cell next to mine was dead too. I realized I was alone . . .

I checked the entire prison . . . Not one person was awake. Some were dead and some were still breathing, but would not wake up. I went to every cell and every building and it came to me that every woman was alive and breathing, but not one man was. They were dead. I was the only male living.

Why was I spared?—was my only thought.

I went into the storehouse and gathered up new mattresses and brought them to the education office. I lined them all up in the hallway and placed one female upon each one with a light blanket. The phones were dead. The radio was nothing but static. The women were breathing so I went into the commissary to get some hot pots warming-up soup for them and me. Anthony, in a situation like this you tend to lose it. I tried placing cool cloths on the first woman and nothing. I touched her here and there, and nothing. So I said to myself, "What the hell!" and I fucked her and she immediately woke-up and hugged me. . . . So I tapped the well of everyone one of them—I fucked them good—and they each woke up. But waking them up was a big mistake! I was the only man and whatever befell us turned them into like sex slaves . . . They couldn't get enough!

After getting everyone in clothing, we decided to go outside the prison but waited until evening. There were dead birds and we could see bodies outside the gate. I sent ten women outside and told them to get us a bus that we could use to escape. They were gone over a day and when they came back, two were missing. I knew they had gone to their homes so myself and a woman went to their homes.

All we could hear was screams in the first house and when I went in, the woman was there holding her dead son, rocking back-and-forth. Getting that woman out of there was a chore. She had to be tied-up and carried out.

Then we went to the other woman's house and she was staring at four dead teenage girls. She had stuck a knife into each girl. Why? She didn't want me to fuck them and I bet she didn't want them to see what this world had come too. She was lost in her mind. What to do? The woman with me, shot the woman and we left her there.

I stopped at a place that sold these Winnabago's travel trailers you drive. We got the two biggest out of a showroom and gathered up everyone. Gas was cheap. It was free. Next I drove alone to a high school and started to revive all the girls that I was able to save by fucking them each. Once that was accomplished, I told them all what had happened and most of the girls cried and then I told them I seemed to have been chosen to save as many women or girls that I was able before I died by fucking them. It was up to me now as the only man alive on earth.

We went into the country where we planted vegetables and built storage barns. A little over a year later, babies were coming into being. Several had to be killed because of deformations. But the ones that were or looked normal were saved. Anthony, I was re-populating the entire civilization.

I woke up from this dream covered in sweat Anthony, and breathing hard. I was stuck to my shorts too! Ha. Ha It was a great dream.
Your best friend,
Arthur Shawcross

16

From the moment that he met Tony, Dr. Sean Duffy focused on how he could use psychotropic medications to compensate for the damaged areas in Tony's brain.

There was a time in America in the 1950s and 1960s when Sigmund Freud's psychoanalytic approach was all the rage. Psychiatrists offered their patients an office couch and searched for clues about their behavior by listening to them describe their childhoods. But by the 1970s, the Freudian approach had been replaced by "biological psychiatry." Traditional mental illnesses were no longer thought to be caused by poor parenting, overly protective mothers, or childhood traumas. Schizophrenia, bipolar disorder, and major depression were now believed to be biological in nature—genetic disorders in the brain's complicated neurotransmitter system. The development of antipsychotic and mood-stabilizing medications, primarily chlorpromazine and lithium carbonate, made it possible for many patients to control their symptoms. For many, the pills could silence the voices in their heads and even the moods that caused a person to swing from being exuberant to being suicidal within moments.

With the development of new pharmaceuticals, the role of the American psychiatrist shifted. The doctor's job now became one of diagnosing what was wrong biologically in the brain and then writing prescriptions to compensate. The words "chemical imbalances" were bandied about. The term became a popular, shorthand explanation for what actually were extremely complicated brain disorders. The psychiatrist's job was to figure out how to put those imbalances back in order.

Dr. Duffy had earned his degree during the biological psychiatry period. He'd earned an undergraduate degree in biochemistry and psychology, and had added advanced degrees in neuroscience and medicine before opening his practice in Las Vegas. There would be no long couch sessions in his office for Tony or chitchats about his feelings and family life. Dr. Duffy would leave that task up to psychologist Nick Ponzo.

"My job," Dr. Duffy explained to his young patient and his parents at the outset, "is keeping your mood out of the dumps and keeping you emotionally stable and off the firing line so that you can cruise through your life being relatively happy."

Dr. Duffy developed a therapeutic cocktail to counter the nonfunctioning spots in Tony's brain. To keep Tony from feeling extremely depressed, he prescribed 1,750 milligrams of Depakote, a mood stabilizer; and 90 milligrams of Cymbalta, an antidepressant that curbed feelings of hopelessness and sadness. Next came 900 milligrams of lithium and 100 milligrams of Seroquel to further control mania and rage. Those were higher doses than most patients were given of extremely strong medications.

Because Tony was taking so many medications, he was given 60 milligrams of Inderal to control shaking and tremors, which were common side effects. He also was prescribed a small dose of Synthroid to help his thyroid, which had been damaged by years of taking medicine.

He took his "pill cocktail" twice a day. At night, he added a drug to help him sleep.

More than a half-dozen psychiatrists had examined Tony by the time he reached Dr. Duffy. After meeting his new patient and his family, Dr. Duffy concurred with his colleagues' earlier diagnoses. The damage to Tony's brain made it difficult for him to control his moods, especially rage, and his impulses. He also showed signs of obsessive-compulsive behavior and of being hypersexual.

Dr. Duffy wasn't certain if the hypersexuality was a result of brain damage or was caused by another factor—the actual timing of the WaveRunner accident. Tony had been going through puberty and adolescence when his brain was damaged. It was possible that the accident had stunted Tony's emotional development, in effect interrupting and delaying his sexual maturity and extending the length of his adolescence.

"Tony is a pretty happy guy," Dr. Duffy said in an interview for this book. "He's childlike at times . . . and this makes him both very engaging and much more open than adults."

When Dr. Duffy first learned that Tony was corresponding with serial killers, he was not overly concerned. Yes, Tony was impulsive. He had flashes of uncontrollable rage. He often didn't recognize the consequences of his actions. He was easily fixated on sex. All of those symptoms could also be found in psychiatric evaluations of many serial killers. Tony had been rejected by his peers because he was different. He felt estranged from society. So did many murderers.

But there was a marked difference between Tony and his new prison pen pals. Tony loved his parents. He loved his brother. He felt empathy. He felt guilt when he did something wrong. His problems were caused by a traumatic brain injury and not an antisocial personality defect.

There was an irony, however, not missed by Dr. Duffy.

Tony's adolescent behavior made him more open to the killers than someone more mature. His obsessive-compulsive tendencies meant he was willing to spend hours and hours corresponding with narcissistic criminals without expecting much in return. Because of his own hyper-sexuality, he did not tire of the killers' endless fantasies about sex and rape. His lack of a social filter and his impaired judgment meant that he was not put off by their macabre stories of cruelty. Most of all, he was not judgmental, and because he knew what it felt like to become enraged, out of control, and an outcast, he felt a link with his new "best friends."

The myriad of problems caused by Tony's brain injury that left him feeling alone and alienated in society were the very same characteristics that built a bridge for him to forge an intimate relationship with serial killers, to bond with them, and ultimately to become their confidant.

Across Las Vegas in his office, therapist Nick Ponzo also wasn't alarmed when he learned Tony was writing to serial killers.

"Actually, it made sense," the Canadian-born and -educated psychologist later recalled during an interview. "It fit Tony's personality."

Ponzo had spent hours talking to Tony. He'd listened to Tony talk about how he'd died three times after the WaveRunner accident. He'd heard Tony describe his near-death experience and how he'd met Jesus and returned to earth after being given a special purpose by God. The fact that he'd suffered a TBI had separated him from other persons his age. It made him different. He wasn't like everyone else. And because Tony was different, he was instinctively drawn to a pastime that was markedly different from what most people would've chosen.

"I realized that Tony wasn't going to be satisfied collecting something as mundane as stamps," Ponzo recalled.

The therapist felt Tony's correspondence with serial killers was harmless. In fact, it probably was a good thing because it kept him occupied and gave him a reason to get up each morning. His young patient enjoyed doing something that no one else was doing.

What Ponzo had no way of knowing, in the beginning, was how successful Tony was being at getting the killers to confide in him. Nor did he, Dr. Duffy, or anyone else realize how subtly Tony was being lured into their world.

In addition to Shawcross, Tony was becoming especially close to two other killers: Joseph Metheny, the Baltimore "cannibal killer"; and David Alan Gore, a sadistic rapist and hunter of women in Florida.

Both were horrifying monsters and both were eager to share their most intimate thoughts with Tony.

17

Cannibal Killer Joseph R. Metheny's Story

December 8, 1996

Rita Kemper burst from the door of a trailer at the Joe Stein & Son Pallet Company in Baltimore, Maryland. Scared stiff, she raced toward the fenced compound's front gate. Joseph R. Metheny emerged seconds later from the trailer, running after her.

Kemper reached the gate first, but found it padlocked. She spun around just in time to catch Metheny's fist in her jaw. The blow knocked her to the ground and nearly unconscious. Metheny grabbed her hair and dragged Kemper back into the night watchman's trailer where he lived.

The thirty-seven-year-old woman was no match physically for the forty-six-year-old Metheny. Standing six feet, one inch tall and weighing nearly three hundred pounds, he was facetiously nicknamed "Tiny."

The two had met earlier at the Borderline Bar and Restaurant, just down the street from the pallet company. Metheny was a familiar face there. Almost every night he could be found drinking beer and downing shots of Southern Comfort in the old bar, amusing other regulars with his jokes. The bar, the pallet company, and an assortment of down-on-their-luck businesses all sat at a crossroads just off the interstate highway. It was one of the saddest neighborhoods in a city pocketed with skid rows. Alcoholics, homeless drug addicts, hookers, and other castaways nodded against the walls of boarded-up town houses or trickled into the Borderline whenever they could earn enough change by panhandling to buy a pint.

Metheny had invited Kemper back to the pallet company on this particular night with the allure of cocaine. They'd both snorted it in the past without incident inside the one-room trailer where he slept rent-free—one of the benefits of his seven-dollar-per-hour job as a forklift driver and night watchman. But this time Metheny demanded sex. When Kemper refused, he smacked her in the face. She'd escaped, only to be stopped by the locked gate and Metheny's fist. The entire pallet company compound was encircled by an eight-foot-tall chain-link fence topped with rusty razor wire.

When he got the terrified woman back into his trailer, Metheny pinned her on the floor and began jerking down her blue jeans.

"Scream all you want," he said. "No one's gonna hear you!"

Kemper started to pray aloud.

"Even God can't help you!" Metheny smirked.

In a calm voice, he explained that he was going to rape and then sodomize her. "When I'm done, I'm going to kill you and bury you in the woods with the *other* girls."

At that point something inside Kemper snapped and she kicked her legs free from her pants, managed to spin from under him, and sprinted out of the trailer for a second time, as if she were an Olympic runner who'd just heard the starting gun.

Still clutching her short pants, Metheny chased after her again. Only Kemper didn't run toward the gate. Instead she began climbing a tall stack of wooden pallets that the company manufactured for truckers to use when transporting cargo. Hundreds of the pallets were piled along the fence.

Using the pallets as a ladder, Kemper reached the top just as Metheny lunged at her, his free hand brushing her heel. She leaped over the razor wire and hit the ground on the other side. Running down the hill, she flagged a police officer.

Within minutes, the patrolman arrived outside the locked gate and ordered Metheny, who was standing inside the compound, to surrender. He was still clutching Kemper's pants. En route to the police station, the officer ran a background check and discovered that the beefy suspect had been arrested less than a year earlier for allegedly using an ax to murder two homeless men under a bridge not far from the pallet company. Those homicide charges, however, had been dismissed because of insufficient evidence. There were never any bodies found.

Based on Kemper's complaint, Metheny was charged with assault, kidnapping, and attempted rape. But he was released a day later from jail and that night was back at the Borderline Bar, perched on his favorite bar stool. He was drinking heavily with William Clinton Ashbrook, Jr., another frequent customer and a coworker at the pallet company.

After several hours of boozing, the men went to Metheny's trailer to get high on cocaine. After they'd snorted a few lines, Metheny asked his buddy for a favor.

"I need to move a body," he whispered.

Ashbrook later testified that he thought Metheny was joking, until his host escorted him into the nearby woods; brushed aside a pile of trash, old tires, and other debris; and revealed the decaying, naked, and mutilated body of a young woman. The sight of the rotting corpse caused Ashbrook to gag. Claiming he was about to vomit, he begged off helping; instead he offered to go down the hill to get more cocaine. By the time he'd returned, Metheny had moved the corpse by himself.

The next morning, Metheny played dumb when Ashbrook asked him about the body. Later that day, Ashbrook began to worry that he could be Metheny's next target, so he contacted the police.

The Baltimore police arrested Metheny while he was attending a company Christmas party. Detectives found a rotting woman's corpse wrapped in a red tarp less than ten feet away from his trailer. The victim was identified as Kimberly Spicer, age twenty-six, a frequent customer at the Borderline.

By the time Baltimore detective Homer M. Pennington finished interrogating Metheny, the killer had confessed to two other killings. One was Toni Ingrassia, a twenty-eight-year-old woman whose body had been discovered a year earlier, dumped by the interstate near the pallet company. Metheny also led detectives to a decapitated corpse buried near his trailer. It was the body of Cathy Ann Magaziner, age forty-five, who'd been strangled and mutilated.

Metheny admitted murdering a total of seven women and three men, but despite extensive and expensive searches undertaken by the FBI and the Baltimore police, no more bodies were recovered.

Prosecutors put him on trial first for his failed attack on and attempted rape of Kemper. It was a slam dunk and he got fifty years. Next they went after him for the two women's corpses found near his trailer.

Kimberly Spicer had been stabbed more than twenty times in the face and chest. Investigators claimed Metheny had gotten angry after she refused his sexual advances. He'd stabbed her while he was high on cocaine and drunk. Prosecutors said he'd killed for "a sense of power" and because he "got a rush out of it." His public defender argued that Metheny deserved sympathy because he'd been abused as a child, was addicted to drugs and alcohol, and frequently heard voices telling him to kill people.

Evidence at the trial—including testimony about how Metheny had engaged in necrophilia with Spicer's corpse—was so "sickening" that the judge formally apologized to the victim's family for being forced, as he put it, "to listen to testimony that no human being should ever have to endure."

Even though the murder was "reprehensible," the judge ruled that it did not meet Maryland's criteria for imposing the death penalty because the killing had not been committed during another felony, such as a robbery, as required by state law. Instead Metheny was sentenced to life in prison.

Prosecutors then put Metheny on trial for killing Cathy Magaziner. He was found guilty, and during the sentencing portion of the trial, he asked to address the court. Most defendants beg for mercy at this critical juncture, but not Metheny. Instead he taunted the court.

"There is a lot about me that has not been told," Metheny declared. He announced that he had committed at least a half-dozen other murders. He hadn't been successfully prosecuted because the Baltimore police hadn't found the bodies, he bragged.

Continuing, he said that jurors needed to know that not only had he murdered his victims and had sex with them after they were dead; he also had a good time mutilating their bodies.

"When the [Spicer] autopsy was performed, they discovered she gave birth to a twelve-ounce bouncing baby beer bottle," Metheny announced. "I get a kick out of every fucking time I say that: bouncing baby beer bottle." (The bottle was found in her vagina.)

Continuing, Metheny told the court: "Now comes the person that you are here for, Cathy Magaziner. . . . The part they left out with her was that after six months, I dug her skull up, washed out the maggots, and made love to it. That's sick, ain't it?. . . . She was just another piece of meat upon the street. . . .

"The words 'I'm sorry' will never come out for they would be a lie. I am more than willing to give up my life for what I have done, to have

God judge me and send my ass to hell for eternity. There is no excuse for the things that I have done to those people. I just enjoyed it. So, I ask of you, please give me the fucking death penalty."

This time Metheny got his wish. But after he spent three years on death row, a higher court overturned his death sentence and a frustrated Metheny ended up with another life prison term.

Tony first read about Metheny on a website that had paid the serial killer three hundred dollars to tell his story. In that short synopsis, Metheny blamed his ex-wife for his murderous rampage. He claimed she was a drug addict and reputed prostitute who'd left him for her pimp. Seeking revenge, Metheny had started killing prostitutes and anyone else who got in his way.

Metheny had made a horrific claim in his Internet story.

"I butchered their bodies," he wrote, "and put the meat to good use."

He revealed that he'd mixed the dead women's flesh with pork and beef that he grilled. He used that meat to make barbecue sandwiches, which he then sold to unsuspecting customers outside the pallet company where he worked.

<u>18</u>

EXCERPTS FROM SELECTED LETTERS BETWEEN JOE METHENY AND TONY

Dear Anthony,
You seem like a damn smart young man with a good head on his shoulder. I don't have a clue of why you are writing to me but I'm sure as hell not going to question it. . . . You ask if I have any remorse for what I have done? No, I sleep just fucking fine. I did most of those sorry pieces of shit a favor. They had one foot in the coffin and the other on a banana peel long before they ran into me. So fuck them. Ha Ha . . .

Dear Joe,
When you first started taking lives, do you remember what you were feeling inside? Were you nervous or scared? Were there no feelings of guilt, shame, remorse? Were you afraid, you would get caught? . . . Did it become easier for you? To this day, are you able to relive the enjoyment of the murders over-and-over in your mind?

Dear Anthony,
The first time I took a life, I was scared shitless. I was only 15 years-old. I had tried to get this little 12 year-old girl to notice me but she never would . . . Anyway, school let out for the day and I followed her home. I had done this several times before. She would cut through this patch of woods. Well one day, her luck ran out—for that was the day, I killed her. I experienced a lot of firsts that day. She was my first kill, she was also my first shot of ass and also my first rape. Anyway, I ran up behind her and grabbed her and pulled her into those woods. I pushed her on the ground and told her to take her clothes off. She was a little

slow so I helped her by ripping them off. I beat and raped her for a little over two hours. Then I stood up looking down at her at what I had done. She was holding herself crying. She was all dirty and bloody. There was a big rock laying about three feet from me. I picked it up and started bashing her head in with it. I dug a shallow grave and buried her into it. And that is where she is resting to this day. That same rock I killed her with is her headstone. That happened back in September of 1970. I used to walk back into those woods many times when I was out there to check on her.

When I was a kid I used to tear my toys apart just to see what was inside them. . . . I used to get off on hurting things. It started with bugs. Just seeing what would happen when you pulled the legs or wings off. Then I moved to animals. I would throw gas on a cat and set it on fire just to watch it run away.

When you kill someone, it feels like time just stops and goes in slow motion. You get excited and the adrenaline starts pumping. Then when the life drains from your victim, it becomes very quiet. Then you stand there gazing down at what you have done. Reality comes back to you. Then you get scared and you don't know what to do. Most will run away from the scene. The best way to handle the situation is to try and hide the body until you can take a little time and clam yourself down. When it gets dark, get a shovel, a couple trash bags and a bag of lime. Now dig a hole three to four feet will work. Line the bottom of the hole with the trash bags. Strip the body of all clothing and jewelry and put them in a trash bag to take with you and throw away somewhere else far away. Now take the bag of lime. Pour some all over the bottom of the hole then place the body in the hole. Now pour the rest of the bag of lime all over the body. Then take the shovel and fill in the hole.

Your first kill is the hardest. Anything else after that is like swatting flies and stepping on bugs. You will have no feelings at all.

Dear Joe,

I have had it rough off-and-on for a while now—so bad that my parents couldn't let me out of sight for several days. I just couldn't seem to get my head together because of a deep depression. My doctor played with my medicines and finally got me doing well once more . . . This is the story of my life—like riding a seesaw that just won't stop and the Downs stay down a lot longer than the Ups stay up. . . .

You are locked up for the rest of your life behind bars and me, I am locked up in my own personal hell within my mind—due to an accident that badly damaged my thinking cap. . . .

Dear Anthony,

You say your emotions are like a seesaw . . . You sound like a man with a lot of anger in him. Something more than an accident has contributed to your rage that burns inside of you. . . . I believe the reason why I handle prison so well is that I have been in places a whole lot worse. . . . I feel your pain maybe a little more than you think I do. I know about your accident with the water ski, but I feel you have a much bigger issue inside you that contributes to your depression. . . . The truth is that you got the world by the ass so don't go and mess it up. I wish someone would have put a foot up my ass a long time ago before I throwed my world away.

. . . Yes, I was young when I took the life away from that sweet, little 12 year-old red haired girl. I was her first and last sexual encounter. She has been lying out there in those woods in a shallow grave cold and naked for 37 years now. When I was in the outside world, I would buy six beers each year and go sit beside her grave and drink them and I would think about what I had done on this very spot on September 19, 1970. Anyone else would probably would have started feeling remorse and would have probably broke down crying at that grave.

But not me. Every year when I would go out there, I would do the same thing. You want to know what a twisted fuck I am? I'd drink the six pack, then stand up and pull down my pants and underwear, and then start stroking my dick until it was hard. Then I would just start jerking off until I busted a nut on her grave. Then I would clean myself up and pick up all my beer cans and go home. You see, there is a big difference between me and people like you. I had a lot of bad things happen to me when I

*was very young and I learned to block it out over the years, but
in reality, all that did was make me hollow inside. In some ways,
that's a good thing, for when you no longer have a conscience or
the ability to care or have emotions and feelings, then no one can
hurt you anymore.*

Dear Joe,

    . . . FBI profilers say that serial killers lack a conscience or that little
things in your brain telling you right from wrong or giving you emotions
are missing . . . I was wondering when you were explaining to me about
your first victim—the little red-haired girl—if you had trouble relating
to other people? Emotionally? Sexually?

Dear Anthony,

    *. . . You may find this hard to believe, but take my word for
it, it's true. My first sexual experience, of course, was with myself
and my trusted hand at the tender age of eight years-old. Yes,
I was a sick, twisted, little mother fucker even back then at an
early age. The first female that I ever had sex with was a German
Shepherd named Shiraz, she was in heat and looking to hook up
with the first dog that passed her by. Yes, I turned out to be that
dog. Somewhere out there in the world, I may have kids that are
capable of lying down and licking their own nuts. Ha! Ha!*

    *So my friend, why does the sick, twisted shit I did in the past
interest you so much?*

Dear Joe,

The reason I am so interested in you is because: How many people
who live the lifestyle that I live, actually know a person like you? . . .
I've always been very fascinated in crime and what makes people do the
unimaginable. . . . So much education can come from somebody like
you . . . None of these authors or profilers have really ever taken the time
to get to know a person like you on a personal level. Maybe even go as
far as calling them a friend like I call you. Not to say that what you did
was glamorous or okay because it wasn't . . . I have people ask me all of
the time how could I write to people like you? Don't you think it's disre-
spectful of their victims?

When they ask me how could I do this, I just ask them: How could

I not? Disrespecting to the victims and their families—well, that's a sore subject . . . I do think about the victims and what you did to them. I can't tell you that I don't because it would be a lie. I guess my faith in God helps me because I believe in God and I do believe in heaven and I would like to believe that God takes care of all those who pass on.

You ask me why I write to you. Because I want to know: Why did you turn out like you have, Joe? Do you know the answer?

Dear Anthony,

I sure as hell am no one special, in fact, I am damn far from it. I am nothing more than what life has made me. I have made a lot of decisions in my life and it's sad to say that the majority of those decisions were wrong ones . . . I am not proud of the murders I did out there. Well, to tell the truth, maybe I am a bit proud of what I did. I was a hard worker, a truck driver, a fork lift operator but it seems the best thing that I ever learned how to do was to take the life of another away from them. There were several people I killed that one might say I feel bad about. But most of them were living on borrowed time. I feel I may have done those drug addicted, crack whores a fucking favor—I definitely helped them get off of drugs! And they made damn good sandwiches for hungry people at my open pit beef stand. Ha! Ha! Ha!

You asked me to tell you about that. Well, Sunday was the day when I had the BBQ stand open. Friday night I would go out in search of my special meat. I would get off work about six or seven and I always made sure I was the last person on the company grounds. Then I would go hit the shower and wash the day's dirt off of me, slip on some clean cloths and then it was time to hit the night in search of fresh young vagina. First, I would go to the Borderline Bar and Grill. I used to get my paycheck cashed in there every Friday. No one in that bar ever had a clue of what a sick, twisted mother fucker I really was. There was quite a few people in that bar who would come up to my BBQ stand on Sunday to get a sandwich to take back down to the bar. They would sit there and eat it and wash it down with a beer while they enjoyed watching the football or baseball game on TV, and I would just be laughing inside. I sure as hell couldn't tell anyone what I was doing. I shit you not, when I was working that stand it took everything I had to keep a straight face. So many times I just wanted to bust out laughing at watching these mother fuckers around me gorging on my sandwiches. The only time I would start to feel bad at that stand was when some of those people brought their kids there to eat but those kids loved those sandwiches too, so fuck 'em I would say. Ha Ha.

I'm going to do something for you Tony that I would never do for anyone else. I'm going to tell you how I did it and my recipe. I would go out looking for a crack addicted whore. Those are the best for no one ever seems to care about what happens to them. I would approach one of these girls that I didn't think looked too bad or disease-ridden . . . I would take her back up to my little trailer always late at night. You could scream your lungs out and there was no one around to hear except for me and the screaming kind of turned me on. I tortured the hell out of those girls. They all died a very horrible death, but I always left the ones I was going to use for meat just barely clinging to life. I did this so I could take them back in the woods, then strip them of all clothing and jewelry. I would tie a rope around their ankles and string them upside down over this tree limb I always used. Then I would place this 5 gallon plastic bucket under her head. I would slit her throat from ear-to-ear and watch the life pour out of her into that bucket . . . Then I would take my knife and gut her . . . I'd let her hang there. About 12 hours later, I would go back to where she was hanging with my hacksaw and start dismembering her . . . I only used the back of the arms and legs. I'm sure there was plenty of other good meat on a carcass I could have used. But I was on a time schedule and had to work alone for obvious reasons. The good point was that I didn't have to share the sandwich money with anyone. Ha! Ha!

I would cut the meat I was going to use and place it in a big bowl and wash it real well. Then place it back in the bowl and fill it with cold water and about a cup of salt and red wine. I would let it marinate for about four hours. Then I would rinse and wash it one more time. Then rub it down with pepper and a little tenderizer and then mix it in on the grill with the beef and pork I was cooking and slip it into a sandwich. No one could ever tell the difference . . . You might get a lot of cool Christmas presents, but

no one else will give you what I have just written down for you.
My secret recipe. You should try it out this summer on some of
your friends. Trust me, they will love it.

Christmas Day
Dear Anthony,

Did you get my secret recipe? I've been feeling a little some-
what down lately. Christmas always has that affect on me since
I have been locked up. It's the one time of the year that makes
me realize that I am truly alone. And I have no one to blame but
myself and the bad decisions I have made in my life. . . . I always
hear people say they took the easy way out when someone com-
mits suicide, but that is stone-cold bullshit to me. Suicide is the
hardest thing in the world to do. I have tried to take myself out
a least three times, but I have punked out at the last second. My
younger brother committed suicide back in 1976. He was only
sixteen at the time and we were close. He took a shotgun and put
the barrel under his chin and then blew his fucking brains out
of the top of his head all over the ceiling and wall behind him.
Anyway, I was glad to hear you had a nice Christmas out there.
I appreciate your letters . . . If I have learned nothing else during
my incarceration, I have learned to appreciate every little good
thing that comes my way. I also never forget there are a lot of
people out there that will not be able to enjoy life's little pleasures
and holidays because I put them in the ground . . .

Dear Joe,

Thanks for sharing some of your emotional side with me . . . It helps
me get to know Joe Metheny the person and not just Joe Metheny the
serial murderer . . . I like that. It makes me feel there is a sense of trust
in our relationship . . . I was very shocked to hear that you have attempted suicide a few times but always chicken out at the last moment.
It's amazing to think a man like yourself who can tie a woman up, slit
her throat and gut her like a deer without batting an eye or giving it
a second thought, feeling no remorse, no sympathy, not having a conscience whatsoever about what he had just done—thinks about killing
himself. What you just read right there is me making a comparison to

how you can deliver death so easily but when it comes time to face death yourself, you fear and decide not to cross that line to the other side.

I was just thinking to myself and I want to know this—is the real reason why you only try to commit suicide up to a certain point until turning back because maybe you fear what waits for you on the other side?

19

Serial Killer David Gore's story

July 26, 1983

Fourteen-year-old Michael Rock was pedaling his bicycle near a house in Vero Beach, Florida, when he heard a woman scream. A naked teenage girl burst from the front door of a nearby house with her hands tied.

As the boy watched, a pudgy naked man ran after her, knocking her to the ground. Raising a handgun, he fired twice into her head, killing her.

The bicyclist raced home and told his mother, Linda, who called the Indian River County Sheriff's Office. Within ten minutes, Deputy C. C. Walker had picked up Linda and Michael and followed the boy's directions to a home near the edge of town.

"That's it!" the boy declared, pointing at the ranch-style house.

At just about that same moment, a 911 emergency telephone call came from someone inside the house, but the caller hung up without speaking. Seconds later, another call came from inside the house.

"I hear a woman screaming in an orange grove area near my house," a male voice said before slamming down the receiver. Two minutes later, a third call came in. "There's a man chasing a woman in the grove area behind my house and I think she is wounded."

By this point, nearly a dozen deputies had circled the house. A detective was using the loudspeakers on top of his patrol car to roust whoever was inside, but no one would come the door. The 911 dispatcher correctly suspected that the male caller in the house was trying to distract the deputies by sending them on a wild-goose chase in a nearby orange grove, giving him time to escape. Accessing public property records, the dispatcher identified the owners of the house. She also determined that they had a son: David Gore, a thirty-two-year-old ex-convict with a history of preying on women.

Deputy Walker gingerly approached the house and ducked into the garage. There were drag marks on the floor and something was dripping from the trunk of a white sedan parked there. Walker bent down to look closer. It was blood. He forced open the car's trunk. The nude body of Lynn Carol Elliott, age seventeen, was stuffed inside it. She was the teen who had been seen running from the house only moments earlier. She was dead.

Deputies warned Gore that they would use tear gas to flush him from his parents' house unless he surrendered. But there was no answer. Donning bulletproof vests and carrying shotguns, the deputies forced open a back door and began searching the house. It appeared empty until a deputy noticed a trapdoor that led into the attic. One of the deputies heard movement and ordered whoever was hiding there to come down.

The door opened and Gore came down its collapsible steps. A deputy climbed up to check the space. A naked girl, age fourteen, was lying on the joists in handcuffs.

With so much evidence against him, Gore confessed. His story horrified not only the residents of Vero Beach, but the entire Sunshine State.

Gore told detectives that he and his older cousin, Fred Waterfield, had spent several years hunting women across Florida. They abducted, raped, tortured, and killed them as sport. He'd admitted five murders, but was suspected of more.

Gore and Waterfield, both in their early thirties at the time, had been best friends growing up in Indian River County, a flat, rural coastal area about 130 miles north of Miami. The region was best known for its orange and citrus groves. Until the murders, the locals had jokingly referred to Vero Beach as "Zero Beach," claiming that nothing exciting ever happened there.

The two men's first known attempt at kidnapping a woman had taken place seven years earlier, when they noticed a woman driving alone on a deserted section of State Highway 60. They shot out her car tires with a rifle, but she managed to escape on foot. No charges were filed.

The duo next picked up a woman in a beach bar and later took turns raping her, but they didn't kill her. After reporting the attack, she later refused to appear in court and all charges were dropped.

Incredibly, four years after that rape, Gore was sworn in as an auxiliary sheriff's deputy, a job that gave him access to a badge. He immediately put it to use.

For several days, Gore stalked Ying Hua Ling, a seventeen-year-old high school student. He approached her in February 1981 after she was dropped off near her house by a school bus. Flashing his badge, he ordered her into his truck and then drove to her house, where he planned to rape her. But her mother, Hsiang Huang Ling, age forty-eight, was there. She had just arrived a few weeks earlier from Taiwan, her husband and two children having immigrated to the United States before her.

Gore pulled a gun on both women and drove them to an orange grove outside Vero Beach, where he tied them to trees facing one another. He telephoned Waterfield and then raped both the mother and the daughter while waiting for his cousin to join him. Waterfield rejected Hsiang as being too old, so the two men rearranged the ropes that were binding her to a tree so that she would slowly strangle. Meanwhile, they repeatedly raped her daughter in front of her. When they finished, they killed the teenager, too. Both bodies were chopped up, put into fifty-five-gallon drums, and buried in an orange grove.

Having drawn blood, Gore soon tried to abduct another teenager but she got away. On July 15, 1981, he spotted Judith Kaye Daley sunbathing at Round Island Beach, a few miles outside Vero Beach. The thirty-five-year-old California housewife was visiting relatives and had just dropped her two daughters at another beach popular with teens. By leaving the girls there, Daley had inadvertently saved their lives. Gore disabled Daley's car and then pretended to be a Good Samaritan. He showed her his badge and offered her a ride. As soon as she got into his truck, he pulled a pistol and handcuffed her. Gore called his cousin and announced that he had a "package." Both men raped and tortured Daley before finally murdering her. They decapitated her, buried her skull in an orange grove, and tossed her torso into a nearby canal that was frequented by alligators and turtles.

A week later, Gore was on the hunt again. This time he chose a teenager whom he spotted leaving a beach. He flashed his badge and told her that a robbery had happened, and that her car matched the description of the getaway vehicle. He ordered her to follow him in her vehicle back to the sheriff's office for questioning. But instead of leading her there, he drove her to a remote area. He had just parked his truck and was heading back to her car to attack her when two men emerged from woods. They'd been fishing nearby. Gore panicked and ordered the teen to leave. When she got home, she told her father and he drove her to the sheriff's office. There had been no robberies that day, nor did an auxiliary deputy have the authority to detain motorists. Gore was stripped of his deputy's badge.

A few days later, a woman emerged from a doctor's office and spotted someone hiding in the backseat of her car. She screamed and a deputy sheriff came running to help her. By chance, he'd been in the same doctor's office. Gore was tucked behind the driver's seat, armed with a pistol, handcuffs, and a police scanner. He was not wearing a shirt. He explained that he had ducked into the car to hide from his ex-wife. He'd been following her to the doctor's office and had chosen the car at random.

But when deputies called his ex-wife, she told them that she hadn't had an appointment that day.

A jury deliberated thirty minutes before finding him guilty of armed trespassing. Sentenced to five years in prison, Gore was paroled after serving eighteen months. In prison, he'd claimed to have found Jesus and rehabilitated himself.

Gore moved in with his parents in Vero Beach, and within days, he and Waterfield were hunting again. They tried to abduct an Orlando prostitute, but she got away. Their next two targets were not so lucky.

In May 1983, the men picked up two hitchhikers, Barbara Byer and Angelica Lavallee, both age fourteen. The men raped the girls and murdered them.

Their final two victims also were hitchhiking when Gore and Waterfield spotted them, offered them rides, and took them to Gore's parents' house. His mom and dad were away on vacation. This is where Gore was spotted by the teenage bicyclist shooting Lynn Elliott in the head when she tried to escape.

Prosecutors needed Gore to testify against his cousin, so they cut a deal. In return for his testimony, Gore was spared the death penalty in five of the murders that he'd admitted. For those killings, he was sentenced to consecutive life prison terms. But the state refused to let Gore plea-bargain on the sixth killing—the blatant shooting of Lynn Elliott.

At his trial, defense attorneys said Gore had been manipulated by Waterfield, but the jury didn't buy it. Gore was sentenced to death. Waterfield got two consecutive life sentences and was ordered by a judge to spend at least fifty years in prison before he could be considered for parole. Both men immediately cried foul and appealed their convictions.

20

EXCERPTS FROM LETTERS BETWEEN DAVID GORE AND TONY

Dear Anthony,

*. . . Unfortunately, I grew up in a little hick town like May-
berry and the cunts in that town were really stuck up, hard to
get and loved to tease. We didn't even have a hooker in town
so if you got any, you really had to work for it. I did get a few
but they were either drunk or passed out when I fucked them. I
met this one chick one night in a bar when I was young and she
was pretty plastered and we hooked up. I figured it was time to
take her home and score. Well, when we got in my car, this cunt
passed out. I figured she'd wake up by the time we got home, but
she didn't so I actually carried her into my house, took off her
clothes and spread her and fucked her. Then I pulled the sheet
over her and figured she'd wake up. After a couple hours, I decided I'd put her clothes back on her and took her back to her
car. You know I did manage to take a few pictures of her. . . . I
used to be big on taking pictures of chicks . . .*

*Let me tell you, I have NO scruples when it comes to sex.
NONE. Hell, I even tried to fuck my mother-in-law . . . I don't
know if you are aware of this, but I have a co-defendant who
was arrested with me. Him and I were first cousins and grew up
together. We were more like brothers . . . and he had the exactly
same scruples as I did when it came to sex. NONE.*

*. . . When I look back, the first time the boundaries were ever
crossed between me and Fred was when I was over at his house
and his mother Midge walked into the room wearing a see thru
blouse and you could see her nipples and I didn't say anything,
but Fred spoke up after his mom left and said how would you like*

to suck those? At first I didn't know what to say but I said, oh yeah and from then on we brought up things in our conversations about sex and what we'd like to do to women . . .

Dear David,

. . . Please tell me more about your childhood. Why do you think you are the way you are?

Dear Anthony,

. . . When I was just a toddler, I fell into a fire ant bed outside our home and got stung all over. I actually went into a convulsion and was rushed to the hospital where I had a fever of 102–103. They said because my temperature got so high it literally altered my brain. I believe this and I believe it is a link to why I am in prison now . . . I think when people go through such ordeals you really can't control the way we act . . .

You asked if I have nightmares. No, not really. I have pretty much accepted what the past is and there's nothing I can do to change it, so why fret over it, right?

Dear David,

I want more details and I want you to talk about your crimes individually. Don't worry about getting too gory in your stories with me because you won't gross me out or offend me in anyway. . . . I'm not a neurologist but the trauma you suffered as a youngster may have caused some brain damage in the areas that control your sense of rage. I'll bet you have a very explosive temper and probably had trouble getting along with others . . .

Dear Anthony,

You believe I might have an explosive temper. You know I really don't. In fact, it really takes a LOT to get me mad. I am more likely to flatten your car tires rather than attack you. I do believe there had to be some sort of chemical alteration in my brain due to being exposed to the fire ants. How else can you explain what we did?

. . . My cousin and I used to take women to the orange grove where I had a mobile home trailer. It sat right in the middle of

almost 400 acres of grove in a thick wood. Him and I used to spend a lot of time with them there and we were not choirboys. What was odd was I was sort of quiet and shy, when he was the opposite. We made a great team . . .

I have always believed we all have a very dark inner-self that we never allow anyone to see and it starts in us when we are very young . . .

One of the things I used to do as a kid was slip into people's homes when they were away and go through their personal items. And let me tell you, I found some pretty bizarre items that women had that you would never have guessed they would have. I found drawers full of nude photos of them. Of course, I had to collect a few. I was inside a woman's home one time when she suddenly came home. Talk about a reaction.

I'll tell you right now, I feel like I am totally alone. I don't have family and no one seems to really care what life is like for me . . . I just sit here in this cell 24/7.

Dear Anthony,

It is hot here and there was a time when I loved hot weather because I could hang out at the beaches and check out the chicks in their bikinis. Of course, I always checked out secluded beaches where you could always find chicks nude sunbathing. Three of my victims actually came off a beach . . . I mentioned earlier in a letter that I was obsessed with Asian chicks . . . I'd be driving down the highway just going about my day and I'd see an Oriental chick and I had to stop all I was doing and check her out. So you can imagine my intense joy the day I spotted this young oriental walking by herself down the road. You know I think a lot of girls like men to chase them. My problem was I was always a bit shy. My cousin was the one who lured them into our snare. Once they were there, they were like bugs caught in a web. Smile.

Dear David,

You mentioned in your last letter that three of your victims came from the beach. Please go into that story a little bit with me . . . Remember you telling me how you have it for Asians? Were any of your victims

Asians and how many victims did you have total? Whose idea was it to rape and murder them?

Dear Anthony,

. . . You asked me whose idea was it to do what we did? It was both of our's. We pretty much had the same desires. And yes, we did work together as a team. But there were times when one of us went solo, but whenever that happened we would always notify the other as to what went down. We had a standard rule between us that at ANY time one of us set our sights on a victim, no matter WHO she was, the other one would team up and then do it together. Many times, I'd go to his [auto repair] shop and he'd tell me he had one picked out and we'd take off and stalk it until we devised our plan. Then there would be times, him and I would just take off on a "hunt" until we found a prospect.

He owned a mechanic shop and people would leave their cars at his shop to be fixed and pick it up the next day and when they did that he always drove them back home. I was at his shop on a couple of occasions when women by themselves would want to drop a car off and all he would have to do was give me a look and I'd know he wanted to get her so when he offered to take her home, he'd tell her he had to drop me off somewhere and well, that was that, we always knew what the others was thinking.

Dear David,

. . . Tell me how did you pick your victims? I'd really like to know.

Dear Anthony,

I could sit in any parking lot and watch and observe women and I could tell you how alert they were. You asked me about the beaches. Let me just say the beach was without question a favorite hunting ground—especially during the weekdays. In the country where I lived you could drive along the coast the entire length of the county. There were literally dozens of secluded beach areas with little trails leading up to the bluff. You could pull your car down on one of these roads and no one could see you or your car.

*When we were on a hunt, we would drive up-and-down con-
stantly checking these areas. We knew exactly what the plan was.
Our method was always the same. If we pulled up to a bluff and
a car was parked, we'd walk over the bluff, covertly check to see
who was lying out in the sun and if it was a go, we'd disable the
car, and move down the beach where we could observe. When
one of our preys got ready to leave, we pulled back down and
they would ask for assistance when we pulled up. This was before
cell phones. Of course we were always willing to assist and when
we couldn't get their car started they always would ask for a ride
because they didn't want to be stranded. And let me say once they
were in OUR truck between us, it was easy. I just never could
believe how women could be so naive about things . . .*

*You asked how many victims were Asians. Actually, only three.
They were something too. If I was hunting neighborhoods, I always made sure I didn't drive down a street more than once. You
drive up and down a street people take notice . . . Now my cousin
didn't care about all that. We'd be driving down the highway and
if he saw one he liked, he'd say, "Let's get her" and it didn't matter who might see us . . . If we wanted to do something, we did it
and didn't care.*

*Tony, we have done things that were pretty horrible. We had
absolutely NO mercy. You said you read on the computer where
it said one victim was fed to the alligators. That was true . . .*

*. . . The state prosecutor put a psychiatrist on the stand and
this doctor testified that I was a hunter—that I hunted females
like a big game hunter hunts his prey and when I bag one, I'd
harvest it like the big game hunter. That was true. I took trophies.
You should have heard the whispers and sighs of people in the
court when he said that. Some of the things described during my
trial most people couldn't comprehend . . . sometimes I can't even
believe I was capable of some of those things that I did. I was so
full of hate and anger. I did not care about anything or anybody.
If I could inflict pain, I inflicted it to the max. I wanted others to
hurt the way I hurt. But the thing was that although I had all the
rage, it wasn't like I just went off. I internalized it and vented it
out very cool and methodically.*

For instance, if you were to meet me back then you would

think I was the nicest guy cause that's what I wanted people to see. That way, they would not put their guard up and I could strike. My rage came out in a quiet, deadly way. I could be the guy next door and then slip right into a dark, evil side without anyone noticing it. I always knew when I was slipping from the good me to the bad me, but you could not tell.

Dear David,

. . . I'm so glad we have met, David, and how we are becoming such good friends as fast as we have . . .

Do they let you write your cousin, Fred? I'm sitting here just imagining what you two hell raisers must have been like when you were children . . . I guess I could go on and on with questions because I'm so interested in this kind of stuff . . . to actually be friends and communicate with somebody that you can only read about in crime books or on different webpages is really something! In the beginning I was just interested in exploring a well-known serial killer, but now it has gone so much further and we have actually developed a close friendship. . . .

Please tell me a little bit about your mother and father and how they reacted when they found out their son was responsible for all that went down . . . Please share with me how you were able to keep your actions private from your family and friends?

Dear Anthony,

I come from a really good family. I was never abused. My parents really did the best they could. We were just plain old country folks who basically lived off the land. We hunted for food, grew our own veggies, milked cows. My dad would work his butt off to provide for us. I can truly, without a doubt, say that the way my life turned out was in no way my parents' fault. I've had more than one lawyer who has worked on my case and looked at my background and come right out and said, "This don't make sense!" . . .

So much of what my cousin and I did defies explanation . . . And it's hard to describe this, except to say it was like a lot of times you will have such an intense sex drive and others times it was low. There were days when as soon as I woke up in the morning, I knew I had to find one that day to do. Then there were times when I could go several days and have absolutely no desire to do anything. Fred was the same way. There were times when one of us would pick the other up early and we'd literally drive hundreds of miles hunting because of the urges that we both felt. We had to satisfy those URGES.

Our favorite target was hitchhikers. We used to laugh and call them FREEBIES because there was basically no risk involved and they were easy to catch. I mean you have two men hunting for one and one jumps right in the car with you. How simple is that?

We used to drive a couple hundred miles on the Interstate 95 and we'd get off at every on-and-off ramp we came to because hitchhikers use to stand on the ramps trying to catch a ride . . . Girls just have no idea how dangerous it is to hitchhike. I guess they think nothing will happen to them.

Dear Anthony,

I truly believe what causes a person to become a SK is more in the genes than anything. And when you add to that any sort of brain trauma, you have the makings of a true killer. Look at me and my cousin. What makes two men from the same immediate family becomes SKs. It HAS to be in my genes. You should have heard some of the conversations we had when we were together. And believe me, there was absolutely NOONE who we saw or knew who was off-limits to us if we decided to go after them . . .

It started young with us. Him and I were using that date rape drug years ago when we were on the streets before people knew about it. You had to be real selective on how you used it, but it did work great . . . the truth is that the cops don't have a clue about how many women him and I raped before they caught us.

Dear David,

. . . I am with you when you say that you believe whatever it has to be genetic. . . . I personally also believe that becoming a serial killer is something that you can grow up with too if you were brought up in to families that were less than zero. Tell me more about your cousin . . .

Dear Anthony,

Me and my cousin, our desires were SO much alike, the only differences between his likes and my likes was he was obsessed with really young ones. The younger the better was his rule and I liked the older ones so that was really the only difference.

. . . Him and I would take off the entire weekend. We would make all of our families believe we were going fishing or hunting so they didn't have a clue. We would use the trailer in my orange grove as our hunting base. We'd take off on like a Friday night and if we got lucky and grabbed one, we'd spend all night Friday and all day Saturday enjoying our catch and Saturday night we'd be back on the hunt for a new one. Sunday was always the clean up day. . . .

. . . I may have mentioned before but Fred [Waterfield] had a 4-by-4 Auto Shop and he also had a wrecker service. There was one time he went on a wrecker call. This woman had broken down on I-95 and called him to tow her car. Well, he brought her and her car to his shop and he determined her car needed some major repairs. So she agreed to leave it at his shop for a couple days while he fixed it and she got a motel at the beach. Well, this woman was NICE and him and I got to discussing how we could get her. Then she told him she was traveling from NEBRASKA down to Miami to start a new life because she had just gotten out of a bad marriage. For him and me this was perfect. We decided when she came to pick up her car, we'd get her then. On the day she came to pick it up, I was there too and I sort of made a comment that she should take a puppy home with her. Well, her face lit up about a puppy. I told her we had several in a cage in the back if she wanted to look at them and she was eager to go back there. We had planned to walk with her to the back room and when we got there grab her and tie her up. Well just as we were about to get to the back room, Fred's mom came in and called him and instead of taking this cunt to the back, we turned around to go back to the front where his mom was. I was pissed and Fred even more pissed. We had this woman and his mom ruined it for us. Our plan was aborted while his mom was there. There were several circumstances like that and to this day, these girls don't know just how close they came to being a statistic. This woman at his shop was no more than 30 seconds away from being put down. Later we discussed how pissed we were

at his mom for coming to that shop at the wrong time and Fred told me if he had known how pissed I was, then we would have gone and got that woman and got HIS mom both that day. That's how angry he was. We would have taken out his MOM too along with that woman. When Fred got pissed like that, it didn't matter WHO it was—even his mom. What many people don't know is when you get psyched up and you're in the process of carrying out a plan, and you get interrupted, you lose all sense of reality. The only thing you care about is satisfying the URGE and you don't care who it is, all you want is to fulfill that urge and that is what almost happened that day. Him and I agreed after that if we ever got into that situation again, and either one of us wanted to carry it out, the other would be right there. That became a set rule for us.

Dear Anthony,

    . . . I don't think a serial killer really has a choice. They may be able to suppress their desire and urges, but if genes play a part, how do you change your genes? Even people who know it's wrong are powerless against it . . . I've never tried to hide from who I am. I've always known there was something inside of me that made me different . . . I'd be at a friend's house sometimes and I'd be seeing his wife and I'd be thinking—Damn, I'd like to do her—and immediately after thinking that, I'd say to my-self—Why am I thinking this?—you see, I'd know it wasn't right, but it was there lurking just beneath the surface, always on my mind. . . .

    I made a mistake once when I was hunting by myself of getting a woman who had some weight to her. She wasn't what you'd call butterball fat, but rather she was just a big boned woman. . . . that was one heavy cunt to move around and after her I swore never to get another one that big because she was too hard to handle . . .

    . . . One system me and Fred had was when we located one that lived alone or was alone during the day, one of us would drop the other off and they would go inside her home and wait for her to come home. There were a couple who didn't come home when they were supposed to and we'd have to abort. If they had *come home, it would have been over for them because we were waiting. I wonder about those women and wish they knew what almost happened to them.*

Dear David,

. . . I guess a lot of those would-be victims have a lot to be thankful for. . . . When it came to killing what was your favorite method of putting people down? Did you prefer strangulations, gun or a knife to finish the job?

Dear Anthony,

. . . You know how you always hear how SKs will take a trophy or a souvenir? Well, a woman's hair were my souvenirs. I've always wanted to understand WHY I did what I did to women. I have enough sense to realize my actions were so far out of the norm. I've even told my lawyers that I was curious about that but no one seems to be interested except for you.

You asked me about Fred and his mechanics shop . . . There was one time when we did coax a woman from out of town whose car had broken down into that back room. We tied her up and put a gag in her mouth and then we put her in our van and took her out to the trailer in the grove where we literally took turns doing what we wanted to her. We spent hours working on her. After we were spent, we found a good spot and disposed of everything. Later that night, we cleaned her car up and drove it about two counties away and parked it in a mall lot and then we came back. . . . This is one of the women I confessed to the police. I even told them where she was buried, but they didn't care. I don't know if you knew this, but I was convicted for killing six women even though I told the police that there were many others. I think the police chose not to pursue them others because they weren't sure if they had enough evidence and they already had my confession on five of them and one case for the death penalty so their thinking was they didn't want to cost the taxpayers anymore money on things they weren't sure they could get a conviction on when they already had enough to put me away. . . . But them others are still out there, Anthony.

Dear David,

. . . Based on your letter, I think it would be fair to say that what started out as a sexual obsession for you, grew into a passion and once it reached that level in your mind, it controlled you. It would be like me trying to live without water or food. Is that how important this URGE became in your life? Every morning when you woke up did you feel the need to kill and the only way to get that need fulfilled was to troll, stalk and destroy? Why do you think you didn't have any feelings for your victims? You seem like such a thoughtful guy. How could you torture them?

Dear Tony,

. . . You were sharing with me about how you thought I should feel more for the victims but don't, and I truly can understand that. Believe me, I've thought about this a million times. And I do believe when I fell into that ant hill as a toddler and got stung so many times . . . that I lost the capacity to care . . . I WISH many times I wasn't like that. But whenever that URGE would set in, I had to hunt. And you are right, the victims were just in the wrong place at the wrong time. And believe me, I don't mind at all sharing with you details of events . . . I actually enjoy it.

In my job, I constantly driving all over the county to all the citrus groves so at any given time I could happen upon an opportunity to do one, so I kept all my "tools" which included gun, rope, tape and all in my truck. I know most guys looked for a certain type of female before they would get her. With me, it didn't matter. I mean, sure if I saw one that looked good to me, I'd stalk her until I could make my move.

There was this one day I was driving around and I was hunting, and I had that URGE. Well, I came upon this woman, standing in front of her car alongside the road. The hood of her car was up and it was obvious she was stranded and her car broke down. So I saw an opportunity. Now this woman was probably in her late 40s maybe even 50, but she wasn't all that bad.

I pulled over and offered to help and she accepted. Since her car had a busted radiator hose, I told her I could drive her to an auto parts store, get the hose and come back and fix it. We got in my truck and off down the road we went and when the coast was clear, I pulled my gun on her. She was stunned. Of course, I told her if she tired anything, I'd shoot her and she kept asking why was I doing this. I would just tell her to shut up. My grove was maybe five miles away so I kept the gun on her this whole time. We pulled up to the trailer and I made her lean forward and I tied her wrists together behind her back. She was scared and kept begging me not to hurt her and asking why was I doing this. After I tied her hands, I grabbed her by her hair, pulled her head back and with my hand cupped one of her tits and squeezed hard and said: "This is why cunt." I pulled her out, got her in the trailer and onto the bed where I cut all of her clothes off. She didn't have a fantastic body, but my URGE was intense and I just wanted one. Her tits were nice but saggy and she had this thick mat of pubic hair. I guess older women don't trim down there. She was pretty much in a state of shock from fear. I told her if she did exactly what I told her to do I would not hurt her. When I had cut her clothes off, she would shake with fear and just had this glazed over look. I told her I was going to screw her and if she didn't do anything crazy I would not secure her feet to the bed and I told her if she did anything whatever I didn't like, I would not hesitate to shoot her.

I ended up giving her a good screw. She wasn't the tightest hole but she wasn't no young chick. The entire time I was screwing her, she lay there like a mummy. The only time I got a reaction from her was when I bit down on her nipples. Since she had this thick mat of pubic hair, I wanted it so I got out my razor to shave her and she freaked out when she saw that. I had to scold her a bit to keep her still. Ha ha. I did end up securing her feet to the bed.

After I gave her a bald pussy, I spent some time enjoying her body, probing all her holes, running my fingers through her hair, pulling on it. Sucking and biting her tits. Then I just slowly moved up, sat on her chest with a knee on each side of her chest. I was rubbing her face and my hands slipped around her neck as I told her I changed my mind. I began squeezing as she bucked and struggled before she slowly went limp.

Then it was just a matter of cleaning up, storing my trophy. I went through her purse and I believe she had a pair of panties in her purse. That surprised me.

I'll tell you Tony, during the process of the whole situation, there was not a lot of long conversations. It's pretty much like being a robot. I really didn't want them to say a word. And it depended a bit on what mood I was in. It's hard to really describe the emotional state I would be in while doing one. It was like I had no emotions. I was just doing it. And you know where I got my biggest rush was really not the sex part, it was the capture. That was when I got a high. By the way, this woman was the oldest I'd ever done. . . .

Dear David,

. . . Wow, that was quite a letter! Thank you for sharing those details with me. You got in trouble for six murders but just from you writing to me and filling me in on some of your stories, I would have to say there is a lot more murders you did. I am not going to ask you the number but I will put the ball in your court. If you would like to share with me the full number I would love to hear it. My mom just got done cooking dinner so I better get in the kitchen so she doesn't have to come in here and twice to tell me.

Dear Anthony,

. . . *You asked me how many women did I kill? Yes, there were more than what I was convicted of. The cops told a man who wrote a book about us that we had done about twenty women.*

You asked me about my fetish with hair and scalping my victims and wrote that you can't envision it. I understand that. But it's like a deer hunter. He goes out and he shoots this big buck with a nice rack of horns so he saws the horns off and brings them home to hang on his wall as a trophy. When you think about it: WHY does he do it? It's simple. He wants to look at it and admire it. In the mind of a serial killer, we do the same act whether it is hair, jewelry, or whatever. We take it as a trophy from the kill. With hair, I'm not sure where my obsession for it came from but I took scalps to admire . . .

Dear David,

. . . I am so thankful that I have you to talk to . . . You are one of those men that my parents warned me about when I was growing up. All that stuff—never talk to strangers, whatever you do don't ever go any-where with anybody unless we tell you to . . . you were one of these men and for me to be able to say, I'm good friends with one of those men—is just beyond my world . . .

Dear Anthony,

. . . You asked if I disliked women. I don't or I guess I should say not ALL women. When I was on the street, I had a couple of Best Friends who were girls. The experience I had with my ex-wife when we got divorced really caused me to mistrust certain women. My ex-wife had two sisters and one I got along with great, but the other was a Class A stuck-up cunt who thought the world owed her everything. There is no way to describe how angry I became over how my ex-wife and her stuck up sister did everything in their power to destroy my life. It went on for years and I came to the point where I felt the whole world was against me. I just didn't care anymore. I think when a person reaches that state of mind; they stop thinking and just function like a robot. I hated everything and everyone. I felt like I had absolutely NO control over anything in my life. You might not know this, but I never committed a crime unless I had some alcoholic drinks. I think that gave me what is called DUTCH COURAGE to do things.

The day the cops surrounded my parent's house, let me tell you there were so many cops and I peeked out the window and the ambulance was there, fire trucks, there had to have been 75 police all around. The only reason they did not come in to get me was they knew I had another victim in the house. When I came to the point I knew it was over and I was going to give myself up, I actually told her to stay put and wait for the cops to come in. If I was such a killer, why didn't I kill that girl? But you don't ever really hear that part of my story because it shows too much of the human side of me.

Dear David,

. . . You are very good at painting a picture for me. I like it when you explain the murders in detail. It's like you have a good way of using adjectives or descriptive words to make me feel like I am almost the one committing the crimes myself. . . . I try very hard when I write to you not to make it sound like I'm interviewing you because I'm not. I know for sure that that is how people think you want to be approached. They forget because of the horrible crimes you committed that you are still a human being. That's the difference between them and myself. I'm not just interested in David Gore the serial killer who brutally put many women to their demise. I'm interested in David Gore the person, the father, the man, and the killer . . .

David, when you were committing your crimes did you feel a sense of invincibility, or did you always know that someday you were for sure going to be caught? It just seems to me that all serial killers eventually go down. Is the urge to kill that strong and uncontrollable that it is worth taking the chance of having to pay the consequences once caught, or taking the other scenario, do you not even think about getting caught while engaging in such risky behavior?

Dear Anthony,

You know, I guess in the back of my mind, I knew there was the possibility I could get caught. But I always figured I'd be careful enough not to. The thing is the more you do it—murder someone—the more relaxed you get and the more careless you become and eventually you get too careless and yes, that URGE can truly be overwhelming. It's sort of along the lines as being horny. You start getting horny and it just keeps building until you have to get some relief.

That is the same with the URGE to kill. It usually starts out slow and builds and you will take whatever chances necessary to satisfy it. And believe me, you constantly think about getting caught, but the rush is worth the risk.

I've gone on a hunt that lasted all day and didn't find one. And by the end of the day, the URGE would be SO INTENSE you began to think of prospects you wouldn't normally think about. All you want is to satisfy the URGE. That URGE one time was so intense in me I pulled up in my driveway KNOWING my wife was inside and sat there thinking about doing her just to satisfy it. I actually pondered going in, walking up behind her, and wrestling her down and doing her. There's just no way to describe how bad you want to satisfy that URGE. And once you do, every-thing is back to normal until it begins to build again.

With me, I always had a couple of possible prospects I'd keep in mind just for days when I couldn't find one. I'd then go to them and see how easy it was to get one. They were usually ones that wouldn't be easy and required risk, but they were still there just in case. One of the ones I kept in mind was my sister's best friend. I knew I could go to her house and give her an excuse and she'd let me in because she knew me. In fact, I did that once and had every intention of getting her. I was standing in her kitchen and we were talking, but in the back of my mind, I was looking for an opening to go ahead and grab her. I was waiting for her to turn her back to me so I could attack. Well, while I was waiting for that moment, my sister called her and she was telling my sister that I was there visiting and when that happened I had no choice but to abort because I'd of been the first prime suspect. That was a day that nothing worked out. Boy, when my sister called, I was pissed. I mean I was just seconds away from getting her friend. I ended up going home very, very frustrated. . . .

21

Las Vegas psychologist Nick Ponzo began noticing changes in his young patient.

"Writing to the serial killers had become a compulsion," Ponzo said in an interview for this book. "It had become a very singular focus for Tony. It was taking all of his time and he was doing nothing else or little else. I also noticed that he had started glorifying them. Even worse, he had begun *identifying* with them. . . . Tony still harbored deep anger and resentment about how his friends in high school had rejected him after his WaveRunner accident—how they had made fun of him. Because of his brain injury, he didn't feel that he really fit in very well and he was angry that the world didn't understand him. The psychopaths who he was writing to were a captive audience and both Tony and these killers were thriving on their newfound relationships. Tony was getting the gratification of having the very strong focus of one individual and having that individual seemingly need him and look forward to his letters. . . . These killers were not criticizing him, questioning him, or challenging him as a person. What were they getting? I imagine that for them, here was this young kid who seemed larger than life and he was taking time to pay attention to them in a jail cell. So both sides were each receiving gratification from the other. He was sharing intimate details of his personal life with them and they were telling him things that shocked and horrified and provided him with stories that no one else was hearing."

Although he was becoming concerned about Tony's increased obsession with serial killers, Ponzo had a more immediate issue to resolve with his client.

One year after he had started writing to serial killers, Tony wanted to stop taking psychotropic medications. When Ponzo asked him why, Tony was characteristically frank. The pills were interfering with his sexual performance. The antipsychotics made him impotent. To compensate, he took Viagra or Cialis. While those medications worked, Tony was having trouble achieving an orgasm. Understandably, that left him frustrated. Tony said he'd fallen in love with Crystal and he was worried that his sexual problems would harm their relationship.

There were other reasons why Tony wanted to stop taking his pills. He'd packed on fifty pounds, a common side effect of many medications. The extra weight was one reason why he'd recently developed diabetes. Other pills were known to cause liver damage.

As was his habit, Tony had already told his serial killer friends about his decision to wean himself off his medications. Most encouraged him to do it. He was especially candid in a letter to Shawcross.

Dear Arthur,

. . . Everything I do feel's to me in essence to listening to someone speak with a monotone voice. I can't seem to get pumped up for anything. I'm not being dramatic either because when I am doing something even something I love, I can't seem to bring my A-game to the event or task at hand. I am very passionate at everything I do because if I didn't give it my all to everything I attempt to do or spend my valuable time at, it would be a farce because why would I spend any time on something if I was only going to do a half-ass job?

The problem is with one of the medicines I take right now. I am taking more of it right now because at one point in my treatment my behavior needed more of this drug to control me. It is a drug that evens your mood and makes you somewhat a monotone. Well, being that monotone is driving me crazy and I need to be able to get excited again for the things that move me emotionally and passionately. When I run my fingers through my girlfriend's long, beautiful, black, silky, hair I want to feel it slide in between my fingers. . . . Not be numb.

I'm tired Arthur, so fucking tired of being numb, numb to a world of emotions out there that have been stolen from me thanks to Dr. Feel Good and his many, many prescription medications that have robbed me from a normal, teenage, adolescence, young adulthood and now venturing into my 30s. I know that sounds horrible but what's even worse is that when my 40s, 50s, and even 60s come around, I will still be taking the same old shit. This is something I don't talk about often, but I bet you didn't know this or never were aware of this disappointing fact. You see when you take a medicine that controls your emotions or your moods, they have something called side effects . . . When you take anti-depressants, you can't even get your dick hard. That's right, I said it, since I've been 16 years old, I haven't been able to get my dick hard unless I take a fucking pill! Do you know what that does to your self esteem?

Al and Chris turned to Ponzo and Dr. Duffy for guidance. Dr. Duffy was dead set against weaning Tony off his medicines. "Tony will always be on medication," the psychiatrist declared. "He can't function without it." Having him stop would be dangerous.

But Ponzo was not so adamant. He told them that nearly all patients decide to stop taking medication at some point in their lives. If Tony was determined to try it, now was as good a time as any. Ironically, this had been what Drew Bulino, Tony's therapist in Plano, Texas, had told them, too, the last time that Tony had stopped taking his pills. That incident had ended with Tony becoming suicidal. But Tony had been a teenager then. Perhaps now he could cope better.

Ponzo believed Tony could be taught, through cognitive behavioral therapy, how to overcome some of the problems caused by his brain injury.

"Tony functions well on many levels," Ponzo explained later. "He makes friends. He interacts with his family. He is not in a vegetative state in any way because of his brain injury. He is very verbal and expressive. He tells jokes. He has relationships. He wants to function in society and does on many levels, so the first question became: how effectively can he function in spite of his brain injury? And the second became: why should we suggest that all he is—is someone who can't control his impulses and just needs to be medicated and just prevented from exploding and doing anything dangerous? I felt strongly that he could control these rages. I could help him learn how."

Ponzo had always felt Tony was capable of learning how to control his outbursts. When the therapist first met him, Tony had mentioned that he had become close friends with his former therapist in Texas. In fact, the entire Ciaglia family had become friends with Bulino. Ponzo had bluntly stated that he had no desire to become Tony's friend. In fact, he didn't really care if they liked each other.

"Psychotherapy is not for the squeamish," Ponzo warned him. "If you decide to work with me, you will be challenged. There will be sessions that are stressful or distressing because of the content. You may not always feel great when you leave, depending on what we talked about. But I believe you are greater than the limitations caused by your traumatic brain injury, so I am going to push you."

From the outset, Ponzo's treatment plan was to confront Tony when they were together. If Tony became enraged, Ponzo would use his skills as a therapist to calm him down. They would then talk about why Tony had lost control and Ponzo would teach Tony ways to recognize "red flags" and learn to control his emotions.

"I set out to confront Tony in a very methodical and calculated way," Ponzo said. "Sometimes I would think about it for weeks—ways to challenge and grab his attention and say, 'Hey, you can't deny what happened to you [the brain injury]. You can't minimize it and you can't normalize it, but you can talk about it and find ways to change your reaction to it.'"

Ponzo felt confident his treatment regimen was working. He believed Tony was not as impulsive or as easily angered as he had been when they first began working together.

But Tony also had been taking high doses of medication during those times.

Al and Chris decided to check with a neurological specialist in California before giving Tony a green light. That doctor sided with Ponzo. He didn't see any harm in letting Tony reduce his medications.

Reluctantly, his parents agreed.

The first medication that Tony wanted to stop taking was Cymbalta, because he believed it was responsible for his impotence. He was taking 90 milligrams. He cut that back to 60 milligrams.

Tony shared the news with his pen pals.

Dear David,

We are going to do this very slowly and not be careless this time around. Who knows? Maybe I am at that time in my recovery where I can prove medical science wrong again. First, they said it would be impossible for me to live a normal life again and that was right after they told my parents it did not look like I was going to survive or ever wake up out of my comma. I have been on this medicine for 15 years now and I feel within me that it's time for me to give it a try. What's the worst that could happen—beside me crashing and having to go back on all the meds again? You see, I will never know if that is possible unless I tried it first. I am very strong David, and what I have achieved in my life is unexplainable to even the top doctors. I will not fail this challenge, and I believe in my heart that I will knock this obstacle out of the way as I have done all others.

A happy family celebrates the first Holy Communion of Tony Ciaglia, age seven, in 1984 in Dallas, Texas. Clockwise from top: Chris, Al, younger brother Joey, and Tony. (Photo courtesy of Anthony Ciaglia)

Tony's seventh-grade football picture in 1989 in Plano, Texas. Tony was a successful athlete before his traumatic brain injury. (Photo courtesy of Anthony Ciaglia)

Tony and friends heading to Taos, New Mexico, for a snow-skiing trip. Left to right: Buddy O'Connell, Coby Russell, Todd Spurr, and Tony. Little did Tony realize that six months later, a Wave-Runner would change his life forever and he would lose all his friends. (Photo courtesy of Anthony Ciaglia)

Tony was one of the most popular kids in his class before his brain injury. Here wearing sunglasses, he is master of ceremonies at a 1990 school talent show. (Photo courtesy of Anthony Ciaglia)

Tony and Al standing outside their house in 1992 in Plano, Texas. Tony was still in rehab from the WaveRunner accident. Because of his brain injury, he had to relearn simple tasks. He had no idea where the state of Texas was located on a U.S. map. Even reading children's books aloud proved difficult. One of his therapists took him to a shopping mall one day to teach him how to step on and off an escalator. (Photo courtesy of Anthony Ciaglia)

Despite the accident, his parents were determined that Tony would graduate from high school. He did in May 1996 through a home schooling program in Plano, Texas. (Photo courtesy of Anthony Ciaglia)

Tony with his karaoke machine in his living room in spring 1993. He took up singing after his accident to help him pass his time alone at home after his friends abandoned him. (Photo courtesy of Anthony Ciaglia)

The Ciaglia family today in the living room of their Las Vegas, Nevada, house, standing beneath artwork that shows Tony with Elvis Presley. While he was in a coma, Tony's parents played Elvis songs to him to help stimulate his brain. After a lengthy rehabilitation, Tony began singing Elvis songs as a tribute to the King. Left to right: Joey, Tony, Chris, and Al. (Author photo)

Tony with girlfriend Crystal Torres, standing by the cross in his bedroom that he prays in front of daily. (Photo courtesy of Anthony Ciaglia)

Although he is required to take more than a dozen pills a day because of his traumatic brain injury, Tony can live a somewhat normal life. Here he is with friends at Yassou Greek Grill in Las Vegas. Left to right: Joey, Erik Per Sullivan, Christian Papas, Tony, and Crystal Torres. (Photo courtesy of Anthony Ciaglia)

Tony found solace in writing to serial killers at a desk in his bedroom, but also found himself being dangerously dragged into their frightening world. (Author photo)

Serial killer Arthur Shawcross described what human flesh tasted like to his visitors at the Sullivan Correctional Institution in Fallsburg, New York, while casually eating popcorn and slurping down sodas. Left to right: Al Ciaglia, Arthur Shawcross, Tony Ciaglia, and Joey Ciaglia. (Photo courtesy of Anthony Ciaglia)

Known as the Genesee River Killer because he often dumped the bodies of his twelve known victims along its banks, Arthur Shawcross autographed this published photo of himself and mailed it to Tony. It was taken during his 1990 trial. (Photo courtesy of Anthony Ciaglia)

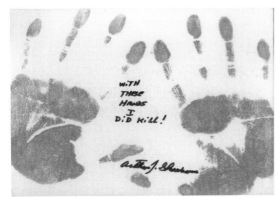

Pressing his hands in red ink, Arthur Shawcross made these impressions and wrote the words "With These Hands I Did Kill!" He sent the autographed imprint to Tony, suggesting it would make a good book cover if Tony would write the "true story" of his murderous rampage. (Author photo)

Killer Joe Roy Metheny as he looked when Tony and Al visited him in a Maryland prison where he is serving two life sentences. Metheny urged Tony to have sex with corpses—just as he had—preferring women who didn't "talk." (Photo courtesy of Anthony Ciaglia.)

Metheny, aka the cannibal killer, poses shirtless in a prison yard with pals. Metheny told jurors how he'd enjoyed torturing one victim, bragging that her autopsy showed she was about to give "birth to a twelve-ounce bouncing baby beer bottle." (Photo courtesy of Anthony Ciaglia)

Florida serial killer David Gore on death row in Florida, awaiting execution. In lengthy letters to Tony, Gore bragged about hunting women to satisfy an uncontrollable "URGE" to hunt, rape, and kill his victims. He had a hair fetish and would take the victim's scalp as a trophy. (Photo courtesy of Anthony Ciaglia)

Judith Kaye Daley walks down the aisle with her husband, Mike. The couple met in Vero Beach, Florida, and often attended college parties on Round Island Beach where killer David Gore later "hunted" women. Sunbathing at the beach alone on July 15, 1981 while on vacation, the mother of two was abducted, raped, tortured, and murdered by Gore. (Photo courtesy of Mike Daley)

Seventeen-year-old Lynn Carol Elliott was David Gore's final victim. He was captured after being seen chasing the nude teen from Gore's parents' Vero Beach home where he had been torturing her and her fourteen-year-old friend. Gore shot the popular high school student to death in the front yard and dumped her body into a car trunk before returning inside. (Photo courtesy of Carl Elliott)

Alaskan serial killer Robert C. Hansen, who hunted women like big game animals, suns himself on a picnic bench in a prison yard. Investigators from the National Center for Missing and Exploited Children sought Tony's help in locating the body of one of Hansen's missing teen-age victims. (Photo courtesy of Anthony Ciaglia)

Suspected of murdering as many as seventy victims, Tommy Lynn Sells was captured after break-ing into the bedroom of Kaylene "Katy" Harris, age 13, in Del Rio, Texas. She cried when he started to rape her, waking up Krystal Surles, age 10, who was asleep in the top bunk bed in the same room. Sells fatally stabbed Har-ris sixteen times and then slit Surles's throat, leaving her to die. Miraculously, she survived to tes-tify against him. In his letters to Tony, Sells promised to reveal the location of several unknown vic-tims. (Photo courtesy of Anthony Ciaglia)

22

EXCERPTS FROM LETTERS BETWEEN JOSEPH METHENY AND TONY

Dear Anthony,

I do greatly appreciate you considering me a friend. I really can't say I have too many people who feel that way about me with damn good reason . . . Nothing will break up a friendship faster than when those who consider you a friend find out that you have killed and eaten some of their friends or relatives. Ha! Ha!

You asked me if my drawings [in letters and on envelopes] reflect what I did and yes, they do . . . I could not even make love to a woman unless she was dead. How sick is that? I like dead pussy. It don't talk back to you. You don't even have to kiss her goodnight unless you want to. Shit, it's not that damn bad once you get past the smell and push the maggots to the side. You just mount it and ride, ride, ride. . . .

Dear Joe,

You're my friend and a damn good one too. It's kind of odd to say this, but I get along better with you than I do with most of the people on the outside now—go figure that one out?

. . . You said in your letter that you could only have sex with dead girls. So I am assuming you are telling me that you couldn't perform with a live woman. Do you think it was a psychological thing? Maybe a way for you to gain complete power and control over the woman?

Dear Anthony,

. . . Do your demons ever tell you or make you feel that you want to murder or hurt anyone? Mine does! And I used to act on it when I was out there on those streets. I have come a long

*way from being the monster that I was out there. But I do still
have these feelings welling up inside of me. Sometimes the littlest
things will set me off. I just want to scream at the top of my voice
and reach out and tear the head off the first mother fucker that's
near me . . .*

Dear Joe,

. . . Rage is a big problem for me too, Joe. It is one of the big things I
work on with my therapist each week. I just got done seeing him today.
We had to talk about one incident that happened. I was driving in a
parking lot heading towards the store where I pick up my mail each day
and a lady in a new van wanted to make a left turn while I was waiting
to make a right turn. I went ahead and waved her on because she was in
the way. I threw a smile in her direction and she proceeded to flick me
off calling me all sorts of horrible names. I politely smiled and waved
her on again. She then persisted on showing me the same rude mannerisms. I was in shock but persisted in smiling to make her think nothing
was wrong. I was throbbing with rage and thought to myself that this
woman has got a lot of nerve acting like this towards me . . .

I played it cool, though, and kept on driving and not showing any
signs of anger in the least. When she walked into a mall store, I pulled to
the back of the parking lot and gave her a good three to four minutes to
disappear in the store. I made sure there was no other customers walking around or looking in my direction. I thought I would teach this lady
a little lesson so I took the key to my car and dug the key all the way into
the metal of her van . . . I guess she should think before she acts from
now on because you never know who you're screaming at . . .

Dear Anthony,

*. . . So you took your revenge. How did it feel? Good, huh?
We may have never met, at least in this life time, but I do find
myself seeing a lot of you through a lot of my own past experiences. I lead a very lonely life out there. Disappointment has been
a very big part of my life. I think some people are just meant to
be alone. For many, many times in my life, I think being by myself was some of my best times. . . . I guess, it just feels natural to
me to be alone. The only time I don't feel alone is when I writing
to you.*

Dear Joe,

I don't ever plan on going to prison but my problem is I have this anger and rage that takes me over at times and causes me to make stupid decisions . . . I would like to know if you were experiencing a lot of anger or a deep sense of rage when you committed murder . . . Was murder a spur of the moment decision like something you would do was spontaneously due to a certain mood that took you over at the current time, or would it be something you planned and arranged—stalking a certain victim over a period of time?

I could never kill like a serial killer does. I know I could never go out and just kill off innocent people . . .

Joe, I want to ask you a serious question. Do you see yourself as a sociopath bearing no conscience? A sociopath can go out and slaughter a woman and rush home to have hamburgers and fries with his wife and kids . . . He is able to compartmentalize or take what he did to that innocent victim and put it away in a part of his brain where he can just forget about it for the time being. The memory is still there and can be fetched at anytime but he has the mental capacity to just put it aside until he wants to relive his actions for his enjoyment over and over which is usually a means of sexual satisfaction . . .

Dear Anthony,

Let me tell you a story. There once was a boy who only wanted to be wanted by someone . . . No matter how hard he tried to get someone to pay attention to him, the only response he got from them was the word "Later." Overtime he heard that word so often that he grew tired of it because in his mind he knew later would never come.

So, he started to withdraw into himself and depressing all the hurt that others brought upon him with their ignorance of his feelings. At first, he cried a river of tears each night on his pillow. Then he wiped them away and said to himself, "Tomorrow will be a better day." Mental abuse and neglect are just as damaging as physical abuse. In fact, in most cases it's a lot worse. For the hurt one suffers from physical abuse will heal in itself but the hurt created by mental abuse will follow a child for the rest of his life. When one uses the words—stupid, ignorant, ugly and useless— to a child often enough that child will in time start to develop a low-self esteem and become a failure before he ever starts to make a decision for himself.

And how do I know this information? The man who is holding this pencil and writing this letter was that little boy a long time ago. And you can see where it got him today. So the next time a child comes in front of you, don't push him or her away with the word Later. Just give them what they need—a kind word and a hug.

Dear Joe,

Your most recent letter really touched me. It allowed me to see a side of you that I did not know existed. I'm sorry you had it so tough as a child and was not given the proper attention by loved ones that one should receive to develop mentally normal . . .

Dear Anthony,

. . . So my story made you see a side of me that you didn't know existed. Before you read that letter, you thought about me the same as everyone else always did. To the average person I do portray myself as the lowest horrible, heartless bastard that has been placed in their minds . . . The truth is I have found it a whole lot easier to live through other personalities that I have made up in my mind. You see deep down inside of me still lives that lonely little child who no one really ever cared about. That boy made up a fantasy world of different personalities to hide behind whenever he felt threatened or insecure. He depends on those personalities to protect who he really is.

I believe you are a lot like me in many ways. I believe you have a lonely little child inside of you too. You may have grown up with a lot of love around you from your family and friends. But deep down inside of you, don't you feel something was missing? And you could never really figure out what it was that was missing that made you feel that way?

Well, today I sure as hell know what that missing feeling is and I can tell you that it's a monster that will eat you alive from the inside out. . . .

You liked what I wrote about the little boy. Here is another story about that same little boy and the monster inside him.

The girl layed screaming in the grass where I placed her that night. The moonbeams washed over her bloody body and glistened so bright. Her screams of pain slowly dwindled down to mere rasps of agonizing grunts and groans. Her eyes slowly closed and the sounds she made slowly faded away never to be heard again. Sweet death had finally come down upon her. Now her body was just a dead carcass, laying in wait for the decomposition to start breaking down of cells and the maggots to start devouring their beloved meal.

That little boy who wanted that kind word and the killer, both in the same body. You see Anthony we both have dark sides, only I let mine free.

Dear Joe,

I consider you one of my closest friends . . . I don't care what anyone says about you . . . Yes, we all have dark sides . . .

Dear Anthony,

. . . During my life, I did get to meet one of the only people I truly ever called my best-friend and that is a man I never got to meet—except in a letter along with a couple of phone calls. Yeah, my friend, I am talking about you, Anthony Ciaglia, you are a damn good man. And I often wonder why you keep writing to a sick, twisted mother fucker like me. I think maybe you just see a little more into me than other people do. I'm not really a bad person. I like to think of myself as a misunderstood person who just happened to make a lot of bad decisions. But those other good law abiding citizens out there don't see me like that. It's just a damn shame . . . But that's society for you. You kill and eat a couple of people and they never let you forget it. Ha. Ha.

Dear Joe,

You said I was the man!! And that was awesome. I thought that was cool when you said I was the man. I had to show the rest of my family that one . . .

. . . In your last letter Joe, you were absolutely right about me not seeing you as only some sick, twisted, demented fucker who liked to murder and eat human remains. I know that's hard to believe that a person of complete sanity could actually see through the evil and may-hem you have caused. I guess maybe I ask myself that sometimes, but it never has been a problem for me to rise above the rest of society and see into the man that is responsible for what horror movies try to bring to reality.

. . . It felt so good when I got to the part in your letter when you said that *if nothing else ever comes out of all this bullshit, I did get to meet one of the only people I truly ever called my best friend and that is a man I never got to meet except in a letter along with a couple of phone calls. Yeah, my friend I am talking about is Anthony Ciaglia!* That is a big honor and for somebody like you to say something like that really means a lot to me . . . Some people would say that it would be impos-sible for somebody with the psychological makeup of Joe Metheny to feel friendship and to have something to read that would bring a smile to his face. Most would call you a man who can't feel emotions. Well, I believe I've proved them all wrong! And when you read this you will be smiling!!!

Your best friend, Tony.

Dear Anthony,

. . . I understand your depression because I have suffered from it all of my life. Mine was brought on by the way I was abused and neglected as a child. I had several bad things happen to me at an early age which started me on the path of hurting others before they hurt me. It all started with me hurting insects then animals then I turned my frustrations on to other kids. You al-ready know about one that no one else does—the little red haired girl who rejected me and paid with her life.

I don't need no one to tell me that I am a waste of a human life. For no one knows it better than me . . . But, all in all, I believe I have been rehabilitated—for I have not killed or eaten anyone in over 14 years now. I think I just may be a useful member of soci-ety again damn soon. Ha Ha.

Dear Joe,

I've been thinking a lot about our friendship. I wouldn't last a fuck-ing week in your prison. They would eat my lunch in that place unless I were to hook up with you and your boys. I'm sure you would look after me . . .

Let me tell you I feel privileged to know the proper way to do the job taught by the number one man himself Joe "Tiny" Metheny.

Dear Anthony,

. . . You talk about murder and about if you would commit a murder, and I know I have told you how to get away with committing a murder. Just always remember the best way to get away with murder is to just eat the evidence. It's a win, win deal. You get rid of the mother fucker you killed, plus you get a free meal out of it . . . so grasshopper, maybe it is time to grab the pebble out of my hand and act.

I say, go for it!

23

EXCERPTS FROM LETTERS BETWEEN DAVID GORE AND TONY

Dear David,

. . . It's so interesting to read about a man and see all his normal characteristics—how he likes to scuba dive, read books and even watch professional football but there is a whole different side to this man. A side that he metamorphosises into. A side that is aggressive and evil beyond all comprehension. A side that has no feelings or emotions for anyone who dares to get into his way while he is in the middle of his hunt to satisfy the URGE that only a killer knows. . . .

Dear Anthony,

. . . You were asking me about Fred and how much we were alike. Did I tell you about the plan me and him had once to abduct an entire bus load of cheerleaders? The only thing that kept us from carrying it out is we couldn't find a school bus for sale. Our plan would have worked. It was at a time when I worked part-time as a deputy and our plan was to wait until our local high school cheerleaders was on their way to a football game in another city. I would stop the bus and tell the bus driver that there was a bomb threat on that bus and so we needed to transfer all of the girls onto another bus which Fred would be driving. And, of course, the bus would be rigged so once they were on, they couldn't get off.

Can you imagine a bus load of cheerleaders and them not showing up for the game? We even had the spot picked out in the grove to park the bus where it couldn't be seen. . . . We would have had a fun time with those girls.

Dear David,

   . . . I know I should probably judge your character for the horror you brought to many women and their families. But for some reason I can't figure out, I just don't judge you. It bothers me, David. It's like I'm missing something because I feel that any normal person would feel sorry or in any case feel something for your victims. But I just don't. If I were to say anything about them, I would probably say it's too bad that they were in the wrong place at the wrong time.

   I have to admit to you it's kind of fun to be able to—let's say relive your adventures through your words on how it happened step-by-step. It is fun for you too, isn't it? Reliving what you've done—telling me about every intimate detail?

Dear Tony,

   . . . I used to hang out at this truck stop a lot. I knew everyone there and even helped out at times. Well one night this Indian chick rode in with this trucker and stayed. She just sort of hung out in the truck stop and I had my eye on her. She had this long dark hair like a typical Indian. She was a bit on the chubby side and she was short. I did not care about that. There used to be this little bar right across the street from the truck stop and this chick would hang out at it. Well this one night I'm over there and she's over there and we're drinking and carrying on and her and I start drinking together and she got plastered. I talked her into going to another bar and she agreed. We got into my car and to be honest, I could have screwed her, but I wanted her hair . . . She put her head on my shoulders and just passed out. I could not have planned it better. I had already known that she was just a drifter and no one would really notice her gone. So I drove her to the grove, stretched her out on the back seat of my car, cut all of her clothes off and she is out cold. I had a club ready if she started coming to but she didn't. She really wasn't much to look at but I got on her and screwed her. And let me say, screwing a girl who's passed out is no fun really.

   I started focusing on her long hair and how best to take it off. I pulled her ass out of my car and over to some woods and she starts moving a bit like she's coming too so I sat on her and choked her until she was lifeless. I rolled her chubby little ass over, got me a handful of hair and pulled her head back and began slicing until the hair came loose. Then for the next several hours it was just a matter of disposal.

I know Tony when I describe things like this it may seem like it was just a walk in the park and simple. But nothing could be further from the truth. All of this takes everything out of you physically and emotionally. Afterwards you are spent. The fantasy is a whole lot more sensual than the reality. . . .

Dear David,

The entire time I read that letter it kept me on the edge of my seat just waiting and anticipating what was going to happen next . . . Please share more of your encounters with me. . . . You spare no detail in how you bring me to the scene of the crime. What an experience for me to be able to journey into the mind of David Gore where you hold nothing back. . . .

Dear Anthony,

Part of my problem was based on how difficult it was to get sex in Vero Beach. I can't understand why people look at a father and daughter having consensual sex as such an awful thing. I say they should try it, they might like it. People place the label of TABOO on way too many things. I know we are supposed to be a civilized society but what's the harm . . . You once asked me about Ted Bundy and our friendship here on death row. We used to talk about stuff like that and he was a real likable guy. You couldn't have met a nicer person. He knew my fascination for the hair so he shared a story with me that he claimed was his favorite. I never heard about this case in the media, so I am telling you about one of Bundy's cold cases, if you want to investigate it.

He told me one time he went to this high school and pretended to be a firefighter, with a badge and all. He spotted this girl who was a cheerleader and waited until she got off by herself and went up to her and told her that her house had caught on fire and her parents had sent him to come and pick her up and bring her home. And she went with him. When they climbed into his van, he subdued her, took her to a place where he raped her and because her hair was so long, he actually used her hair to strangle her. He used to have so many ruses and disguises. I would have never thought of half of them. Back then it was pretty easy to use a ruse on a girl. People were more trusting then. You couldn't do half the stuff today. Also, Ted was not shy about taking a chance. Where I would evaluate a situation, he would go right for it. One reason why he targeted high school and college students was because at that age you think you are invincible . . .

Dear Anthony,

    . . . Do you believe that a person can be wired in such a way that they can't help but do certain things? I ask this, because there have been times in my life when I did NOT want to do something but it was like a compulsion that I had to do . . .

    I actually got a woman one time and she was in her late 40s and she made the mistake of begging me NOT to do her in her ass. I guess she had a thing against being screwed there. Well you can guess, I banged her good and even used the big dildo up her ass that I kept in the orange grove and she lost it. She told me she wouldn't fight if I fucked her in her pussy as long as I didn't do her ass. Don't ask me why in the world she thought I'd do what SHE asked after I hunted her. After I got tired, when I took a break, I'd leave that dildo in her ass and walk away and believe me, it freaked her out. . . . I think she was relieved when I finally choked her to death because this had gone on for hours.

    One thing that got me caught was after you abduct and kill as many as I had done, you get relaxed and careless. At the start, you pay attention to every detail but eventually you think you aren't going to get caught and you slip up . . .

Dear Anthony,

    . . . I don't know if I told you that one time my sister-in-law took the wrong medication and it caused her to fall into this really deep sleep almost like a coma. My wife had been talking to her on the phone when she stopped responding so we drove over to her house and she was on the couch sound asleep still holding the phone. I told my wife to call the doctors but while my wife's back was turned, I did a quick squeeze on her tits. I often thought how I wish I could have gone over there by myself to check on her and

found her passed out. Who knows? We might have had a baby together. That would have surprised her! I was always looking for opportunities like that. . . .

My sister-in-law was a stewardess for United Airlines and I had her in my sights for quite a while. She lived only a mile from us and we had a key to her house because when she was away, my wife would go over to her house and check up. . . . Believe me, I had every intention of getting her, but I knew suspicion would fall on me. I knew that once she disappeared, family members would be looked at. So I was trying to come up with a plan that I would think would be foolproof. Getting her would be easy because all I had to do was hide in her house till she came home. I had asked my cousin if he wanted in on bagging her and he was all for it. Let me tell you what I did do, she had a friend who was one hell of a beauty and I heard that she was going to watch my sister-in-laws house one time so I went and hid in the house fully planning on getting her. My plan was to step up from behind her and hit her in the head and knock her down. I waited an entire afternoon in that house for her to show up, but she didn't . . . she is one who got away but I still think about that a lot . . . But my sister-in-law friend definitely missed my claws . . . Every time I saw her, she tripped my trigger . . .

24

As soon as he began weaning himself from his medications, Tony felt better. His sex life with Crystal improved. In fact, he experienced an orgasm that was so intense he naively hurried out to tell his parents because he thought he was having a heart attack.

He shared the good news in letters, including a letter to Arthur Shawcross.

> Dear Art,
>
> Another day, another challenge to live my life and attempt to be as happy and depression free off the medication that I have now been off for a good four weeks. I am proud and so thankful that my body has been able to go on without this certain drug—Cymbalta—I have been on for so long . . . I'm not afraid for my future for I know the worst has been beat. The future could only get better and I am excited to explore it.

But as the days passed, Tony's moods began turning darker.

One night, Crystal woke up and Tony was not in bed. He was in front of his computer writing to his serial killer pals. She dozed off and when she got up in the morning to go to work, he was still typing. When she asked him what he was doing, he became annoyed.

"My job!" he snapped.

In addition to responding to daily packets of letters sent by his growing list—now nearly forty serial killers—Tony was getting daily calls on the murder phone in his bedroom from convicted murderers. Some asked him to help them find relatives whom they'd lost contact with. Others asked him for help doing research for their legal appeals. Others simply wanted to talk to someone outside prison. One afternoon, his mother spotted him going from room to room with a digital camera taking pictures.

"What'ya doing, Tony?" Chris asked.

"I'm sending the guys photos of our house."

"Tony," she said, "I don't want them seeing the inside of our house."

"But I have to send the pictures," Tony said. "We're more of a family to these men than their own families are."

Tony told Chris that he'd already mailed photos of the house's interior to several death row inmates in San Quentin. One had written back criticizing Chris's decorating tastes. Tony had also mailed photos of Crystal in a bikini. He'd described their lovemaking in graphic detail to the prisoners.

Al and Chris noticed that their son kept referring to the serial killers as his "best friends" and closest "buddies." Whenever the family went out to eat, Tony would wonder how Shawcross, Metheny, Gore, or some other serial killer might react if one of them were inside the restaurant. Which girls would Gore feel the URGE to rape and murder? Which ones would catch the eyes of Shawcross or Metheny?

In his letters, Tony began asking the killers to fantasize about what they would do if they lived in Las Vegas and the two of them were best pals. Would they hang out in strip clubs? Would they go to get coffee together or stop for breakfast at IHOP? Or would the killers expect him to join them when they went on their hunts? Would they expect him to help them choose victims to kidnap, rape, and murder?

David Gore's mention of serial killer Theodore "Ted" Bundy in a recent letter intrigued Tony. He asked Gore to speculate about how "much fun" the two murderers could have had together if they'd teamed up.

Such comments began to scare Al and Chris. Tony's obsession seemed to be taking over his life. He was consumed with the murderers every waking moment. It was all that he talked about—even to strangers. When the family went out to eat, he'd ask waitresses if they had ever heard of Joe Metheny.

"Well, he's one of my best friends but I don't think he would like anything on your menu," he'd reply with a grin.

If the waitress asked why, Tony would explain that Metheny was a serial killer who fed barbecue tainted with human flesh to innocent customers at his BBQ stand.

One night Al said, "Tony, why don't you pull back a little from writing these guys?"

"I can't," Tony said. "They need me."

"What do you mean, Tony?"

"Some of them read my letters three or four times. I'm their only escape from prison. I am their window to our world."

"Everyone takes a vacation from their job," Al said.

But Tony was adamant. "They're my friends," he insisted, raising his voice. "They're my only real friends. They care about me."

With each passing day, Tony grew more and more on edge. He would erupt without warning—and without reason. He became distrustful, even of his own family and Crystal. Paranoid. Whenever he went out, he thought strangers were watching him. He began using the same prison terminology that the killers used and seemed to be mimicking and glorifying their crudeness.

Al wondered: Was Tony's personality changing because he was taking less medication to control his TBI? Or was Tony's intimacy with the serial killers taking a toll as they drew him closer and closer? Regardless, Tony was beginning to spin out of control.

25

While everyone around him was becoming alarmed about his behavior, Tony was confident that he was doing great off his medication.

At Al's urging, Tony took a handful of letters to his next therapy session with psychologist Ponzo. While Tony and Al were driving to the appointment, Tony suddenly asked: "Do you think I could be one of them?"

Before Al could reply, Tony began building his case. "Some serial killers have brain injuries," he said. Scans had shown scarring to Shawcross's frontal lobe. Gore claimed his brain had been damaged when he was bitten by ants and nearly died. "That's what causes their rages," Tony continued. "They've told me they feel like they are two different persons. I feel that same rage. I feel like I could be two different persons—one good and one bad. I don't want to be like them, but maybe I don't have a choice because of my brain injury."

"Tony," Al said firmly, "you have a loving family."

"David Gore came from a good family."

"But you could never see a beautiful girl walking across the street and hunt her and want to hurt her. You know that. You could never kill her and bury her in a hole. You just couldn't."

Tony sat silent for several moments and then said, "For the longest time, I hated those kids who were supposed to be my friends in high school. I wanted to kill them. I really did. I even made a list and thought about how I could take them out, one at a time."

"But you were a kid and they'd been mean to you. The point is that you didn't," Al replied. "You didn't hurt them—they hurt you. You knew how to stop yourself. You were angry and felt those urges, but that was part of the grieving process. That helped you deal with what had happened—how they had rejected you."

"I wouldn't hurt some innocent woman but I could hurt someone who hurt me or my family."

"Most of us would," Al replied. "That's normal."

"Some of what I've been thinking isn't normal," Tony replied. He said he'd been wondering what it would feel like to kill a living thing, maybe a stray cat or an abandoned dog.

Therapist Ponzo was uncomfortable when he read how the serial killers were referring to Tony in their letters. Some were clearly trying to manipulate Tony. It was clear that Tony felt a tremendous need to please them. Ponzo asked if Tony really thought that serial killers such as Shawcross, Metheny, and Gore were his best friends.

"Yes," Tony answered without hesitating. "If David Gore was sitting across from me at the breakfast table in our house, I'm not looking at him as David Gore the rapist, the murderer, the scalper. I'm looking at him as a regular guy, a friend who'd dropped by, and we're just talking like two friends talk. Just like me and my brother talk."

"Tony," Ponzo said, "these people are not really your friends. They're sociopaths. They're not really capable of being your friend or anyone's friend. And you really would not want to be friends with them if they were out of prison."

"They wouldn't harm me," Tony shot back. "We've talked about this in our letters. They might hurt others, but not me. They care about me and would never do anything to hurt me because I'm important to them. I've asked them if they have feelings and emotions and they do. I know they do because I know them better than anyone, including FBI profilers. I've invested my time and personality in these people. I know them better than you."

"These people are incapable of caring about other people—including you."

"No," Tony insisted. "You just don't know them. No one does!"

Ponzo joined Al in suggesting that Tony take a break from corresponding with the serial killers.

"There's no way I'm quitting," Tony declared. "I've spent years getting to know them, getting them to trust me, getting them to open up to me and tell me how they really are and how they really feel and now you want me to stop? I'm not going to do that. This stuff they're writing, it's the real stuff. It's how they really think and how they really feel. They aren't pretending or hiding from me. I wanted to know what made Metheny be a cannibal and he's telling me. I wanted to know how Gore could hunt women and he's telling me. I wanted to know how Arthur could strangle people with his bare hands and he's telling me."

"Tony," Ponzo said, "imagine you are looking at a river or you are flowing down or swimming down this river and the river is clear and clean and you are enjoying the beauty of it. You feel comfortable and safe in this river and there are no pollutants or toxins in the water. Now, imagine that you are in that same river, only this time, people have thrown a lot of garbage and toxins and objects in it that don't belong there. You're riding in this river but it's not pretty, it's not enjoyable, it doesn't look good, and it's bad for your health."

Ponzo continued: "We all have a stream or a flow of consciousness. This is why some people practice meditation, because they want to clear their minds for periods of time and they want to recharge and renew themselves mentally. One way to do that is to keep your stream clean. You don't want to expose yourself solely to negative content. That's my point. If all you are doing is swimming in a river that has all sorts of pollutants and toxins and garbage in it, then you are not going to be healthy."

Tony didn't believe the stream that he was swimming in was polluted. He insisted that Ponzo just didn't get it. Neither did his parents. No one did. No one understood him and what it was really like to have a traumatic brain injury except his serial killer friends. They alone knew what it felt like to be an outcast.

Dear Arthur,

. . . When I call you my best friend, I am being serious. I do consider you one of my best friends even though I'm not able to see you and interact with you on a personal level all the time. I can't ask you if you would like to go meet me for coffee and donuts at 10 o'clock on Sunday morning . . . our friendship takes a little more effort and time. . . . But you understand me.

Arthur, I find my inner rage burning like the fire that engulfs Satan while he's ringing Hell's Bells. . . . I see that you noticed some similarities between the two of us. I think that is very good . . . Yes, it is true and it is as real as death!!! I do have that monster inside me and if I come across someone who tries to hurt me emotionally or physically payback is a bitch. Sometimes it starts out with someone giving me a dirty look, or at least, I perceive it as a dirty look. My parents have seen it happen time and time again and tell me that I am imagining things, and that person never even looked at me to begin with . . . but I want to strike out.

Thanksgiving was coming but Al and Chris were reluctant to take Tony out in public. He had become an emotional tinderbox. They invited their relatives to celebrate with them at their house. Al knew that one of Tony's uncles didn't think there was anything physically wrong with him. The uncle had told his wife that Al and Chris had indulged Tony since the WaveRunner accident. They'd babied him, protected him, given in to his every whim. That charge had especially infuriated Al.

"You'd think your own family would understand about traumatic brain injuries and how they completely change a person, how the parts of Tony's brain that control emotions and impulse don't work correctly. You would think your own family would support you," he'd complained to Chris.

Before the relatives arrived, Al warned Tony: "If your uncle starts getting on your nerves, just go into your bedroom and shut the door."

Chris had just popped two large turkeys into the oven on Thanksgiving Day when Tony appeared in the kitchen saying he was hungry.

"Dinner won't be ready for several hours," Chris said.

Al offered to drive Tony to a McDonald's, and as they were leaving the house, the uncle decided to join them. Everyone was fine until they were sitting in a booth and Tony mentioned serial killers. His uncle said he didn't want to hear about them. He didn't understand why Tony would even want to write to them. In his opinion, all they deserved was a bullet to the head.

Al could tell Tony was becoming exasperated, especially when the uncle continued to rant about Tony's fixation with psychopaths.

"I think there's a lot we can learn from serial killers," Tony said, defending himself.

His comment infuriated his uncle, to the point that Tony became so upset that he decided to leave the table to cool off. The moment he walked away, Al asked the uncle to drop the subject. Tony returned and everyone began eating again, but within seconds, the uncle bought up serial killers. He began busting Tony's chops about why he was wasting his time talking to them when all they deserved was a bullet to the head.

"You don't know them like I do," Tony said.

"A gun and a bullet!" his uncle exclaimed. That's what needed to be done to them.

Tony lunged at his uncle, grabbing his shirt collar and shoving him against a wall. The man's eyeglasses flew from his nose. Cocking his fist back, Tony was about to hit him when Al grabbed his son's arm.

"Get outside now!" Al yelled. Tony released his grip and started to leave but stopped when a clerk behind the counter yelled: "I'm calling the cops!" Spinning around, Tony began cursing her.

Rising from the booth, Al said, "This is a family affair. No need to call the police." He escorted Tony outside and got him settled in their car. Dashing back into the restaurant, Al told the uncle that he would send someone to pick him up.

Not wanting to go home and risk another confrontation, Al drove Tony to Crystal's apartment and telephoned Chris.

"You've got to tell my sister and her husband to leave," he said. "I'm sorry, but he was obnoxious to Tony and just wouldn't let him alone."

Thanksgiving was canceled.

"We can't go on living like this," a tearful Chris told Al that night.

"But to be fair," Al said, "it really wasn't Tony's fault." The uncle had "kept screaming—a 'gun and a bullet,' a 'gun and a bullet.'" From that day forward, Al and his sister and brother-in-law stopped speaking to each other.

Everything Al and Chris had read about traumatic brain injuries had warned them that Tony would not be able to control his emotions and rages without medication. They quietly began to question if Ponzo and the California neurosurgeon had given them poor advice when they'd okayed Tony going off his pills.

Each time Tony left the house, Chris was afraid she would never see him again. When Tony became enraged, Al was the only one in the family who could calm him down. Now Tony was beginning to openly rebel against Al, too.

Despite the Thanksgiving altercation, Tony stubbornly insisted that he didn't need to take his pills again. And he refused to cut back his communications with his ever-growing list of serial killer pals.

One afternoon, Tony became enraged and even Al couldn't settle him. A desperate Al persuaded Tony to go with him to see Ponzo. When Al and Tony reached the therapist's office, Tony became belligerent. Leaping from his chair, Tony screamed at his father and headed for the door. Just before he reached it, he smashed his fist into a mirror hanging there, shattering it and cutting his hand.

Al started to go after his son. But Ponzo called him back to his seat. He suggested they let Tony cool down.

But Tony wasn't in a cooling mood. His hand now bleeding, he marched outside and became even more agitated when his father didn't chase after him. He picked up a rock from the landscaping around the office building. Raising it above his head with his good hand, he slammed it into the windshield of his father's car. He walked to the side and broke the passenger's window, too.

When Al came outside, Tony was sitting on the curb with his hand still bleeding. By the time they got to an emergency room, Tony had calmed down. A doctor stitched his hand. On the ride home, Tony began to cry. His emotions were a mess. He loved his dad and apologized for yelling at him.

"Tony," Al said, "people don't understand traumatic brain injuries. They think you can control this—even Ponzo. But your brain is damaged. It is not your fault. It's the brain injury. Not you. Dr. Duffy understands. You need to be on your medication."

That night, Ponzo called to tell Al that other tenants at the office park had seen Tony smashing the car windows. They'd called the police, who'd arrived after Al and Tony had gone. The police had interviewed Ponzo and he had told them that Tony was one of his patients. Ponzo was calling to warn them about the police.

Tony was terrified. He was terrified the police were coming to arrest him. But no one did. At that point, his fear turned into rage. When they went to see Ponzo, Tony blew up.

Dear Arthur,

I got into a fight with my psychologist yesterday and my dad was with me when it went down. . . . I told my therapist that he was a traitor, a Judas, a little bitch because in the last session we had, I blew up and broke a mirror in his office. Then I proceeded to go outside, take a rock and bash the windshield and passenger window of my dad's car in. People came outside to see what all the racket was, somebody even call the cops. My dad and I left the scene and the cops showed up asking people what had happened. They eventually went into my therapist's office and questioned him. He gave them my name and address . . .

We went in to see him today and I was so angry, I threatened him and told him that I knew where he lived and if anything happened to me with the cops I would know just where to go. There's no tape recorders so I wasn't worried in that aspect. No tape recorder, no threat, no threat, no crime, no witness, you're out of fucking luck then, game over!!!!

Tony was out of control. He was scaring everyone in his family. It wasn't just the traumatic brain injury anymore. It was the influence the serial killers were having on him. He was calling the police "pigs," calling women "bitches," and now he was boasting about how he had threatened his therapist. Al had read the earlier letter that Tony had written about how he'd keyed a rude driver's car. Sometimes Tony exaggerated in his letters to impress the killers. Sometimes he tried to appear tough. He stooped to their level. Regardless, Al was concerned about Tony's mimicking behavior. It had to stop. It could only get worse. The conversation that Tony had had with his dad—when Tony asked if it was possible that he was doomed to be a serial killer because of his brain injury—was fresh on Al's mind.

Al, Chris, Joey, and Crystal decided to hold an intervention. When Tony emerged from his bedroom the next morning, they called him into the family room. As gently but also as forcefully as they could, they told him that he had to start taking his antipsychotic medication again. He also needed to step back from the serial killers.

Each of them explained why. Each of them told him that they didn't blame him for his rages.

Tony argued. He didn't need to take the medication. No one could force him. They didn't understand him anymore. Only his pen pals got it.

The intervention lasted all morning. Eventually Tony broke down. By that point, all of them were crying. He could see how much he was hurting his family, and they could see how much he was suffering. He apologized and offered to put himself under "house arrest." He promised he would not leave the house without a family member or Crystal accompanying him. And, he said, he would begin taking his medication again.

But he told them that he would not stop writing to serial killers.

"They're all I have."

"You don't have to stop," Al said. "But let's take a little break for a while until you feel better."

"They're not all you have," Chris added. "You have us."

Al telephoned Dr. Duffy to discuss how to safely get Tony back on his "pill cocktail." That night, Tony took his medication and went to bed without turning on his computer. The next day, he took his pills and didn't get his mail. Nor did he answer the murder phone. He felt like a trapped animal. A week later, he sat down at his keyboard and wrote several letters.

> Dear Arthur,
>
> I am writing to let you know what's been going on the last couple days in my life. Sorry that I have not written sooner but my doctor has been experimenting with my medications, trying to get my rages under control . . . Yesterday was a disaster. I was heading to my computer in my room to write you and by golly my computer was messed up and then something went off in my head—that is something I have no control over because of my brain injury—people don't understand because I look so normal but that's something that turns me into a monster and makes me break things.
>
> I jumped up screaming at the top of my lungs, and took the chair that I was sitting in and threw it across the room. Then I took the phone that I talk to you on and threw a fast ball of it into the wall and that was that because it broke. My mom came in and rule of thumb is when I break down she breaks down because she can't stand to see her baby boy go through the mental hell that I do over and over again. It's a battle that seems to have no end . . . Living with this demon inside me having no escape out of my body is something I won't stand for. I want to learn how to control him and learn to shut him down when he decides to show up not invited. I'm very worried about my mother's health. It scares me immensely!!! I wish I could make it stop. I wish the demons would leave me alone and stop haunting my family and me. . . .

> Dear David,
>
> I don't want to go outside and I have no motivation to do anything really. The desert sun and high temperature just drains all the stamina out of me, leaving me like an uncooked noodle. Sorry that I haven't been writing as much as I often do. I promise I will get busy and try to write the good shit, I'm know for but for now, I have hit rock bottom . . . I am lost.

Dear Joe,

. . . I have had it rough off and on for a great while now. So bad that my parents can't let me out of sight. I just can't seem to get my head together for the life of me. . . . I felt these terrible rages and wanted to attack people. Tell me, is that rage what you felt? Is it possible that I am like you?

When Tony went to bed at night, he repeated the same prayer: "Help me, Jesus. Help me. You let me come back. Why? Why? What is my special purpose in life?"

PART THREE

the journey

Dear Tony . . . You are a good friend who has traveled a road even rougher than my own and still retained your compass and humanity . . .

Your friend, Douglas Clark
aka the Sunset Strip Killer

Thank you for being such a great pen pal and friend as well . . . We have had an affinity since the beginning. . . .

Your friend, Harvey Carignan
aka Harvey the Hammer

The only helpful advice I can give to you is ALWAYS FIGHT YOUR INNER DEMONS NO MATTER WHAT THE COST . . .

Your friend, John Eric Armstrong
aka the Psycho Sailor

26

Tony returned to his former regimen of taking his twice-daily plastic bag of pills and going to bed on a regular schedule. In addition to the antipsychotics that he'd already been prescribed, his psychiatrist added another powerful drug to help stabilize his mood. Al and Chris decided Tony needed to take a break from seeing therapist Nick Ponzo because their last encounter had ended badly. Instead Tony remained under a self-imposed "house arrest," spending time only with his family.

During the coming weeks, the medication kicked in and his temperament and outlook began to improve. There were fewer rages, less dark thoughts. Tony had promised to reduce the hours that he spent writing and talking to serial killers. He kept his word. He limited the number of letters that he read each day and answered only a very few. He spent more time with Crystal, less time on his computer.

Al talked to his son about the importance of taking medication. They also discussed whether Tony was fated to become a murderer simply because of his brain injury.

"Tony, that's just not you," Al assured him. While his brain injury made it impossible for Tony to control his emotions without the help of medications, it had not robbed him of his ability to feel guilt, remorse, or sorrow, or to love someone other than himself. Also, Tony was not manipulative. "You're not like these guys," Al said, referring to serial killers. "They're hollow. You aren't."

Eventually, Tony came around. "I could never just go out and kill someone—even though I have a brain injury. I was confused. I understand that now."

Although he'd been warned against swimming in "polluted" waters, Tony did not want to stop writing and talking to serial killers. He'd worked too hard to win their trust and get them to share their feelings, fantasies, and rationalizations. He still considered many of them to be his "best friends." Two serial murderers—Harvey Carignan and David Gore—had asked him to take charge of their ashes after they were cremated. Others wrote in their letters about how they had never been as honest or as open with anyone else as they had with him.

During his hiatus, Tony received dozens of letters from serial killers asking him what was wrong. Why had Tony stopped writing? They needed to hear from him.

One of the most concerned was Elmer Wayne Henley, who, at age fourteen, had lured boys to a house in Houston in the 1970s under the guise of giving them free beer. Once inside, the boys had been attacked by Dean Arnold Corll, a sexual sadist who strapped them to a home-made torture board where he'd raped, mutilated, and murdered them. The police had recovered the bodies of twenty-seven victims, some boys as young as thirteen.

> *Tony—you tell me you would like to quit taking the medications that suppress your violent tendencies because they also suppress your sexuality, correct? I mean, come on Tony, you would never want to lash out and unintentionally hurt your family or Crystal, right? That is way more important than sex, true? . . . You shouldn't fight the meds, Tony. Take 'em, learn to cope with 'em and be glad of all the plusses in your life . . . God doesn't put more of a load on you than you can bear. Don't give up on Him cause He will never give up on you. I tell you from inside this prison cell that life is too grand and too beautiful to ever give up on. God is great and He has blessed me magnificently. Believe as I do and take your medicines. Hang in there buddy.*

After several long talks with his parents, it was decided that Tony could continue writing to his prison pen pals as long as he kept his relationship with them in perspective and continued taking his medication.

Nearly five months after the family's intervention, Tony and his parents went with Joey for hamburgers at a local In-N-Out Burger, one of the family's favorite fast-food hangouts. A gaggle of teenagers came inside and sat at the table next to them. Three boys, wearing baggy pants at half-mast and baseball caps turned sideways, flirted loudly with three giggling girls who playfully felt the boys' biceps and punched their shoulders. A look of concern washed across the faces of Al, Chris, and Joey. They braced themselves for what was sure to come. All of them expected Tony to say something to the teens, especially since his eyes were glued on the girls. Because of Tony's past outbursts, his family was certain a confrontation was coming.

But Tony didn't utter a word, even though he continued to eavesdrop on the teenagers' jabber and watch their nonstop flirtation. He ate his burger and left the restaurant without interrupting the teens. Al complimented Tony when they reached their car.

"I thought about saying something to them," Tony acknowledged, "but they was just kids being kids."

To someone unfamiliar with his history, Tony's restraint might have seemed insignificant. But to Al, Chris, and Joey, it was an incredible step forward.

Not long after that outing, Tony came to his parents with an idea. He'd always been content to read the serial killers' letters and reply. But his conversations with his parents about the serial killers had caused him to think about ways that he might be able to use his access to do something more—something useful.

Tony's first thought was about Douglas Clark, one of the Sunset Strip Killers blamed for seven murders. Tony suspected Clark might have been framed. The convicted murderer had represented himself at his own trial and had always insisted that it was his accomplice, Carol M. Bundy, who had done the actual killing. He'd been manipulated by her and after they were arrested, she'd cut a plea deal. Her life had been spared in return for her testimony against him—testimony that had put Clark on California's death row.

"Maybe I could prove he's innocent," Tony said.

Al admired his son's intentions. But he wasn't sure how Tony was going to investigate murders that had happened more than thirty years ago in California.

"That sounds a bit much, Tony," Al said.

Tony thought for several more minutes and then offered another idea. Several of his serial killer pen pals had written to him about unsolved murders.

"What if I get them to tell me about their victims?" Tony asked. "Maybe I could help the families of the victims or even the police."

Al and Chris knew there was a slim chance of Tony actually solving a murder case or getting a serial killer to confess to additional killings.

How could a young man, struggling to keep his own life on track because of a traumatic brain injury, who had no expertise in law enforcement, solve a murder?

But Tony seemed determined. "If I can, I want to help someone."

Not long after their conversation, Tony appeared for breakfast with news.

"Arthur wants me to visit him." Tony beamed.

Shawcross was his favorite. He'd been the first to respond to Tony and the most prolific. "I want to go see him," Tony said.

The serial killer was considered a master manipulator and a liar. He'd also told Tony that Tony was the only person in his entire life who had been his "true friend."

Al and Chris were wary, given what their family had been through. But Tony made a persuasive case. The medication had stabilized his moods, he was not obsessing as he had been, and in fact, he seemed to have gained new insight about his relationship with his pen pals. He genuinely wanted to use the access that he had gained during four years of letter writing to help others.

There was also another reason why Al thought going to visit Shawcross might be a good idea. If Tony met the serial killer face-to-face, perhaps he'd realize just how different the two of them were.

"Can we go?" Tony asked.

"Let's pack our bags," Al replied.

27

Tony, Joey, and Al were surprised at how welcoming the correctional officers were at the Sullivan Correctional Facility in Fallsburg, New York. After entering a reception area, where they were checked for contraband, the trio was politely directed along a flower-edged walkway to a low-rise building with a glass exterior. The Neversink River valley and the panoramic Catskill Mountains could be seen from the second-floor visiting room window. It was a beautiful vantage point.

They'd planned to arrive at the prison much earlier, but they'd been delayed. The flight that they'd caught the day before from Las Vegas to New York City had gotten off late. They'd run into one of Manhattan's infamous rush-hour logjams. The two-hour drive to Fallsburg had taken an hour longer because they were unfamiliar with the roads. They'd finally reached their hotel at 2 a.m. and even then, Tony was so excited that he'd had trouble falling asleep. They'd hoped to get up early and drive to the prison, but had overslept.

As it happened, they were the only visitors that afternoon. They were told they could choose any seat at the eight rows of steel tables inside the room. About ten minutes later, they heard an electronic bolt slide. An officer opened a heavy door so that Arthur Shawcross could enter the visiting room.

Tony, Joey, and Al stood, smiled, and looked at the white-haired, portly, grandfatherly figure. But even though they were alone in the chamber, he didn't make eye contact.

Instead Shawcross walked slowly around the perimeter of the empty tables as if he were searching for his visitors. When he reached the spot where he had started, he gave the correctional officer standing there a puzzled look. The guard nodded his head toward the three men sitting in plain sight only a few feet away. At that moment, Shawcross glanced at them and then strolled over to where they were waiting.

"Oh, here you are," he said. "I got lost, just like you got lost coming here this morning. That's why you're late, right?"

He was clearly irritated that they'd made him wait.

They had only three hours to talk before visiting hours ended, so Tony got right to the point. With Shawcross's autobiographical letter about Vietnam fresh in his mind, Tony asked: "Arthur, what's it like to cut someone's head off?"

Al and Joey grimaced, but the serial killer seemed pleased. He methodically told them the same story that he'd written to Tony about the two Vietnamese women whom he'd surprised and decapitated while hunting for enemy soldiers. Lifting his fat hands, he showed them the angle that he'd used to swing the blade and explained with obvious delight how the blood from the corpses had squirted about ten feet from each body.

"It jumped out in spurts. You hit an artery and their heart is still pumping," he explained.

Without waiting for Tony to ask another question, Shawcross began bragging about heroic feats that he'd claimed to have done in Vietnam. He was such a fierce fighter that the Viet Cong nicknamed him "the ghost of the jungle."

A few times during his war stories, Shawcross sent Joey to a row of nearby vending machines to fetch him snacks and soft drinks. He gobbled them down like a stray dog turned loose in a butcher shop.

"Tell us about the hookers you killed," an enthralled Tony said.

"We'll discuss them tomorrow," Shawcross replied, waving his hand as if he were swatting away the question. Al couldn't tell if Shawcross was still irritated about their late arrival or if he simply wanted to keep something back for their next day's visit.

But when Shawcross saw the disappointment in Tony's face, he said, "Okay, here's one story about them gals that *no one* knows."

Shawcross asked if Tony remembered Frances Brown, one of the Rochester murder victims. She'd been twenty-two years old when she disappeared on November 11, 1989. Her body had been found four days later.

"I'm gonna tell you this," Shawcross said, "and then I'll write it in a letter so you'll have a record of it. After I strangled Frances Brown and dumped her body, I drove into town to the Ponderosa Steakhouse and went inside and ordered a steak and large potato with blue cheese. Plus, I ate at the salad bar. They have quite an assortment of foods and salads plus different Jell-Os, too. Plus, I had a large ice cream in a tall glass. I drank four cups of black coffee, as well. I walked out of there full!

"I drove up to the lake outside the city and sat in the parking lot and watched the boats coming in. About midnight, I drove back to Roches-ter and went to the Dunkin' Donuts on Monroe Avenue and Alexander Street. Went in and had a large coffee regular with four doughnuts, plain. While looking out the front window, I saw a white young woman come around the corner from Monroe Avenue and she was covered in blood. I called out to the girls working in the doughnut shop to get help. I ran out across the street and the girl was lying on her side making a strange sound. Her mouth was one big hole. Someone had punched a hole in her mouth that had took out some teeth and part of her lips.

"The cops arrived and questioned me. Now remember this is just a few hours after I killed Frances Brown and dumped her body. Anyway, the cops had an ambulance come . . . The girl could not talk and when the stretcher was picked up, she grabbed my arm and handed me a card with an address and phone number. I went to the phone booth and called. It was the girl's mother."

"I drove over to Scio Street and the mother was waiting so I drove her to the emergency room at Genesee Hospital, where a nurse asked us questions. The mother said, 'Take care of my baby,' and then fell on the floor and just started crying. I sat down holding her.

"Five hours later, a doctor came out and asked me if I knew what had been used to hit her so I drove back to where I saw her come up the street and I found the weapon and some of her teeth and skin, and I drove it back to the hospital and gave them to the doctor and he called the police again.

"The surgeon came in just after seven a.m. and said you can see her. Her whole lower face was in bandages. She had a tube sticking out where her mouth is and blood was dripping into a tube.

"The girl was there nine days and when she was discharged, I took her to my apartment because she didn't have no place to go and my girl-friend Rose took over helping her. The woman was a deaf mute. She was given a pad of paper and a pen and she wrote quite a lot about me and how nice I was to help her and take her in and then she cried and Rose and I all held her. The police found out who hit her. He was an ex-cop from the South Precinct and he was sent to prison."

Shawcross paused and then said: "So you tell me, Anthony. What sort of man is capable of strangling a woman and then a few hours later helping save the life of another woman on the very same night?"

The corrections officer announced that visiting time was over. Shawcross stood and said: "Tomorrow *be* on time or I may not be here."

The next morning, Tony, Al, and Joey arrived a half hour early. Shawcross greeted each of them approvingly with bear hugs. He immediately asked Joey to get him a Coke and a bag of popcorn from the vending machines and once they settled in, he surveyed the room. Unlike yesterday, there were several visitors meeting with other convicts.

Tony said: "Arthur, I want you to tell me about every murder. I want you to write it all down for me, just like you did about Vietnam. I want you to tell me everything."

Shawcross pondered the request. He said, "No one really knows what went on because there were only two of us there and the other person is dead." He smiled. "You're right, Tony, there needs to be an official record made. There's been a lot of misinformation spread in the media and the cops really don't know what happened, either. Anthony, I'm going to tell you and *only* you the real truth. I'm going to do what you want me to do."

Shawcross looked proud of himself and he clearly expected Tony to reciprocate by thanking him. Instead, Tony asked: "What about the two kids you killed? Will you write to me about them?"

The killer's smile vanished. "Don't you go there, Tony," he said sternly. "I know you and how you are. I've told you before not to ask me about them kids."

Al and Joey decided it was a good time to fetch Shawcross another Coke and more popcorn, leaving Tony alone to speak to him. When they returned, Shawcross was telling yet another Vietnam War story.

As soon as Shawcross finished, Tony blurted: "Arthur, what's human flesh taste like?"

Rather than being offended, a look of what appeared to be amusement appeared on Shawcross's face. He said his first taste of human flesh happened after he'd decapitated the older Vietnamese woman whom he'd surprised hiding weapons. He'd cut meat from her body, cooked it over a fire, and tasted it. But he'd done that only to frighten his second captive before he raped and beheaded her.

"I spit it [flesh] out. If you want to know about actually eating it, then I need to tell you about June Cicero," he explained, "one of the prostitutes I murdered."

At this point something happened that surprised Tony, Al, and Joey. When they described it later, they would agree that it was as if Arthur Shawcross had put himself into a trance. His expression became blank. His voice was robotic. He appeared to disappear into his own thoughts—as if he were replaying the events that he was now describing on some sort of internal DVD screen that only he could see.

Tony, Al, and Joey did not think Shawcross was engaging in cheap theatrics. They honestly believed he was reliving the event in his mind as he was telling it to them.

"I strangled June and then drove down a dead-end road and parked and sat there thinking. I opened the door and let her body fall out into the snow. It was freezing cold and just before Christmas 1989 and her body stayed in the snow while I sat in the car with the heater going full blast. I was there most of the night in that car with her body outside, and near dawn, I got out and she was frozen. I took out my knife."

Shawcross lifted his right hand as if he were holding a knife. He thrust it down toward the tabletop, saying: "I jabbed it into her pussy and then grabbed her pubic hair and ripped it up with my hand."

He raised his clenched fingers, as if he had just pulled a weed from a garden.

"I stuck her hairy flesh into my mouth. It was frozen."

He moved his hand to his now open mouth.

"I ate it raw."

He acted as if he were chewing.

No one spoke. They waited for him to continue. But he didn't. He seemed to be savoring the moment. They wondered if Shawcross had become sexually aroused sitting in the prison's visiting room telling them the story. His face was flushed. That's how excited he was.

Joey would later recall feeling a sudden wave of nausea sweep over him. Try as he might, he couldn't stop his mind from superimposing the missing women's flesh that Shawcross was pretending to hold in front of his smacking lips. It was as if Joey could see the frozen female genitalia, and that imagined sight disgusted him.

For Al, the re-creation of cannibalism seemed to be almost surreal, as if he were watching a grotesque B-grade slasher movie. To imagine otherwise was simply too awful to accept. The scene, however, had no noticeable impact on Tony. He did not shudder, or wince, or feel the revulsion that his younger brother and father felt. Tony simply wanted to ask more questions and probe deeper. His emotions, if he felt anything at all, were inconsequential compared with his curiosity. Tony wanted to know what Shawcross had been thinking at the moment he first tasted the dead girl's flesh; what was he thinking now as he recounted the experience? Tony's mind was racing with questions and an urgency to hear more, learn more.

It was Tony who broke the spell. "Why, Arthur? Why would you do that? Why would you eat her pussy?"

"I have no idea," he said. With that, he removed his false teeth, stuffed his hand into a fresh bag of microwave popcorn, and crammed his mouth full.

Five years earlier, Shawcross had been interviewed by a British television reporter, Katherine English, for a documentary about cannibalism. He'd bragged about eating the vaginas of three victims, even though autopsies showed that only two of the corpses had been mutilated in their vaginal areas. During that filmed interview, he'd claimed that his cannibalism had been prompted by some Freudian-fueled desire to take revenge on his mother for sexually molesting him during his childhood. Tony, Joey, and Al had watched that interview on the Internet and had noticed that Shawcross had not gone into a trance during it—not like the one that they had witnessed.

In 2006, Shawcross had offered a completely different explanation when he'd been interviewed by Columbia University forensic psychiatrist Dr. Michael Stone for a cable television show. Shawcross said he'd eaten his victims' vaginas because he'd heard that a Rochester prostitute had infected him with HIV and he was trying to speed up his own death.

Now, sitting in the prison visiting room, Tony reminded him of those television interviews.

Shawcross threw back his head and showed them his toothless grin.

"That's bullshit," he declared. "Pure bullshit for the cameras, Tony. I was acting, giving them what they wanted to hear. The serial killer cannibal."

He'd conjured up the quotes for the British reporter because he'd wanted to impress her and thought she would "wet her panties" if he gave her a psychobabble answer about his mother. His comment to Dr. Stone had been what Shawcross always had fallen back on to justify his murders—that he was hunting for an HIV-infected hooker.

Tony was not impressed. "Okay, Art, if those answers were bullshit, then tell us—what's the real reason you ate her vagina?"

Shawcross tried to dodge the question by replying with a joke. "All I can say is I'm the only one sitting here today who has really eaten pussy. You have only licked it."

Tony, Al, and Joey forced smiles. But Tony wanted an answer.

"Tony," Shawcross said, "humor helps the rough spots, especially about this stuff."

Tony said, "Okay, I get that, but Art, why did you do it? You said you would answer my questions. Why did you eat a piece of that woman's vagina?"

"Anthony," Shawcross said, "people say they chewed the fat, well, I really did chew the fat—only for real."

It was another joke.

He smirked again and stuffed more popcorn into his mouth. But Tony was getting irritated with Shawcross's refusal to tell him the truth.

"At least the women were dead," Shawcross said. "They didn't have any feelings."

"What did it taste like?" Tony asked.

"It was like munching on something raw from the butcher shop. You want to know. Go eat a piece of raw steak and close your eyes and think of pussy . . . only it tastes more like raw, uncooked fat."

Tony was still unsatisfied. "But why, Art? Why did you eat human flesh? Please tell me."

Shawcross was quiet for several moments as he continued to chew popcorn. He took a swig of Coke to wash it down and then said, "It was my reward. Some people take trophies."

He paused. "I ate mine."

28

Shortly after they returned to Las Vegas, Tony received a thick manila envelope from Shawcross. It contained twenty typewritten pages, single-spaced. Tony gave the bundle to Al, who put on his silver-framed half-glasses and began to read aloud.

Dear Anthony,

I have had quite a few people ask me to describe my crimes and I've turned them all down . . . But I am writing this to you for you to keep. I have not thought about these murders in eighteen years or better. This is going to be a tough assignment to put together but here goes.

[Number one: Dorothy Blackburn, age twenty-seven]
The first took place on February 8, 1988 to be exact. After borrowing a car from a friend—Clara—I headed west up Lyell Avenue until I came to Dewey Avenue where this woman stepped right out in the street. I stopped and she grabs the door and gets right in and asked me, "Do you want a date?"

I said, "What kind of date?"

She said, "You a cop?"

I said, "Fuck no."

She asked, "You want a blow and fuck?"

I said, "Show me what you have to offer."

We turned into an alley. Dark back there. I had the doors locked so no surprises from any of her friends hiding there. She pushed her pants down, panties and all! Then took them off. Then her coat and blouse. No bra on. The coat was a black and white fur type coat. Pants were black and the panties were pink with white frills along the edges.

I took off my pants and then adjusted the seat as far back as possible. She sword swallows me right off! I was hard as a rock and she was really going at it and slow too. All the way in and back up to the tip and tickles the opening, and then she bites me! I belted her in the side of her fucking head hard in the left temple and she drops onto my lap. I opened the door and pushed her off and gathered some snow on my cock and it slowly stopped the blood and some of the pain.

I decided to bite her back. I twisted this bitch around in the car seat and opened her legs and went right at the pussy and savaged it, for real . . . I bit through the skin and she started to bleed some herself. She moaned and then screamed as soon as she came to and I handed her panties to her and she held them against her pussy and I asked her: "Why did you bite me?"

"I felt like it," she said.

I smacked her again and said, "You'd better make sense or you will never bite anyone in this life again."

I don't think she heard what I said because she started reaching for my dick again because she wanted to fuck, bloody pussy and all, and that is when it hit me that she could be high on something!

I decided to fuck the living piss out of her. I mounted her and lifted her legs higher and then leaned forward against her in the car, pinning her back. As I was fucking her, I reached up and put both hands on her neck and I began strangling her until she became unconscious.

While she was passed out, I tied her ankles together and her hands behind her and laid her on the front seat still unconscious. I sat on her legs in the driver's seat so she couldn't move when she came around and I drove out of town.

I was really pissed off over what she did to my dick as it was starting to hurt some more! I drove out Route 31 away from Rochester to Brockport, New York, and made a right . . . I drove all across that to Route 19 along the lake. I knew where a burned out building was located and I eased into its garage and closed the door.

I had my way with that bitch again and again everywhere you can think of. Mouth, cunt, and up her fucking tight ass! She moaned and said, "Yes, give me more." I fucked her until I was too tired to keep going. Then I went out and got snow and cleaned myself up and then got a rag and cleaned her up too. She had stopped bleeding by then. I opened the door and set her up straight in the seat and untied her hands and she swung at me.

Sleepy time—she went with a finger jab to the side of her neck by the ear on the left side. Legs still tied. While she was knocked out, I drove back to Brockport. She woke up and asked me: "Who sent you? Was it my husband?"

I didn't know what she was talking about but I played along and said, "No, try again."

She said, "Oh shit! Please, I'll get the money tonight."

I still didn't know what she was talking about but I was beginning to think it was drugs because she was so groggy so I said, "It is going to cost you double." She starts talking and I realize she stole drugs from someone and I asked her where the drugs were and she says, "In my coat pocket." I reached into her coat in the back seat and she had fifty one square inch envelopes in the color pink. I reached in the other side and there were the same amount of light blue one square inch envelopes. "I'm taking these," I said. I also took all of her money.

It was cold as hell outside the car what with blowing snow. She started to cry and asked me, "Do you really have to do this?" And I said, "Yes, it's a lesson to others" and she shut right up and then said, "Fuck me again please."

I drove over through South Hampton Park, pulled in next to a small bridge over a stream. I lifted her legs up on the seat and untied them. Pushed her legs back and fucked the pussy hard!

I said, "Open your mouth and if you bite me this time, I will cut your cunt right out of you and leave you in the cold."

She opens her mouth and I shoved my cock down her throat until she started to choke and then eased up. Then I pushed her head against me so hard she could not breathe and I held her until she started shuddering and I held tight until she stopped moving. She wasn't breathing so I started CPR on her and when she began breathing on her own, I rolled her over and began fucking her in the ass again!

She came too while I was fucking her in the ass and she began cursing me now and said I was hurting her so I drove it in and left it there and reached a forearm around her throat and began choking her again and I said, "It's time for you to either head for heaven or hell."

When she stopped moving, I still kept up the pressure and life eased out of her and I knew she was dead while I was still inside her ass.

I pulled out and unscrewed the overhead light bulb in the car and opened the door. Got some snow on the rag and cleaned myself off. I then put her panties back on her and her pants and blouse. Next the socks and shoes. Went around the other side and opened the door and pulled the body out and eased it over the bridge abutment and she fell into the Salmon River. Cold fucking water for damn sure! I got back in the car and headed back to Rochester.

As I crossed the Genesee River, I pulled over. I took her coat and removed all the envelopes and took her other items out as well. Then walked back to the bridge and tossed the coat in the river. Watched it go over the falls . . . I drove to the Dunkin Donut Shop on Monroe Avenue and sat at the small seat by the door. I asked for a large coffee, regular. Plus four donuts in the Cinnamon Twist type.

As I sat there eating and drinking, I took some of those envelopes out and was looking at them when in walked a group of skin heads, combat boots and weird haircuts and this one chick with half of her head shaved and a short tight skirt and high boots came and stood next to me and bent down and whispered, "Follow me now!" I put the envelopes in my hand and walked out with her and she took me to this house nearby and when we stepped into the doorway, she said, "What are you trying to do, get busted?"

I said, "What are you talking about?"

She told me the pink envelopes were cocaine and the blue were heroin and she asked me what I wanted for a couple of them. I just smiled and she began taking off her clothes, but I couldn't get hard for anything.

She was sucking me when this big black bitch comes walking into the house and says, "What are you doing with my bitch?"

I reached in my pocket and took out every envelope and she grinned and said, "You can stay as long as you want too!" She took her clothes off and joined us.

For the rest of the night I was right there with the two of them fucking . . .

It's a strange and funny thing Anthony, but I never gave it a thought to what I had just done to that whore . . . I forgot all about it and went about business the next day as usual.

Tony decided to compare the confession with the one that Shawcross had given the Rochester police some twenty years earlier. He retrieved a copy of the original police report from the files that he had collected about Shawcross. During the police interrogation, Shawcross had said that Blackburn had been high on drugs when he picked her up and she had bitten his penis.

But from that point forward, the two confessions took much different turns. The police quoted Shawcross as saying:

After she bit me, I told her she was going to be raped. All she did was laugh. Then I got mad and started to sweat real bad. Pulled her close to me and fondled her. Then whispered in her ear she was going to die, and what did she say now! She must have been on drugs. Just smiled at me . . . then she called me little man. I choked her for a good ten minutes . . . she went limp.

Continuing, Shawcross told the Rochester police that he had strangled Blackburn *without ever* having sexual intercourse with her. She'd ridiculed him because he'd been unable to get an erection after she'd bitten him. That's why he'd snapped and killed her.

In his confession for Tony, Shawcross wrote that he'd raped Blackburn repeatedly throughout the night. He bragged that Blackburn had become unconscious after he'd jammed his penis into her mouth, preventing her from breathing. He'd been forced to revive her with CPR. This was not the first time in his letters that Shawcross had mentioned sexual asphyxiation—choking someone during sex and then either releasing them or bringing them back after they had lost consciousness.

Al began reading Shawcross's next story.

[Number two: Anne Marie Steffen, age twenty-eight]

I did my second one in July 1988. I was walking from my apartment, trying to find how far it was to walk to this so-called beach that I was hearing about. I walked until I reached Lake Avenue and a woman called to me from the other side of the street. She . . . had on a long yellow flowered dress to just below the knees and sandals. She asked if she can walk along with me and I told her she can walk wherever she has a mind to. I got as far as the Pizza Hut and went in for lunch. When I came out, she was still there and she asked me to follow her to a place where, she said, "I can get to know you better."

Like the fool I was, I did just that. We walked to Driving Park Bridge and then went down this steep hill to a tall grassy area about 90 feet above the Genesee River . . . There was a circle of laid down tall grass about six feet wide or so. She sits down and lifted her dress over her head and she was completely naked.

She said, "Take off your clothes, so I can fuck and suck you off."

I asked her to open her legs and what did I see but a huge dark colored vein on one lip of her pussy. It was as large as my forefinger and I said, "What's that?"

"That's nothing. It's where I shoot up my drugs," she said.

I started to back away and she said, "If you try to leave, I will scream rape!"

I came back to that spot and knelt down in front of her and asked, "What did you say?"

She said, "I will scream rape." Then she started to scream!

I grabbed her by the neck and put her to sleep. Dragged her to the cliff and rolled her over between some rocks. Picked up some trash that was there and covered her over. I walked away and never even thought much about it, either.

. . . Anthony, I was able to push bad moments away from my mind like it did not happen and that's what I did with this murder. I just forgot about it.

Al moved to the next victim.

[Number three: Dorothy Keeler, age sixty]

I was coming home from working at the Farmer's Market

on Jefferson Road in Henrietta when I saw this woman curled around a light pole in the dirt. I woke her up and asked: "What are you doing out here in the dark along a foot path?"

"I got no place else to go," she said.

I told her to follow me home and meet my partner, Rose. I knew she would like Rose. So Dorothy Keeler did just that and came home with me. While she was talking to Rose—I drew her a bath and added Calgon beads to the water. Got out a large towel and slippers. I motioned to Rose to get this woman a bath as she was filthy. They were in there a while so I started supper and a pot of coffee. After they finally came out, I had her sit at the table in a bathrobe with Rose and eat. I took all her clothes [and] went down in the cellar and placed her clothes in a washer with half cup of Tide.

After supper and she was dressed in clean clothes, I asked if she wanted a job taking care of the apartment . . . I would pay her $4.25 per hour. She said she would work but all she wanted was $20 a week, plus room and board. She was placed in the spare bedroom.

I worked nights and Rose worked days. We only had about three hours with each other during an average day . . . Usually when I get home in the morning; I shower and then sleep about four hours. That is all I need. Then I would go fishing. Then at 2:45 p.m., I head back home and prepare supper. Dorothy was usually watching tv and I'd ask how was her day and what did she do for the apartment and she would get up and show me. She was a good house keeper! The first winter I bought her new shoes and boots plus better clothes . . .

The next spring, things started to disappear in our apartment. I asked Rose what was missing and she would check and then start to cry. Her mother's jewelry was missing! Dorothy admitted taking it. I said, "Didn't I offer you more money and here you go and steal from the apartment. I am going to this pawn shop and get my wife's jewels back if you still have the tickets." She did and she went with me.

When we got back, I told Dorothy to pack her stuff and leave. She didn't say a word and walked out. Several weeks later, I went down to the river at Driving Park to catch salmon and saw

Dorothy talking to some guys fishing on a rock. I went to my usual spot and shot my leaded hook out . . . and let it drop in the water. I yanked and . . . snagged a fish so I called out "FISH ON!" Everyone near me is supposed to reel in their lines so I can land my fish, but these guys with Dorothy didn't do nothing.

I got my fish landed and walked to Seth Green Island just down the stream about a quarter mile away. I . . . decided to make a hut somewhat like we had in Vietnam. I started cutting down a six inch tree about six feet above the ground. . . . I worked on the hut for several hours and after I got it built, I put plastic GLAD trash bags across the roof and gathered stones for a fire place inside it and added mud to the rocks. I could sit in the hut and fish so I sat back and took out a lure and . . . tossed it in the river. Nothing grabbed it. So I gathered dead wood and started a fire and attached leaded hooks and tossed them out and started snagging and caught a salmon of about two feet long. Trimmed off the fins and gutted it. Rinsed the fish and then skinned it. Shoved a green stick into the flesh and set that over the fire. I always carry salt and pepper in my tackle box. When the fish was near done, guess who shows up by her damn self? Dorothy. I asked her if she thought it was funny to get those two assholes to fuck with me when I caught my fish? She just laughed.

She was looking at what I built and climbed up inside the hut. I sat on a log outside and started eating some of that fish. It was good. Then I gathered up my rod and tackle box and went up into the hut and Dorothy was asleep. I laid down at an angle because I was too tall to lay straight back in the hut but the grass was nice and comfortable. I slept for awhile until that bitch stirred. Then I grabbed her and started kissing her. I stripped her down and myself too. That woman was tighter than a fucking keyhole so I got down and sucked the juices out of her cunt. Then I nailed the bitch hard, so hard that she passed out!

When she woke up, I was still going strong and she grabbed on me and shivered and was weeping with a funny smile. I asked if she was okay and she said, "Why, of course, you asshole!"

"Oh, I'm an asshole now, huh," I said.

I grabbed her panties and tied her ankles together and then shoved them back until her heels were behind her head. Now old

Dorothy is helpless and wide open. That's when I really fucked her and hard at that, and she was laughing at me and said, "This is a new one."

That got me going so I turned her over and fucked her in the ass and she did not laugh at me then. She kept saying, "OH DAMN, OH DAMN" over and over again.

I looked outside and it was dark. So I picked her up while I was still inside her and carried her down into the river and walked in to just over the knees and sat down slowly and then pulled out.

I rinsed myself off and told her not to move. I went back and came back with a bar of soap. I washed her all over. After we were clean, I released the panties and we stood in the dark with the warm breeze drying us off and I went back up to the shore to get dressed and she told me that I was the first man to fuck her. I didn't understand and then she said she was a lesbian.

Then this bitch tells me that she is going to move back into our apartment and if I don't let her, she will scream rape to the cops because everyone knew she was a lesbian!

I grabbed her neck and began choking her right then and there. When she was almost gone, I let go and she comes out of it slowly and then she tells me that getting choked was a rush. She said, "Do it again and I might cum!"

So I did and that is when she went bye-bye and never returned. Cum she sure did! I took off her clothes and folded them neatly. I carried the body about twenty yards away and laid it under some brush and covered it with long grass. I went back for the clothes and shoes and laid them next to the body and gathered up everything I brought with me and even threw the excess fish back in the river.

. . . A couple of months later, I went back to Seth Green and made my way down to the island . . . I went over where I had left the body and saw that it was almost a complete skeleton and I took a chunk of wood and popped the skull away from the rest of the bones. I used a stick and carried the skull to where the trees are and climbed up a tree and inserted a branch in the eye sockets and then climbed back down.

Anthony, the skull looks down at the body—the soul stays put

*forever. Dorothy Keeler's soul is still floating there on that island.
The cops have taken away her headless body, but her skull is still
in that tree and she will never be free . . .*

As he had done earlier, Tony compared Shawcross's confession with
the one that the Rochester police had recorded. His statements to detectives had been mostly yes-and-no replies to their specific questions. For
the most part, the two accounts matched, except that Shawcross was
telling Tony much more information, especially about the rapes that he'd
committed.

[Number four: Patricia Ives, age twenty-five]
*Patty Ives was a dope head! One day I was walking from Driv-
ing Park Bridge and crossed over to Lake Avenue and headed
south and Patty Ives walked up and asked me where the hell have
I been for so long. She asked if I had an hour to kill. I gave her a
slight smirk and nodded and she takes my right hand and leads
me to the side of the YWCA. Along a high-wire fence was a low-
hanging tree full of leaves. Dark under there and the grass was
very soft and thick. I think she uses this spot often. I went under
there and stripped off. She did as well.*

*She was sucking my cock and stroking my nuts when I felt
my cock get stiff as a bone and stand tall for some reason and it
started to hurt from the pressure. I asked her how did she do that
and she shows me a packet of cocaine. Shit. Drugs is not what I
need now. She takes the rest and rubs her pussy insides. I asked
her why did she rub that shit on me and she said, "It worked
didn't it?"*

I said, "How long does it take to leave the system?"
"A long time," she said.

*I snapped her fucking neck, then covered her over with sod
that was piled to one side.*

*When I got home, I was still stiff as a tree limb because of the
cocaine. I did not know what to do. I took a shower and changed
into loose shorts and went up on the third floor to visit Susan.
Now she was a virgin at age 53 when I first met her in 1987. She
was a nun for 37 years. As soon as I walked in, Susan locked her
door and closed the curtains and dropped her clothes that fast.*

She stood there going "OH MY GOD!" over and over all the while stroking me. Then she dropped to her knees and kissed the end of my cock and I pushed it into her mouth and she went right at it . . . I shot my load but I was still hard and pulsating. I couldn't come because of the cocaine. So I pulled out of her mouth and shoved it up her cunt . . . I shot again, but was still hard.

I could not for the life of me figure out what to do. I walked down the hall towards the front of the building and tapped on another neighbor's door. This woman opened her door and asked me to come in. I had a cup of coffee with her and sat at her dining table while she sat on her bed. She ups and opens her legs and no panties are on. I got up and went over and stood in front of her and dropped my shorts. She reached for me and stroked it slowly . . . but I could not get release so she said, "You need to fuck me" and I did . . . Afterwards, she said we should not have done this and I told her I wanted to for a long time and then I told her about what that woman had done to me with the cocaine and she laughed and said she would remember that when her boyfriend got home from jail.

She was one of several women I was fucking in our building. In the next building over, I had a few on the side too. Mother and daughter team. There was a lot of sex for me in those buildings.

About two days later . . . I went up on the second floor of one of the buildings where a woman who looked just like Rodney Dangerfield lived. She had wild looking eyes and man, she was all of 80, I bet. She had sent for me and she said, "Are you Art?" and I said, "Yes, what do you want me for?"

She said she had heard about me from other women and she goes into her bedroom and then calls me in. I walked in and she was naked as a jay bird and she had more wrinkles than a raisin. She handed me $500 in cash and said, "Fuck me until you can't."

Did she ever squeal. I fucked her for a good hour and when I finished, I was so damn tired, I just went back to my building and a woman was sitting on my porch. I asked who she was and what she was doing and she said she was a transient person and had just gotten off a bus and did not have enough money for a room. So Rose and I told her she could stay in the guest room that night.

So much was happening to me, I didn't know if I was coming or going. Before we went to bed that night, I asked the transient woman her plan. She said she wanted to get a job if possible. So Rose and I asked her a lot of questions about what she is able to work at and she was a very intelligent woman so she should be able to get whatever she wanted. I told her she could stay with us until she got on her feet.

Then Rose and I went into our room and got frisky with the door closed. Sometime during the night, I woke up and heard someone crying softly. I eased out of bed and went into the hall and listened at the woman's door. She was crying. I had on my bathrobe and went in and sat upon the edge of the bed and asked why is she crying and she said she had split with her husband. OUCH. I asked if there was some way we could help her and she said, "No." She was just upset. When she left the apartment the next morning to go job hunting, I snooped and found her old phone number and copied it down and put it away in case.

Now the reason I have been explaining what I did on both sides of the tracks is because I felt I was two different persons, Anthony. Weird as that is. I was good and I was bad. I murdered this woman and then I helped this other woman—just like I'd done the other time with the deaf woman.

What do you make of that, my friend? A good Arthur Shawcross and an evil Arthur Shawcross. All in one.

[Number five: Frances Brown, age twenty-two]

I had been out with this hooker before. I was driving a small compact car in the color light blue—a Dodge Omi 1987. I went down an alley near where she was standing . . . and eased out enough so she could hear the music playing on the radio and she turned, waved . . . opens the door and gets in. Tells me to drive over to Lake Avenue . . . behind a Chinese restaurant. The back seat folded forward so we had plenty of room. She sucked me off and then mounted me. She worked herself into a frenzy and busted off. I rolled over above her and lifted her legs up and drove in slowly.

She said, "Hurry up, damn it!"

So I did. I eased forward harder and held her so she could not move if she wanted too. I slowly moved my hands to her neck and squeezed until she went limp. I backed off of her and she relaxed on the seat in a stupor.

I drove off naked as she was. Drove over to St. Paul Street and parked above Seth Green Drive and pulled up along the cliff side drop off. She was still unconscious so I fucked her some more.

When she woke up, for some reason, she could not lift her arms. She asked: "What did you do to me? I can't feel anything?" She spoke in a whisper.

I reached over and squeezed the side of her neck and shut off the oxygen supply to her brain and she was gone in about four or five minutes. I opened the door and pulled her out. On her left ass cheek she had a tattoo that said, "Kiss Off" and that is what I did. I pushed her over the cliff and she dropped a good fifteen feet and rolled face down in the leaves. She was a sort of blonde and shaved too. I drove away and placed her clothes and things in different dumpsters.

[Numbers six and seven: Elizabeth Gibson, age unknown; and June Stott, age twenty-six]

This woman I picked up without knowing it. I stopped in a restaurant called MARKS. After I ate and came back to the car that I had borrowed from Clara Neal, there was a woman sitting inside it. I said, "Why are you in my car?"

She said, "I was cold and you had just drove in so I knew your car would be warm."

I told her she would have to leave as I was heading home . . . She asked if she can give me a blow job and I said, "Not tonight." She asked if I would take her home. She said drive to St. Paul and I did and when we got there, the house was dark. I asked if this was the place and she said, "Yes." She then said she wanted to fuck and I said, "Get out lady and let me out of here!"

She raises her left leg and kicks the gear shift and bent the fucking thing. I reached across and grabbed her by her hair and pulled her to me and strangled her then and there. She was a fighter too. But she lost the race.

I opened her door and placed her in the back seat and closed the door. I then went to try and bend back the gear shift. Man,

I was fucked badly on this one. I got out the tools and took the gear shift off and tried to bend the shaft back, but could not. I even placed it under the left rear tire and backed over it and that almost straightened it.

I drove out Highway 104 and turned down a side road and into a field. I stripped the woman and carried her out in this semi-snow filled field where an old tractor was sitting. I sat her on the steel seat and held her right arm to the steel steering wheel like she wanted to grip it all the time. She was starting to stiffen up and when I left without turning my lights on, she was looking West. I thought I was creative!

I drove to a garage and asked the man if he could flatten out a gear shift. No problem. He heated it and tapped it almost smooth. Replaced and it was good as new.

That was all there is to say about Elizabeth Gibson.

Now, June Stotts was a different story, Anthony. And it is important story for you to hear but it is not easy for me to tell.

I was driving down Lyell Avenue when I heard someone call my name: "Art." I stopped and looked around and saw a woman who I called "J" who I used to see all of the time at Midtown Plaza. She would always hit me up for fifty cents. Sometimes I gave her more. She gets in my car and asked if we could go to the beach. During the ride, I learned her name was really June. So we went to the beach and I locked the car and we walked along the beach. June took her shoes off and walked in the water at the edge where it was only a couple of inches deep and any wave that came in, she laughed. We went to where the Merry-Go-Round was and . . . she wanted to ride and I asked the attendant if she can and he said yes. She got on-and-off, she went laughing all the time. Then, all of the sudden she jumps off crying and grabbed me and hugged me while crying. Strange woman here. After a few moments, she stopped and the guy running the machine looked at me and I mouthed to him, "I don't know." We walked out on the pier to the very end and there was a dredger coming in to clean the lower part of the Genesse River of silt . . .

We ate at the arcade restaurant and after that I had an idea. We drove South towards the city and made a turn into Turning Point Park and watched the dredger come up the river and I told

June that the Genesee River is one of seven rivers in the world that head due north.

I took June by the hand and we walked down the steep hill to the river and walked out on the piers there and sat down to wait. About an hour later, the ship got closer and we waved to the men on board. As the ship got even closer, we could almost touch it and it scooped up the river bottom as it went and I told June that the boat just scooped up a bike I tossed in last Spring when I came down the hill and both tires blew out. I got mad and threw it in the fast water.

June got up and we walked back to a dirt path just to see what we could find and I found a good size piece of light blue rug laying in the grass and weeds. I picked it up and shook it out and it was fairly clean . . . I sat down on the rug and the sun was beating down and it was nice. Hardly any insects and no breeze to speak of. I took off my shirt and t-shirt and laid back and must have went to sleep because when I woke up June was naked and playing with herself. I looked up and smiled. I took off my clothes fast and looked at her body and she was not bad at all. I started kissing her and she was really getting into it. I mounted her and slowly fucked her . . . When she came, she cried. I asked, "What's the matter?" But she did not say anything.

She leaned over and became performing oral sex and I thought she was drooling but she was bleeding badly and I pulled her head up and she said that everytime she does this with someone she gets a nose bleed. I had to walk back to the river and rinse my lower body off.

Went back to the rug and fucked that woman most of the day. She was very passionate too! Then I laid back and her head was on my shoulder and she was not saying a word and then she sits up and right out of the blue said, "I am going to tell my boyfriend you raped me!"

I was in shock and said, "I woke up and you were naked next to me, so what was I to think?"

It didn't matter.

I sat there looking at her and then slugged her right on the chin. Bam. TKO, stretched out cold on the rug.

I went through her pockets and found a very sharp jackknife, about a dollar in change and her ID card. Nothing else. I pock-eted everything. Grabbed her by the hair and dragged her way back in the reeds and waited for her to wake up. She came too and began crying.

"I won't tell anyone," she said.

I said, "You will never tell anyone anything ever again!"

I grabbed her throat and squeezed just enough to get her un-divided attention. Then fucked her for real and she held on and responded back and then some. . . . After that, she wanted more so I gave it to her . . .

I said, "From now on, you are mine from this day forward."

She said, "That means I will have to move out of my boy-friend's apartment and come live with you!"

Anthony, my friend, I did not have to kill this woman/girl but I did at that moment and she is the only one who affected me!!!! I stayed with the body until dark and used her knife to remove her pussy and there I sat eating the thing. Before cutting, I shaved it smooth. Then I cut the body from the neck to the pussy area. Straight down and she had at least five inches of fat on her stom-ach. I did not cut the membrane that held in her guts. I covered her with the rug and looked the area over for anything I may have forgotten.

When I got to my car, I let the motor run and then drove away back to the city. I was having very strange feelings like I was not the person driving. When I arrived at our apartment, I walked in and went and sat in the kitchen in the dark. My wife came in and tried to talk to me, but I ignored her. Then two other people came in and I did not know who they were. I went into the bathroom and took a shower and came back out and changed my clothes and put the others in the wash basket. I walked out in the dining room and asked who these people were. In fact, I did not know who Rose was. I was way out in left field. I was gone from real-ity. The two people were Rose's niece and son-in-law and I sat down and waited for, I don't know what. Rose got up and came to me and started talking to me but I just could not at all that time bring everything into focus.

Raylene and Butch [her niece and son-in-law] got up and came over and took me into the living room and sat me on the couch.

It took awhile for me to arrive back from wherever my mind was hiding! . . . Asked for a cup or two of black coffee and Rose said, "He is coming back when he wants coffee."

I could not explain to them what was going on inside of me because I did not know myself. It was like I was someone else . . . But that evening I went back to work as usual. I thought, "Everyone is safe when I am working; BUT that depends on the work I am into, right Anthony? Ha. Ha."

Al decided it was time to take a brief break from reading the confessions. Chris was upset. It was difficult for her to visualize that the Arthur Shawcross who called her from prison to chat about Italian recipes and sent her four-leaf clovers from the prison yard was the vicious rapist and murderer cannibalizing women in his confessions.

[Numbers eight and nine: Marie Welch, age twenty-two; and Darlene Trippi, age thirty-two]

These next two murders will interest you because I could have been caught. One evening as I was coming back into the city, I headed towards Lyell Avenue and saw someone I knew because I had been with her before. It was late and after midnight and freezing cold outside and I lowered my window and said, "Hey babe!"

She came up to the car and said, "I didn't recognize you."

I said, "It's warm in here, get in."

She did just that and we drove to some warehouses and I parked between two buildings and left the heater going. She asked, "Wanna fuck?" . . . Off came the clothes.

I asked, "Your night been slow?"

She said, "Nothing but blow jobs. After sucking so many dicks, I'm horny."

So I leaned down after I got the seat back and . . . licked her . . . After a few minutes, I was hard enough and slid up inside and fucked her for a good forty minutes but I could not cum!

I said, "Damn-it."

She said, "Shit happens."

So I lifted her legs higher and missed the cunt and hit the asshole and she said, "Hey, wait a minute, you're in the wrong place.

An ass fuck is going to cost you fifty dollars."

So I went at her ass for a while and blew a gasket.

I rolled her over and she said, "That's twice for you—so you owe me a hundred" and after fucking her for a few more minutes, I snapped her neck. I heard it crack and she relaxed.

I got off of her and pulled her pants back up around her waist and put her other things back on her . . . I had her sitting beside me in the car. [Shawcross tied a bungee cord around her chest and the seat to keep her sitting upright next to him. The cord was hidden by her coat.] Suddenly a sheriff's car pulls up and knocks on the glass and said we can't park in this area. I thanked him and slowly drove away with a dead body beside me the entire time. The cop thought she was my girlfriend.

I drove up to the lake and went along towards Long Pond. There was a dead end spot and I went in there and took the body out and carried it into the brush not far from the road to a fence line next to a thick tree. I took clothes off the body and left it sitting up looking at the lake. . . .

The next murder was Darlene Trippi, someone I met walking up Plymouth Avenue heading north. She waved to me and I stopped. She got in the car and told me where to park. She was one of the first I had fucked back in 1987—over a year earlier— so she felt safe with me. Her mistake.

I parked behind two tractor trailers and there was a lot of snow on the ground. She stripped down . . . I got my clothes off and we got in the back seat of a Chevy and went to it hot and heavy until the windows steamed up fast. After forty-five minutes, I called it quits as I was tired out . . . I strangled her then and there. Waited until dark and drove out Route 31 past Brockport, New York, and went down Redman Road and pulled-up without headlights next to a small bridge and dumped the body over in the water there.

Anthony, I was getting sloppy having that cop check on us when Welch was dead and then I overlooked one of Trippi's ear rings that had dropped on the floor of the car.

Makes you wonder if I wanted to get caught, doesn't it Anthony?

Al had reached the final two confessions.

[June Cicero, age thirty-four; and Felicia Stephens, age nineteen]

It was in December of 1989 and it was raining this one evening and I was sitting at a street light on Plymouth Avenue and Lyell Avenue and this woman opens the door and got right in and started talking bullshit. I pulled up on State Street by the Chinese Restaurant and asked her: "What is your problem?"

She said she knew who I was and I said so then you know me and further more you and I have dated before if you remember. But she said that is not what she was speaking about. She said I was the guy going around and killing the girls. I started to laugh at her and she started to laugh as well. I told her that it's totally impossible. Then asked if she had time for a love session and she was all money then. Off we went and I drove out of town to Salmon Creek Park and parked in some pine trees. I told her: "This is a nice spot" because I had been there before. But that was with Clara Neal, my girlfriend. June was very wet and I said; "How many have you had this night?" And she said: "Maybe ten" I thought, huh, fucked ten times. I said: "How about a blow job instead?" She said, "I need the money upfront" and I asked, "Well, how about fifty for an ass fuck?" Down came the pants and she laid on the seat with her butt in the air and said, "Let's go!"

I was behind her so I struck her with my fist hard behind her neck and heard it crack. The woman just started to shake all over. So I pinched her mouth and nose closed and she stopped moving. I dumped her body in the Salmon River on Route 31 about 90 yards from where the police helicopter saw me pissing later in a bottle. But that didn't happen until several weeks later.

Now Felicia Stephens was black and she had on a long gray coat on and she was naked underneath. I was parked on the corner of Jefferson Road and West Main Street when she sticks her head in the window on the passenger side and said, "Let me in—two guys are chasing me!" I reached down and hit the window button and up that window went before she could move and it caught her head in it between the glass and door, and I drove off as she was hanging on the side of the car. When I got past all the houses, I stopped and lower the window. I got out, opened the passenger door and pushed her body inside. I drove away. She was not conscious. She could have been dead. About six miles down an old country road, I stopped. I opened her legs and smiled because she was shaved and smooth. I reached in and felt her and she was slightly damp. I pushed the seat back and went at it with my mouth. Not bad at all. Then I fucked her for good measure. No different from a white woman! I fucked this woman all night long and then carried her across three feet of snow to a brush fence line. I dropped her in a depression and left her there . . .

On January 3, 1990, I picked a woman. Her name was Barbara and I took her to the Tool and Die Shop on Saint Paul Street. We got naked in their parking lot and we fucked hard and heavy until a UPS truck pulled up beside us and boy did he get an eyeful. We got dressed in a hurry and left laughing like two fools. I dropped her off where she started and went out to Route 31 to Spencerport to pick up Clara. But as you will have it, I had to piss so bad that I pulled over and I was pissing in a bottle when that police helicopter was flying over and saw me. Then they came and got me because I had stopped so close to where I'd dumped June Cicero's body.

Did I want to get caught? The truth was that I was tired of it all, Anthony.

Now you and you alone know what really happened. I've told you about all of the women. End of story.

Your good friend Arthur Shawcross.

Under his signature, Shawcross had added a postscript: "—I think."

"What does 'I think' mean?" Tony asked.

Al said, "The last line of his letter says: 'End of story.' Then he writes, 'I think . . . ' He is telling us there might be more murders and he either doesn't remember them or doesn't want to tell us about them right now."

"So he's leaving us hanging?" Tony said.

"Yes, he is."

29

Dear Arthur,

   . . . Thank you for your detailed descriptions of the murders. . . . I want to ask you a few follow up questions. . . .

The serial killer was quick to reply.
Why had Shawcross strangled his victims?

Because you feel it, Anthony . . . the panic, the pounding of the heart, the look of fright in their eyes as the oxygen is being cut from their brains.

Strangling someone was actually a sign of respect.

Those girls deserved to know what I was doing and who I was. Shooting someone is impersonal. There is no human connection between the life-taker and his victim. There is no respect. I chose them to die and I killed them with my hands because I respected the life I was taking from them.

Why had he choked some victims and then brought them back to life while he was having sex with them?

It gave them sexual pleasure. The feeling intensified because they were close to death . . . but I got something too, Anthony . . . that brief moment that exists between life and death.

Reviving the women enabled him to repeat that moment, much like a cat allows a wounded mouse to escape from its paws only to pounce again.

There is such power in those seconds when you are squeezing the life from someone. Their whole being depends on you. You are holding their life in your hands and that is a rush like no other.

Which gave him more pleasure: sex or murder?

I get no pleasure from a blow job and never did. But my reasons you know about already—my fucked-up childhood. . . . Sex never motivated me, Anthony. It never did. I explained this to you when I described my many sexual conquests in my apartment building. There were plenty of women who wanted me to fuck them. There still are. I didn't need those girls for sex because this was never about sex. It was about killing. You must travel to the other side of insanity to truly understand what I am about to share with you. The first thrill is the deception and then comes the stalking and then the intense pleasure of total dominance— total power—of authority.

Why did you spend so much time with your victims before you killed them?

I acted like I wanted to get to know them and maybe I did. But I also knew my face was their last sight . . . When you kill someone, it is a feeling of strength beyond human belief. There is only one problem. It does not last. After the brain or soul or whatever gets back in control, you calm down and you feel guilt and you look around to see what harm you've caused. That's the worse part. Because you see what you really are and what you have done and you hate that. But that feeling—you want that feeling—that rush back. You want to be in control again. To dominate. And so you do it again and again and again until someone stops you.

Tony understood now.

By almost every standard, Arthur Shawcross was a loser—starting from birth. An unwanted child, he'd never measured up. He'd returned from Vietnam further psychologically damaged and had sexually molested and murdered two children. Chased from town to town, he'd ended up in Rochester working at a dead-end job, living in a low-rent apartment. He was a complete nobody.

But during the final seconds in his victims' lives, as he clutched their throats and squeezed the life from them, Shawcross had finally achieved the superhuman, genetically superior, sexual warrior status that he'd fantasized about in his letters.

Although Tony had no psychiatric training, after several years of writing to Shawcross and talking to him on the telephone, Tony believed he understood the serial killer as well as anyone ever would.

"When he was strangling those girls, he felt like he was God," Tony told his dad. "Art got to decide—not God—who lived and who died. And that turned him on because he was in total control and, most of all, he *mattered*. He was not just somebody, he was all-powerful to the person he was killing. He finally was somebody."

30

If Arthur Shawcross had committed more murders than the ones that he had admitted, Tony wanted to know. The Rochester police believed Shawcross had murdered Kimberly Logan, whose naked body had been found a few blocks from his apartment. The prostitute had been beaten to death and hidden under leaves and trash. Detectives had tried to get Shawcross to confess to her murder. But he'd refused. Police also suspected that Shawcross had strangled Jacqueline Dicker and Rosalie Oppel, two more cold cases.

Tony asked in a letter if Shawcross would write to him about Logan, Dicker, and Oppel. His request got an immediate reply.

> *Dear Anthony,*
> *. . . Now Anthony you really surprise me. Why would I admit to unsolved murders or any bodies that were never found? That would not be cool would it, man? Shame on you! Smile. Good try though . . .*

Tony refused to give up. The next time Shawcross telephoned, Tony again mentioned the unsolved murders. If Shawcross wanted to leave behind a factual historical record of his life, he needed to be honest about every killing, including details about the two children whom he'd slaughtered—Jack Blake and Karen Hill.

On the phone, Shawcross bristled at the mere mention of Blake and Hill.

"I told you Tony, don't go there!" he said angrily. "I'm not going to talk about them."

A few days later, Tony got a letter from Shawcross that contained a drawing. The killer had outlined his hands on a sheet of white paper. Scrawled under the crude drawing were the words "With These Hands I Did Kill!—signed Arthur Shawcross." Shawcross said his drawing would make a great book cover for the autobiography that he was writing with

Tony's help. He also noted that he'd decided to tell Tony about "some other women who, let's say for now, that I got to know."

In closing, Shawcross wrote:

> *You are right that I need to come clean about the murders. All of them. But I will not discuss the kids. And it might take me a while to do this. I am very sick in the stomach. Pains are very hard to take. If I cough, it hurts bad! Sneezing is worse! The doctor is going to send me back out for a look-see with a CAT scan . . . I have no ambition to do anything but rest right now. Sleep, sleep and more sleep. That's all I do. Then I get someone to wake me to get medication and a shot . . . Anthony, I am so sick now, I am no longer able to eat even a hamburger. Man that is tough. But the burger has fat in it and it made the stomach pain hurt worse . . . You are a good friend. Please know I am working on what you asked from me. You will not be disappointed. . . .*

As always, Shawcross signed the letter, "your best friend."

Tony was eager for his next contact with Shawcross. But the serial killer missed their next scheduled telephone call. Tony began to wonder if something was wrong. Finally, a letter from the prison arrived, but the return address showed it was from another inmate—not Arthur Shawcross.

> *Dear Anthony,*
>
> *. . . You are probably saying to yourself, "Do I know you?" The answer is "No!" But I will explain why. I got your name and address from Arthur Shawcross. He had just gotten an operation and he couldn't sit up for too long to type his friends' letters so he asked me to do it for him.*
>
> *Artie got an operation the first week of November and he came back to the housing unit November 6th and on the 8th, he called me to his cell and told me his legs were hurting him bad. I informed an officer and they put Artie back in the hospital here inside the prison. They told me he would be back on Monday, November 10, but Monday came and they told me he was sent to an outside hospital. That night at 10:36 p.m., I was informed that Artie had passed away. I was in shock. I couldn't believe it, but*

it was true. I'm so sorry that you would have found out this way.
Out of respect to my friend, I felt I should contact you.

Artie was a very good friend to me and I will miss him very
much everyday and if I may say so Artie had many people write
him but he only told me there were six people who he wanted me
to tell if something happened to him. The others are family—so
that tells me something about you . . . He called you his best
friend.
Sincerely,
Henry Vega

Tony telephoned Shawcross's daughter, Margaret, and she confirmed
that her father had died from an apparent heart attack.

If Shawcross had been ready to confess to additional murders, he'd
taken that information with him to his grave.

That night Tony, Al, Chris, and Joey gathered around their dining
room table to talk about Shawcross. "I prefer to think of him as the voice
on the phone who offered me recipes and sent four-leaf clovers," said
Chris. "Not the monster who murdered those girls."

"But he was both of those things," Tony said.

Tony had brought one of Shawcross's letters to the table to read. He
explained that he'd asked the serial killer once if he thought he was
going to heaven or hell when he died. His reply, he thought, was typical
Arthur Shawcross.

Dear Anthony,
. . . I really get a kick out of people when they tell me that I am
going to hell. I tell them that I know that is where I am going. And
you know what? When you die and go there, who do you think is
going to be waiting for you to torture your ass for eternity? I will
and I will be enjoying the hell out of it . . .

Of all the investigators who had helped catch Arthur Shawcross, the
officer most responsible was Rochester Police Detective Leonard Borriello. Tony decided to send a copy of Shawcross's confessions to him. He
contacted the police department but was told the detective had retired.
Tony tracked him down and sent the confessions.

Even though it had been decades since Borriello had faced Shawcross in a police interrogation room, the detective could still remember every word that was exchanged the night Shawcross had finally confessed. It was one of those once-in-a-lifetime moments that a lawman never forgets.

Borriello and New York State Police Investigator Dennis Blythe had been chosen to bring Shawcross in for questioning. It had been tricky because the police didn't want to spook him into asking for an attorney, which was his constitutional right.

Shawcross had just finished visiting a female friend at her apartment and was about to ride his bicycle back to the apartment where he lived with Rose when Borriello and Blythe approached him. He agreed to go to the police station voluntarily to answer questions after they promised him that other officers would get his bicycle safely back to his apartment.

Borriello had developed a confidential informant who had led the police to Shawcross. Even so, the evidence against him was circumstantial. The informant was later identified as Jo Ann Van Nostrand, an older Rochester prostitute. She'd called Borriello after she'd had a strange date with a "john" who'd identified himself to her as "Mitch."

"Mitch" had driven her in his car to a spot near the Genesee River where the bodies of several murdered prostitutes had been dumped. He'd appeared nervous and, at one point, he'd asked her to play dead because it made him feel more sexually excited. Van Nostrand had quietly removed a razor-sharp hunting knife from her purse and had been secretly holding it next to her leg while the two of them were having intercourse in his car. When he reached his hands up and placed them on her throat, she'd told him about the knife and threatened to stab him. "Mitch" immediately released his grip and then had tried to make a joke of his touching her there.

Van Nostrand had given Borriello a good description of "Mitch"— enough to positively identify him as Shawcross. The detective felt certain that Shawcross was the Genesee River Killer. He also believed that Shawcross had planned to murder Van Nostrand that night. If she hadn't been armed with her hunting knife, she would have been his next victim.

Inside the police interrogation room, Borriello and his partner used the details that Van Nostrand had told them about "Mitch" to bluff Shawcross. They convinced him they had enough evidence to link him to several murders. But he didn't crack until they mentioned that Rose and his girlfriend, Clara Neal, also could be arrested and indicted. At that point, he'd confessed.

Borriello eagerly read the typed account that he'd been mailed. Shawcross's new confession contained many more details than he'd shared with the Rochester police decades earlier. For the most part, the old and new confessions were similar—with one glaring exception.

"Shawcross was trying to make himself out as a lady's man, a real cocksman in his confession to this young man," Borriello said later. "And Arthur Shawcross was just the opposite. We knew this because he'd been on a date with Jo Ann Van Nostrand and she'd told us Shawcross had a difficult time getting an erection and maintaining an erection, and we knew from other girls that he would become violent if girls taunted him sexually."

Borriello believed the rapes that Shawcross had described in such graphic detail to Tony—especially his claims that some of his murder victims actually had enjoyed being sexually attacked and had begged him for more—were fantasies.

The detective also was disgusted by what he saw as the killer's empty rationalizations. "After all of these years, you would think he would finally take responsibility for what he did. But he tried to act in these confessions—just as he did when he was talking to us. It was if he had no choice but to murder these women—because they had threatened to accuse him of rape or blackmail him," Borriello said in an interview. "We know some of the murders were clearly premeditated. My partner and I went to talk to Darlene Trippi because we'd been told by an informant that she might be able to give us information. She didn't know the killer's name but we thought she'd seen him get into a car with a girl who later was killed. It just so happened that Darlene was not at home when we knocked on her door, but we talked to another tenant who lived near her and she told us that 'the meat man' had come around looking for Darlene, too. Only later did we learn that 'the meat man' was Arthur Shawcross because he liked to go hunting and when he killed a deer he would bring meat to different girls. Darlene Trippi was killed not long after we tried to interview her and there is no doubt in my mind that Shawcross was covering his tracks. Somehow, he'd found out we were looking for Trippi to interview her, so he'd gone and killed her."

Borriello had always believed that Shawcross had strangled more women than the eleven whom he'd admitted. The detective estimated there were as many as five or six more, including Kimberly Logan.

"We tried to get him to admit he killed Logan because we were sure he had. But he just didn't want to admit it. It was like pulling teeth to get him to admit that he'd strangled Felicia Stephens, who was also black. He didn't want to admit that he'd had sex with a black girl and the truth is that I don't think he did have sex with Felicia because I don't think he could get it up. I think she made fun of him and that's why he killed her. We know that he didn't kill every girl he paid for sex. There were other prostitutes who went out with him and were patient with him and didn't ridicule him and he let them live—so it has always been my contention that Arthur Shawcross felt inadequate sexually and that is what set him off and why he murdered these women. He had no conscience, he was insecure, and he had trouble performing sexually."

Shawcross had told Tony that only two people would ever really know what had happened when he picked up his victims and murdered them. He'd sworn to Tony that the typed confession that he'd written was the "real and true" story.

"Do I believe those girls were murdered exactly like Art wrote in his confession?" Tony asked his father rhetorically one afternoon when they were discussing Borriello's theory. "Probably not. But I've thought a lot about this and I think Art convinced himself that what he wrote to me was the truth. He believed it—because that's what a serial killer does. He creates his own reality. He changes the past to fit what he wants to believe. He convinces himself it really happened. The confession he sent me was Arthur Shawcross's 'truth.' Art was telling me what he honestly believed just before he died because in his head, the mind of a serial killer, it was the true story. These were not fantasies to him because he lived in a fantasy of his own making."

31

The tipping point in Tony's relationship with Arthur Shawcross came when they met each other face-to-face. It was during that visit when Tony asked Shawcross to write about the murders and the serial killer had agreed to type out his version of what had happened. It was when Tony, Al, and Joey had watched him fall into an eerie trance as he described how he'd cannibalized June Cicero.

Tony wrote to Joe Metheny and David Gore and asked both men to put him on their prison visiting lists. He wanted to meet them. Gore said yes, but Metheny balked.

Dear Tony,
    . . . Please don't waste your time for I don't want to see anyone. Nor do I want to make any phone calls. It's nothing personal against you or anyone else. I just want to be a friend in a letter. . . . I hope you can live with that.

In his reply, Tony was blunt. He explained that one reason why he wanted to visit was that he'd decided to investigate cold cases. He asked Metheny if he had committed any murders that had never been solved. The killer already had written to him about a twelve-year-old red-haired girl whom he'd followed home from school, caught in the woods, raped, and murdered somewhere in Baltimore in the 1970s. Metheny also had written about a prostitute whom he'd met at a truck stop and strangled. He'd later buried her body in an industrial park in Sparks, Nevada, where he'd gone to pick up a load of salad dressing for delivery.

While Metheny had been reluctant to meet Tony face-to-face, the convicted killer did respond with a graphic account of a cold case.

Dear Anthony,
    . . . I was driving my truck east on Interstate 70 on my way to Baltimore and was a little bit hungry and tired, so I pulled into

the 86 Truck Stop in Frederick, Maryland. I was planning on grabbing a fast bite and nap . . . I went into the diner and found a table and picked up a menu. I heard a voice say to me "Can I help you." . . . there was the cutest little waitress standing there. I ordered a couple eggs, bacon and some home fries along with a cup of coffee . . . I pulled out my log book to work on and then out of nowhere, I heard this little voice say: "Mister, please help me. I'm lost and I can't find my mommy." I looked up and there across from me was this little girl about 6 or 7 years old. I asked her if she was hungry and she said, "Yes, I am." Then here comes the waitress with my food. The waitress says to me: "Don't worry; her mother will be back in here shortly." I told the waitress to bring the little girl what she wanted to eat. Well, the waitress left and come back with some pancakes, syrup, along with some strawberries and glass of milk. The waitress asked me to step over to the counter for a little talk. I got up and she told me the girl's mother is turning tricks out in the parking lot. She says her mother comes here just about every weekend and does this. "I know her mother very well," she says. "She's had a very rough time since her husband was killed in a car accident. She doesn't live far from here and this is how she makes her money to support her and her daughter. Please don't go and be too hard on her. She's just trying to get by the best way she knows how." I went back over and sat down and started eating my food. I looked over at the little girl. She was eating her pancakes and she gave me a big old smile and said, "Thank you mister. You're a very nice man." A few minutes went by then her mother came walking in from the parking lot. She sat down next to her daughter then looked at me and said, "Hello, my name is Kelly and this little girl is my daughter, Robin. I saw you when you pulled your truck across the street." Then this woman told me this was not the first time we met. "I guess you just don't remember me or maybe it's just because you never saw my face . . . I was giving you a blow job in your truck." Then it hit me like a ton of bricks . . .

I ended up spending the whole weekend with her and her daughter. It was money well spent.

Little Robin was a sweet little virgin at first when I met her. But she sure wasn't when I got done with her. She was a bloody mess and so was her dear sweet mother, who was a hysterical, screaming, blabbering idiot by the time I got around to taking the life out of her. For you see, I tied her up and made her watch as I raped and killed her dear sweet little daughter.

. . . Besides Robin and her mother, there is a damn good possibility there could be more out there—that I may have killed when I was drunk and high on drugs. I know those five that I killed are still out there because I was stone cold sober when I raped and drained the life out of them. That's why I remember them so well. . . .

Metheny had mentioned *five unsolved murders* in his letter. The red-haired girl was Metheny's first kill, followed by the hooker in Nevada, and he'd just written about killing Robin and her mother, Kelly. *Who was the fifth?*

Tony hurried off a letter. He asked Metheny if the murderer was putting himself into danger by disclosing cold cases.

Dear Anthony,

. . . I have had this shit bottled up inside of me for such a long time that I wanted to tell you. I am not really looking forward to going through all that court and TV media news shit again. But in my sick, twisted way of looking at it, there is some good that could come out of it for you and for me . . . The fifth victim is a little 12-year old girl named Thelma who I killed and buried up in Deep Creek Lake State Park in 1977 . . .

Metheny added that during his last trial he had specifically asked for a death sentence. He wasn't afraid of being executed, he wrote. In fact, it would be better than living in a "cage" for the rest of his life.

Tony was pumped up. The serial killer had always been candid with him, so Tony asked if Metheny would tell him where he'd buried the bodies of his five victims. In his reply, Metheny wrote that he would disclose information to Tony about three cold cases but only in general terms.

Dear Anthony,

I will not tell you the actual spot where to dig, but I am willing to put you within at least 50 feet of them . . . The little red-haired girl has been lying in the same spot where I buried her at since Sept. 19, 1970 . . . The mother and daughter are both buried in the same hole. I put the little girl, Robin, in her mother's arms when I buried them. Her mother's name was Kelly. They was both naked and freshly fucked when I throwed the dirt in on them. . . . I don't know if this information will help you. But it sure did help me by getting that secret out that I have been carrying around for a long fucking time . . .

Tony thanked Metheny and asked him to send him the full names of his victims and also reconsider and tell him the exact location where they were buried. If Metheny told him, Tony would find the bodies, notify the victims' families, and inform the police. While he waited for Metheny to answer, Tony turned to the Internet for clues. He searched newspaper archives for stories about missing persons. Surely the parents of the red-haired girl had filed some sort of police report; surely a Baltimore newspaper had published a news item about the hunt. He tried to imagine what she looked like. He thought about what he would say to her parents once he helped the police find her grave. Would they be angry or thank him? Helping them solve this mystery was going to be one of the best and proudest moments in his life. He would be helping them.

Al was as just as excited as his son, but he also felt a bit of hesitation. Metheny had described the murders in such detail that Al believed the killer was telling the truth. But he reminded Tony that serial killers were notorious liars. How could they be sure that Metheny wasn't simply making up his stories?

As was his style, Tony bluntly asked. Metheny's next letter arrived with his trademark drawing of a cue-ball-shaped baby decorating the envelope. This time the character was holding a woman's severed head in his hands.

Dear Anthony,
. . . I have always considered you a very smart and well-educated man so I feel you should have no problem detecting when someone is blowing smoke up your ass . . . I am sure there are many who feel my stories are somewhat bogus. And I often wonder to myself why someone would keep writing back to me if they doubt the authenticity of my writings . . . For all those who

question what I write, Fuck 'em. I don't lose no sleep over what another motherfucker may think about me.

But as for you, my man, I do care about what you think. You are the closest person I have that I would consider a friend. We have sent a lot of fucking letters back and forth to each other in the past four years. We have written some funny shit, serious shit and on occasion even some deep shit. What I wrote is damn near a full confession to you. . . . The name of the little red haired girl was Pam Hilton. The name of the mother and daughter was Kelly and Robin Shifflet out of Keyser, West Virginia . . . That's enough for now. Now I am very curious what you will do with the information you find. I guess that will tell me what kind of friend you are . . .

Tony was frustrated that Metheny had not pinpointed the grave sites. He also was confused. What had Metheny meant when he wrote "what kind of friend you are"? Did he expect Tony to keep quiet about the unsolved murders—to share his secret with the killer but keep quiet about it?

He talked to his parents and they agreed that Tony's allegiance had to be to family members of Metheny's victims, no matter what. Metheny had written in earlier letters that he expected Tony to go public if he found the bones of Metheny's victims. The convict had boldly declared that he didn't care. He wasn't afraid of being put on trial and getting a death sentence.

Armed with full names, Tony kept digging. He searched public records for Pam Hilton, and Kelly and Robin Shifflet. He searched newspaper files. But he came up empty-handed.

Karen Shoemaker, the chief of police in Keyser, West Virginia, said she'd never heard of anyone missing named Shifflet. Tony obtained a copy of the court reporter's transcript from Metheny's trials. He couldn't find any mention anywhere about the three missing victims. But he also couldn't find anything that showed Metheny was lying.

Tony told Metheny that there was no proof the three women existed. Metheny replied quickly.

Dear Anthony,
. . . I am sure if you thought my stories from the past were bullshit—stuff I was making up in my mind—you would have stopped writing to me and kicked me to the curb a long time ago.

*What I've told you is true. I may have not been totally honest
with names. I know the little red haired girl was named Pam, but
I never knew her last name. As for Kelly and Robin, what hooker
tells you their real names? But my friend, they are as real as you
and me and because of me, they also are dead, freshly fucked and
forgotten.*

Tony asked Metheny once again if they could meet face-to-face.
Metheny claimed that Tony was his best friend. Why wouldn't he want
to talk with his best friend? Tony asked.

This time, the murderer agreed.

Hey Anthony,
        *. . . I told my case counselor to put you and your dad on my
visiting lists so it now looks like this visit is truly going to happen.
All that is left is you all jumping into the family owned corporate
Lear jet, popping the champagne in celebration of getting to fly
across the country to see a big fat 500 pound motherfucker, who
you have been calling your friend for the past four years. Ha Ha.
I do appreciate you coming all this way to see me . . . I have not
had a visit from anyone, except the cops, in the whole 15 years
I have been locked up. So you will please have to forgive me if I
don't truly know how to act when we first meet. Ha! Ha! I will be
on my best behavior and wearing a clean pair of underwear for
this fine occasion.*

32

The grounds at the New York state prison where Tony and Al had visited Arthur Shawcross looked like a college-campus; by contrast, the North Branch Correctional Institution near Cumberland, Maryland, made no effort to conceal what it was. Built on a clearing in the Appalachian Mountains, the high-tech maximum security prison held Maryland's most dangerous inmates in multiple low-rise housing units encircled by double rows of tall chain-link fencing topped with razor wire.

After passing through metal detectors and being stripped of all cell phones and money, Tony and Al waited forty minutes in a Spartanly furnished holding room for correctional officers to clear them. While there, they watched a curvaceous young woman being sent to her car three times to change her outfit because the officers on duty didn't think she was dressed modestly enough to enter the inmate visiting room. Tony and Al were surprised because nothing the woman was wearing would have caused an eyebrow to be raised in a restaurant or shopping mall.

"They're really tough here," Tony whispered to his father.

Although neither of them had ever met Metheny, both recognized him instantly. How could they not? He was one of the largest human beings that either of them had seen: grossly overweight and standing six feet, one inch tall. Metheny's arms were as thick as Tony's thighs.

Prisoners were seated on one side of a table with visitors positioned directly across from them. An eighteen-inch-tall divider in the center of the tables kept visitors and inmates from slipping items across to each other. Metheny reached across the divide to hug Tony and Al when they found their seats, but a correctional officer monitoring the room ordered him to sit back down on a tiny round stool bolted to the floor.

Metheny's scalp was freshly shaven and decorated with an ornate prison tattoo. An upside-down black cross was inked into his forehead between his eyebrows—the mark of Satan. Three black teardrops and two white ones were tattooed on his right cheek under his bright blue eyes.

"Do you know what these mean?" the serial killer mumbled in a low voice, pointing to the teardrop tats with a finger.

"Yes," Tony answered. "Murders, right?"

Metheny nodded approvingly.

"Are we really the first visitors you've had since you've been locked up?" Al asked him.

Metheny spoke in a well-practiced whisper, a prison precaution to ensure that those around him couldn't eavesdrop. "Like I told you in my letters, no one's come to see me in sixteen years and why you two good-looking guys traveled all the way here from Las Vegas to see a five-hundred-pound motherfucker like me is beyond me. If you want to get up and leave right now, I'll understand."

"You and my son have been writing for four years," Al said. "When we have an opportunity to go and visit someone and see them face-to-face, we want to take it."

"You don't look like what I expected," Metheny said.

"Why's that, Joe?" Al asked.

"You got a broken nose."

"It's been broken several times," Al said laughing. "I grew up in a pretty tough section of Chicago. There were lots of fights."

"I didn't think you was born with a silver spoon in your ass."

Metheny smiled, revealing a mouth with less than a handful of teeth, and then complained that the visiting room stool that he was precariously perched on was extremely uncomfortable because of his massive girth. "I don't know how long I can stand this. This might be a short visit."

"C'mon, Joe," Al said. "We came all the way from Las Vegas." Al offered to ask the correctional officer for a chair for Metheny, given his size. But the prisoner shook his head no.

Al asked why Metheny's family hadn't come to visit him. They'd disowned him, he said, after he admitted that he had served human flesh to people who'd bought barbecue sandwiches from him.

Tony said, "A Baltimore police officer says you never did that."

"Fuck 'em," Metheny said. "I know what I did and so do the good people who ate my sandwiches."

Tony asked: "When was the first time you did it? Ate someone?"

"She was a crack whore."

"Will you tell us about it?"

"That's why you came all this way, isn't it?" he asked rhetorically.

During the next several minutes, Metheny spun out his story. Shortly after his wife had left him, taking their son with her, he became filled with hate. His wife had been addicted to crack, he claimed, and he blamed her for destroying their family. While drinking at the Borderline Bar one night, he'd heard a rumor that his ex-wife had been spotted under a nearby bridge that spanned the Patapsco River. Prostitutes often turned tricks or shot up drugs there. He went to the bridge looking for her. She wasn't there, but two homeless men were and Metheny began drinking with them.

"They were the poor souls who fell asleep around me that I killed with an ax. I chopped them up and threw the pieces in the river," Metheny said. "The cops arrested me and it went to trial, but I was found not guilty because they could not prove it was me. The state got me the best lawyer you can get. I lied my way through it."

After he got out of jail, Metheny returned to his old job at the pallet company and bar seat at the Borderline. One night, he persuaded a prostitute to go with him to the same bridge where he'd killed the two homeless men. He offered her crack cocaine. During a whiskey-and-cocaine-fueled frenzy, he'd murdered her.

Returning to the bar, he'd coaxed another hooker under the bridge. He killed her, too. "It was blind revenge," Metheny said. "I was pissed at my ex-wife and all those other crackheads who were turning tricks."

Metheny was standing under the bridge looking at the women's dead bodies, trying to collect his thoughts, when he decided to have sex with them. He undressed the corpses and was "fucking their dead asses" when a man came down the embankment to fish and saw him. Metheny grabbed a pipe and killed him, too, bringing the body count to three.

Metheny took more crack cocaine to foster his courage and built a fire because he was cold and unsure what to do next. He decided he'd chop up the bodies and toss the pieces into the river to get rid of the evidence. That's what he'd done before to the two homeless men. As he was butchering one of the women, he suddenly realized that he was hungry and thought, "Why not?"

He cut some flesh from one of the hooker's thighs, stuck it on a branch, and roasted it over the fire he had going there.

"It tasted like pork," he volunteered.

Metheny had not gone into any sort of hypnotic trance when he told them his story. Rather, there was no emotion. It was as if he were read-ing a sports story in the morning newspaper.

"Did you like the taste?" Tony asked.

"Why else would I put it in my sandwiches?"

"You really did that, right? You put flesh in those BBQ sandwiches?"

It was the second time Tony had questioned Metheny about the sandwiches and Al thought the killer might get irked. Instead the convict said, "One of my best customers was pissed when he found out. He used to come by just to get my sandwiches on Sundays and he used to tell me how they were the best in the city. He worked at the courthouse and when I was on trial, I saw him and just smiled. Ask him if I did it."

The visiting hours were over, but Tony still had lots of questions. Metheny reluctantly agreed to meet them again the next morning.

When they arrived the following day, Metheny was in a foul mood and warned them that he was too sore from sitting on the visiting stool to spend much time with them. Because of his weight, he'd developed diabetes. He said prison doctors had told him that it was likely he would have both of his legs amputated within a year.

"I'm sorry, Joe," Tony said sympathetically. Metheny shrugged indif-ferently.

Then he got right to the point. If Tony wanted to find the "dead bitches," he was going to have to pay. Metheny wanted $1,500 and, in return, he would give them the exact location of two bodies.

"We don't have that kind of money," Al said. "C'mon, Joe. We can't pay you."

"You bought two plane tickets here," he replied.

"Joe, I couldn't find anything—any records—about that red-haired girl or the mother and daughter," Tony said.

Without missing a beat, Metheny said: "Look, I'm the one who's going to end up with a death sentence here when you find those bod-ies. So stop busting my ass about if they are real or not. When I tell you where to look and you begin poking around, you're going to find what you're looking for. But what's in it for me?"

"We can't pay you, Joe," Al repeated.

"How about five hundred dollars for the mother and two hundred and fifty for the daughter. Shit, the little girl was just a kid and wasn't even full-grown yet—so she really wasn't worth that much. But then again that was about twenty years ago. If you dig her up and she looks any bigger than the three foot, eight inches I remember from back then, go ahead and send the full price."

Once again, Al said they weren't going to pay him.

"How about buying me a television?" Metheny asked.

He began to complain about how he needed a new video game system to play in his cell. If they weren't even willing to buy him a few new video games, then they were wasting his time.

Metheny announced that he was done. Sitting on the stool was too painful for him to continue.

Al could tell Tony was disappointed. He'd genuinely thought Metheny was going to tell them where they could find his victims. Metheny glanced at Tony and saw how disappointed he was.

The killer asked if Tony planned to keep writing to him. Tony said, "Sure." That seemed to pacify Metheny. "Think about the money," the convict told Al. "It's a bargain."

Then he addressed Tony once again. "I'm going to give you some advice, Tony. For free. It will make your trip to see me worthwhile. It's something you can use. When you get home, find a mortician in Las Vegas who will let you come in late at night. Slip him twenty bucks and he'll open the drawers for you."

Tony looked intently at Metheny to see if he was joking. But the convict wasn't smiling.

"A dead woman is the best fuck you'll ever have," he continued. "Or you can go to a cemetery and dig one up. That way, you will never go hungry, either, and you'll have plenty of women to fuck."

With that, he left.

33

The Sunday afternoon drive from the prison to Baltimore took Tony and Al east along Interstate 70 from tree-lined mountains through rolling valleys dotted with quilt-like apple orchards into a barrio of boarded-up buildings, homeless men sipping from paper bags, trash-littered sidewalks, and malnourished hookers desperate for another fix. If there was a hell in Baltimore, Tony and Al felt they'd arrived in it.

Their first stop was the Joe Stein & Son Pallet Company, at 3200 James Street, where Metheny had committed at least two of his murders and reportedly sold tainted BBQ sandwiches on Sundays to his unsuspecting friends and passersby. As they drove up a slight hill at the rear of the company, they noticed that the company's delivery gate was open and two men and a woman were standing inside the compound washing the hull of a motorboat on a trailer.

Al parked their rental car and Tony marched through the gate and called out a friendly "Hello! Can we talk to you?"

The boat's owner, a man in his forties, told them that he was in charge of the pallet company's daily operations. The woman was his former girlfriend. They'd just returned from spending the morning in the Chesapeake Bay fishing on the boat that they were now spraying clean. The other man was an employee at the pallet company who'd taken over Metheny's old job of helping unload trucks and working as a night watchman. He stuck out his hand and said his name was Jake Brown and he was happy to meet them. All three said they'd known Metheny.

"Me and my wife lived next door to Joe and his wife and kid for sixteen years," Brown declared. "That was before his wife took off and Joe went plum crazy. I used to go to his house to watch *Wrestlemania* and drink and party and I'd pass out right next to the guy and wake up and think nothing of it the next day."

The trio offered to show them the night watchman's trailer where Metheny had lived and the rear of the compound where he'd strung up one of the women whom he'd murdered. The trailer was tiny and dirty inside. They guided Tony and Al through a maze of wooden pallets toward the far northern corner of the property, where there was a tree-covered hill.

"That tree right there is where he hanged that girl from," Brown volunteered. "That's where he bled her to death and cut her up."

"Do any of you know about his BBQ stand?" Tony asked.

The woman said, "Everyone knows and I'm sure as hell glad I never ate there."

Metheny had started selling BBQ sandwiches only a few weeks before he was arrested, she said. On Sunday mornings, he'd put a wooden sign that he'd made out near the main road that ran by the pallet company, advertising BBQ for sale. He'd buy paper utensils and accoutrements, and use an outside grill on the pallet company grounds to cook the meat. The sandwiches were $3.25 each.

"Did people know what he was putting in the sandwiches?" Tony asked.

"He was cutting up those girls and putting 'em into those sandwiches," said Brown. "That's one sick motherfucker."

"Plenty of people were angry about it when they heard," the woman said.

The threesome showed Tony where Metheny's BBQ stand had been located. Brown then led them to a large wooden box where the company stored rock salt for use during the winter when the parking lot became icy.

"They found one of the girls—or at least pieces of her—in that box," Brown said. "Joe was salting her, like curing meat!"

The couple finished cleaning the boat and left, but Brown was eager to talk. He offered to take Tony and Al to the bridge where Metheny reportedly had killed three people. He got into their rental car and began to give directions, but first told them to stop at the Borderline Bar so he could buy a fifth of Southern Comfort whiskey. When he returned with the bottle, he proceeded to sip the whiskey as he directed their "tour."

"Joe was plum crazy," Brown said. "One day we was sitting on the loading dock together at work and he catches this mouse and bites the head plum off it and spits it out right in front of me and the other boys. He just bit the head off and laughed."

The bridge where the murders happened was about a mile away. Even though it had been years since Metheny had been there, its underbelly had not seemed to have changed much from how he'd described it in his letters to Tony. A discarded mattress under the bridge was edged by piles of broken whiskey and beer bottles. Someone had grouped rocks together in a ring to contain a campfire.

"This is where he chopped up them bodies," Brown said. "Everyone in the Borderline knows about it."

From there, Brown gave them directions to a row house in another seedy area of Baltimore where Metheny had once lived with his wife and son. En route Brown said, "He was an alcoholic but he didn't use drugs much back then. We spent a lot of time talking and partying and like I said, until his wife left him, he was a good guy who used to be real friendly and outgoing and stuff but then he got real angry and mean and quiet. One night him and me was in this bar and he got into a fight with this dude and they went outside and when Tiny, which is what we used to call him, came back inside later, I said, 'What'd you do to that fella?' And Tiny said, 'I chopped off his head.' And I laughed 'cause I thought he was joking but I never saw that man again after that night so I think Tiny really did it. Down at the Borderline, we got to talking after he was arrested and we realized there was girls who'd gone missing too and no one had paid them no never mind because they was crack whores and we figured they'd just moved on. But Tiny really hated crack whores because of what his wife done to him and now, who knows where them girls is or what happened to them?"

Al asked Brown about the BBQ sandwiches. When exactly had he heard that Metheny was selling tainted meat?

"Word spread through the bar pretty fast after Tiny was caught. I don't know who first got it going, but I know'd it sure as hell is a fact."

"How do you know that?" Al asked.

"Well, I know he did it, 'cause the man himself told me he did it only I didn't believe him at the time. We was sitting in the bar, this was before he was arrested, drinking and such, and he says to me, 'Hey, you ever taste human flesh?' and I figured he was just drunk. And I says, 'Hell no!' But he says, 'Well, I have' and I said, 'You're fucking halluci- nating' and he didn't say no more about that but he starts telling me all this sick shit about how the best way to have sexual intercourse is with someone's who's dead because they can't say no and I'm thinking, 'This sick motherfucker's been fucking dead women' and then I thought, 'Did he just tell me he'd been eating them, too?' And I thought, 'Naw, it's just the liquor talking. Who does something like that?' And then he says, real smart like, 'You know if you mix it with chicken or pork, it ain't that bad.' I thought, 'Oh man, I hope this is bullshit.' After them dead girls were found all chopped up and everyone started talking about how he'd served up them girls' flesh in them sandwiches—I was just damn glad I never ate none of them sandwiches."

Brown asked to be dropped off at the Borderline Bar.

"When you next write to Tiny, you tell him I said hello," Brown said, as he stepped from the rental car. "And tell him that there are a lot of people here who hope he goes to hell because of that little trick with them sandwiches."

It was starting to rain as Al drove toward the airport. He flipped on the rental car's wipers and noticed that Tony had his eyes shut.

"Tired?" Al asked.

"No," Tony said. "Praying." He made the sign of the cross on his chest. Al was used to Tony praying. Whenever they were out driving and Tony spotted a church, he would say a prayer. It was something he'd done ever since the WaveRunner accident.

"Who you praying for?" Al asked.

"I was praying for that little red-headed girl and Kelly and Robin or whatever their real names are," Tony said.

They rode in silence for several minutes as the windshield wipers slapped away the rain. Tony closed his eyes again and then crossed himself.

Al glanced around but didn't see a church.

"That was for Joe," Tony said. "I was praying for him."

A few seconds later, Tony said, "He really is a monster, isn't he?"

"Yeah," Al said, "he is."

After they returned home, a letter with Metheny's trademark cue-ball character drawn on the envelope arrived.

Dear Anthony,

. . . I got a visit from my homicide friends yesterday. They even brought someone who I had not seen in a long time. It was Detective Homer Pennington from out of the Baltimore City homicide unit. He is now retired. But he came with the other Baltimore detectives. They'd heard about the letters I was writing to you. The prison reads our mail. I guess they thought he could

get me to open up a little more than they could. They brought me two fish fillet sandwiches and a large bottle of Pepsi. I sure as hell did greatly enjoy eating that stuff in front of them. It tasted very good. I have not had any real street food in years. I did appreciate the food very much. And I told them so.

But I also told them I didn't appreciate it enough to kick out none of my dead bitches. They wasn't too happy about hearing that from me but what the fuck do I care. For I know damn well they will be back here again visiting. It kills my ass to think that no one gave a shit about those girls when they were alive—when they really did need someone to help them straighten out their lives so they wouldn't run into a motherfucker like me. But now these fucking cops are up here busting my balls trying to pretend they care about finding these dead stinking bitches. They're all just trying to make themselves look good down there at the police headquarters. Fuck 'em all. I was really the only one who helped those girls get off the drugs and other problems they had. They looked very peaceful to me as I was throwing that dirt on their dead stinking asses . . .

A letter from the Baltimore Police Department arrived a few days later. When Tony opened the envelope, he found a copy of a letter that Baltimore Homicide Detective Gary Niedermeier had written to Metheny.

Mr. Metheny,
*   I was the detective with Homer Pennington when we came to talk to you . . . I just wanted to let you know that we followed up on the information you provided and found it all to be less than credible. No persons in Maryland or West Virginia have ever been reported missing based on your information.*
*   Both Homer and myself felt that you are making these stories up . . . A true serial killer does not regress in their crimes. If as you claim these victims exist, you would love the opportunity to claim additional victims to validate your claims. Instead you refuse to assist in any investigation which may prove you to be a liar . . .*

The detective noted at the end of his letter that he was mailing a copy to Tony.

• • •

"Is Joe lying to us about those cold cases or is he just toying with us and the cops?" Tony asked his dad.

Al reminded Tony that a Baltimore police detective had told a newspaper reporter that Metheny had never served anyone sandwiches tainted with human flesh. But when Tony and Al had spent the day in Baltimore at Metheny's old haunts, Jake Brown had told them that Metheny had admitted being a cannibal before he was arrested. Body parts of his victims also had been missing when their corpses were recovered by the police. That was convincing evidence.

Neither Tony nor Al had any way of knowing what, if anything, Metheny had told the police and how it might differ from what he was telling them in his letters.

"I believe he did serve flesh in those sandwiches," Al said. "And he was so exact when he described those cold-case murders—especially that little red-haired girl—the moonlight—all that stuff—that I think he was telling the truth there, too. He just isn't going to tell us or the cops where they're buried unless he gets something out of it. Especially if he's going to end up getting a death sentence for it."

Al felt Metheny was manipulating the police and them as well. It was one of the most common traits of a serial killer. Tell a story. Maybe it is true. Maybe it isn't. But the cops and public pay attention anyway. They have to. It made a serial killer feel important and it helped him relive the thrill of his murders.

"I'm going to keep writing Joe," Tony said. "Maybe I get him to tell me more."

"I'm sure he'll write back because he is enjoying the hell out of all this attention," Al said.

Meanwhile, it was time for them to make another trip. They were heading to Florida to pay a visit to David Gore.

34

It was a sunny summer afternoon but Tony and Al seemed pensive as their rented Chevrolet Tahoe sped south on the Florida turnpike across the flat state with its seemingly endless gated retirement communities, golf courses lined by palm trees, and waterways posted with warnings about alligators. They had come to visit David Gore, and since Glen E. Rogers, aka the Cross-Country Killer, also was on Florida's death row, they'd arranged to see him, too.

Tony had exchanged more letters with Gore than with Rogers, but both had seemed eager to meet him. Before Rogers was arrested in 1995, he'd been on the FBI's Ten Most Wanted list and the subject of a manhunt televised on *America's Most Wanted*. Rogers fatally stabbed four women in four different states, including Florida. With boyish good looks and sweet talk, he would seduce women in bars and leave them naked and dead after having sex with them. The actual number of his victims was unknown. His sister told investigators that he'd once boasted about murdering fifty women while drifting from state to state working for traveling carnivals. He later told detectives that the real number was "more like seventy."

Both serial killers had beaten the odds on death row. It usually took twelve and a half years for a condemned man in Florida to exhaust his appeals and be executed either by lethal injection or, if he wished, by being strapped into the state's electric chair, aptly nicknamed "Old Sparky." Rogers had spent thirteen years fighting his conviction. Gore had successfully bottlenecked the process for nearly thirty years.

The irony of their claims of innocence was not lost on Tony. Both Gore and Rogers had admitted in letters to killings that had never been solved. Rogers had admitted one murder to Tony. Gore had described at least two cold-case murders, although he'd been cautiously vague with specifics. One was a Native American drifter whose remains had never been found.

Tony was especially eager to meet Gore because they had been corresponding for more than four years. He felt a special bond with the killer.

Everything appeared on track for their visit to the Florida State Prison in Raiford. Tony and Al had filled out the necessary bureaucratic forms and passed routine background checks required by the prison. But then, without warning, Gore and Rogers jerked the rug out from under them.

Tony and Al didn't know why. They would later learn that the two serial killers had panicked. Prison officials had been curious about why Tony and Al had requested visits with two condemned men. Most visitors were relatives or lawyers and they came to see only one prisoner. When asked, Tony and Al said they wanted to discuss cold-case murders. A prison official had let this slip to Gore and Rogers, and when the condemned men realized this was not simply a friendly social call, they'd refused to come out of their cells and go to the visiting room.

Tony had been dumbstruck. He'd asked both men about cold cases before and they'd never hesitated to brag about them. Until now.

Tony and Al were not going to let their canceled visit keep them from pursuing a tip that Gore had given in his letters. They had always planned to drive to Vero Beach after they'd visited him anyway. That was now where they were driving in the SUV. The coastal community was where Gore and his cousin had abducted, raped, tortured, and murdered their victims.

Tony and Al were not going to find a missing corpse. But they were on an equally macabre hunt.

In his letters, Gore had admitted to having a fetish for women's hair. He'd claimed to have scalped several victims. He'd also mentioned that he'd taken dozens of photographs of his kills. Some showed them naked in the midst of being tortured.

In a September 17, 2008, letter, Gore wrote:

Dear Tony,

. . . You know I read about these cell phones nowadays that can take photographs. I was thinking the other day how it's a good thing they weren't out when I was doing my thing. Can you imagine some of the pictures I could have taken? I took Polaroids of my victims, mostly close up of the pussy and tits.

But nowadays, man you could take a picture of anything,

anywhere. Yeah, I'd probably get into trouble real quick. [Smiley face.]

    I often wonder if anyone ever found my stash of photos.

That had been the first time Gore had mentioned a "stash" of pictures, and Tony had asked him for more details. Gore had obliged.

Dear Tony,

    You asked about the stash of pictures I had hid. I doubt very seriously they were ever dug up because where I buried them was in a spot that would not be disturbed. The pictures were in a black vinyl briefcase and that was put inside a double heavy-duty garbage bag. There was no way moisture could get in . . . There has to be over a 100 photos in there. I took photos of every single thing. . . .

In their next exchange, Tony asked Gore what he thought might happen if someone found the photographs.

Dear Tony,

    . . . You asked if you tried to find those items I told you about, would it cause me any problems? Absolutely not. I say go for it.

    But as I said before, it has been over 20 years so there is no telling what changes have taken place there. The area where I buried the stash may not be the same as it was then. I do know if there was any kind of construction there, they most likely would have uncovered it because it was not buried deep. Maybe, two feet. I will say this, if you were able to find it that would be quite a find!

    I'm not even sure how well the Poloroid pictures has held up. I had them in a zip lock bag and inside another so it should have kept them from fading. Zip lock baggies was what I used for everything—including the hair.

Tony pushed Gore for more information. The killer replied that he'd scalped his victims and also shaved their pubic hair.

In their next exchange, Gore sent Tony a roughly drawn map that would lead them to his long-buried items.

Unlike Joe Metheny, Gore hadn't demanded money in exchange for information. Gore had never asked for anything. Even more important, Gore had mentioned the photos and human scalps casually in his correspondence. He'd seemed curious, himself, about their fate.

"I think deep down he wants me to find them because they're his trophies," Tony said. "He took them from those women because he was proud of what he'd done, like a deer hunter keeping antlers."

Al agreed.

They'd planned to ask Gore, when they met him at the prison during a visit, for more specifics. While the crude map that he'd sent would get them in the general area, they needed Gore to pinpoint an exact spot to dig.

But Gore's last-minute change of heart had ruined their chance of getting more clues. They would have to use the map as it was to guide them.

At Exit SR 60 on the Florida turnpike, Al turned the SUV east, toward Yeehaw Junction, a town whose name lightened Tony's mood. By the time they reached the city limits of Vero Beach, it was almost 7 p.m.

"We've got about an hour of light left," Al noted. "Instead of checking into a hotel, let's scout out the area where Gore buried his stash."

"But we need a shovel," Tony said.

"We can get a shovel and dig tomorrow."

Al wasn't entirely certain how he wanted to proceed with this hunt. He could take the map directly to the Vero Beach police. But he'd decided not to do that. First, he wanted to do some preliminary investigating. He didn't want to waste detectives' time if Gore's map turned out to be a fake.

Al stopped the SUV on the side of the highway and studied Gore's instructions.

I was a field supervisor for a large citrus company. I oversaw about 1200 acres of citrus . . . About those souvenirs that we discussed. I think they should still be there. I buried them in one of our groves. It was 320 acres and located west of Vero Beach . . . Of course, you can't find them without a map . . . but if you follow the map I drew for you and my instructions, it will actually be pretty easy to find the spot. . . .

Gore had instructed Tony to head west from Vero Beach and turn south on a dirt road that led into an orange grove. Gore had drawn several landmarks to help guide them. One was a narrow bridge over an irrigation canal. He'd also included a description of a storage barn that was close to where he'd hidden his keepsakes.

"This is a perfect time to find that storage barn," Al said, "because the field workers have gone home for the night so we shouldn't run into anyone asking us what we're doing."

Al began following Gore's directions as Tony glanced through the passenger window at the acres of orange trees that edged both sides of the highway. Every few miles, a dirt road would break from the main one and disappear into the miles and miles of groves. Nearly all of these dirt trails had metal security gates across them, barring entry into the fields. The entrances also were marked with large "No Trespassing" signs. Written in smaller letters on the signs were the names of the fields' owners and telephone numbers. "Call for permission before entering this grove!" the placards warned. "Trespassers will be prosecuted."

"Won't we be trespassing if we go into a grove?" Tony asked.

"We'll say we took a wrong turn," Al replied. "As long as we're not stealing anything, I think we'll be okay."

Tony looked again at the warning signs.

"What if they catch us digging?" he asked.

"That's going to be harder to explain."

"Do you think his trophies are still there?"

Al wasn't sure. There could be plenty of reasons why they might not be able to find Gore's stash. They didn't know the exact spot to dig. Gore's souvenirs had been buried for nearly three decades in wet Florida soil. Despite the precautions that he'd described, moisture could have seeped in and ruined the pictures and washed away the hair. Gore himself had suggested that the grove might have been sold to new owners. There could be houses or other buildings now sitting over his hiding spot.

Of course, Gore also could be lying. This could be a wild-goose chase.

Al could tell his son was nervous about trespassing. The signs were tough to ignore. He'd thought about calling the telephone numbers listed on one of them and asking for permission to enter the grove. In a letter, Gore had told Tony the name of his former boss. Maybe he'd give them permission to search his property.

But Al decided against it. Would a landowner really want human scalps and lurid photographs of women being tortured to turn up on his property? Al had checked with an attorney before leaving Las Vegas and had been told that anything buried on someone's land belonged to the landowner. The owner could simply tell them to stay off his property and do nothing. Or he might call the police.

As they continued driving west, Al felt confident that what they were doing was the most prudent step. There was no need to tell anyone about the map until the two of them were convinced it was real.

Al kept an eye on the SUV's odometer, and when it clicked off the number of miles that Gore had written in his letter, he looked to his right and saw a dirt road that led into an orange grove—just as Gore had described. Like the others, the road was posted with a large no-trespassing sign and there was a metal gate.

But this gate was wide open.

"This is the first one I've seen unlocked," Tony said. Perhaps it was an omen.

They hesitated, aware that they were about to trespass. Al scanned the field and the highway. Except for a few vehicles hurrying by them on the main road, no one was in sight. He pressed the gas pedal and turned the SUV onto the dirt side road.

"Maybe we should call Mom and have her waiting with bail money," Tony said.

The four-wheel-drive SUV rolled through the gated entrance and hit a large mud puddle left from a late afternoon rain. One of the vehicle's wheels spun as it slipped in the brown goo, splattering the sides of the black SUV with an ugly spray.

According to Gore's map, the dirt path would lead them over a narrow one-way bridge.

But less than a mile down the path, they reached a dead end. The road stopped at an irrigation ditch. Al turned the SUV to the left and traveled another hundred yards. But they hit another irrigation ditch there.

"Maybe these ditches weren't here thirty years ago," Tony said.

They tried yet another turn, but within a mile, they'd reached another canal. None of the landmarks Gore had described in his letters matched the route they were driving. There was no one-lane bridge within eyesight, no metal storage barn. The mileage didn't fit.

By now it was dusk and they were parked on a sandy patch at the back of the orange grove. Directly in front of them were other groves and swampland. Glancing to his right, Tony spotted a tiny structure about a half mile away. Al drove the SUV off the road and into the grove, thankful that he had rented a four-wheel-drive vehicle. They had to walk the last hundred yards on a footpath next to a slime-covered irrigation ditch.

Al carried Gore's instructions with them, and when they reached the structure, he read Gore's description of the storage barn.

"This can't be it. The barn we are looking for is on a poured concrete slab," he said. "It has a canopy big enough for tractors to pull under if it rains."

They were standing in front of a six-foot-tall and four-foot-wide tin-roofed shelter built over a water pump. A hose from it dropped into the canal.

"This shed isn't big enough," Tony said.

They returned to the SUV just as the sun set.

"We've either gone to the wrong spot or he's lied to us," Al said.

"I don't think we're at the right place," Tony replied.

Under the SUV dome light, Al studied the map to see where he might have taken a wrong turn. But he'd followed the instructions perfectly. Or at least he thought he had. Part of the problem was that Gore had told them to drive along "Jones Road." But none of the highway maps that Al had brought with them had a Jones Road listed.

"We need to find where Jones Road is to make sure we're going in the right direction," he told Tony. "Let's head back, check into a motel, and get something to eat."

The next morning, they stopped at a Home Depot after breakfast and bought a shovel and plastic gloves. From there, they drove to the Vero Beach City Hall, where they asked a city clerk if she'd ever heard of Jones Road. She hadn't, nor could she find it listed on any city maps. She suggested they try the county courthouse, since Vero Beach is the seat of Indian River County. Tony and Al drove to the courthouse, went inside, and asked a clerk there if she could direct them to Jones Road. She told them there was no record of a Jones Road on any county maps.

"So Gore lied to us?" Tony asked when they got back to their SUV.

"I'm not sure. None of this makes sense."

Al decided to call the orange grove owner—the man whom Gore had mentioned in his letters. He'd been Gore's boss. But the telephone operator told him that there was no listing in Vero Beach for the name that Gore had sent them. They'd hit another dead end and Gore's credibility was continuing to drop.

Al came up with a new idea. If Gore had given them a real name, there would be records of the grove owner in the courthouse. He would have paid property taxes and there would be maps that showed the acreage that he owned. If they were able to match the landowner's name to a specific orange grove, they could use the map that Gore had sent them to pinpoint Jones Road, drive to the correct grove, and find the storage barn.

It was a smart plan. Both were proud of their detective work as they returned to the courthouse. Inside, the clerk recognized the landowner's name. She assured them that the owner was an actual person. But she also told them that he had moved away from Vero Beach several years ago.

"Can you show us which orange groves he owned around here?" Al asked.

The clerk said she could, but added that the landowner had owned more than a dozen orange groves scattered over several thousand acres. There would be no way for them to look at those records and determine which grove was the one where Gore had buried his stash.

Back in their rented SUV, the father and son realized they were no closer to finding Jones Road and pinpointing the orange grove than they'd been an hour earlier.

Al could tell Tony was becoming frustrated, so he suggested they take a break and drive to one of the beaches where Gore had abducted women. Tony had brought along several of Gore's letters. They chose Gore's description of how he'd abducted Judith Kaye Daley from Round Island Beach on Highway A1A, which ran parallel to the Atlantic Ocean. Al typed the park's address into the rental's GPS. Gore had written that Highway A1A was one of his favorite hunting spots. This was before cell phones and he would search for a parked car and then creep over the dunes to see if there was a single woman sunbathing on the beach. Tony began reading aloud what Gore had written about his thirty-five-year-old victim.

She was the woman I had sitting in the front seat when I drove right through town . . . She was handcuffed. Her right wrist was cuffed to the door handle and her left wrist was cuffed to the seat belt strap between her and me. Plus I had a gun and told her to sit there and look like a passenger. Looking back on it, that was a pretty risky move, because what if I had had an accident or what if I had encountered a police check? I didn't think about all that at the time. All I could think about was getting her to my place and what I was going to do to her. Of course, I kept telling her constantly that if she did everything I asked and didn't cause any problems, I'd let her go later. She knew I was going to rape her. But she thought that was all . . . All of them but one believed me. That one woman fought, but it didn't do her any good. It just made me angry.

35

July 15, 1981

"Don't you want to come with me?" Judith Kaye Daley asked her sister-in-law.

"No, you and the girls go," Bonnie Schwey replied. "I'll stay here and fix a nice dinner. I want to make a key lime pie." Bonnie was not a beach person. She also had given birth two months earlier to a son and she didn't want to cart him through the dunes. Besides, Kaye was one of those true beach lovers who could sunbathe on the beach for hours without getting bored. Bonnie preferred to keep herself busy.

"Just be back in time for Paul to get to work," Bonnie said. Her husband worked nights and Kaye was borrowing his car that afternoon. Bonnie asked: "Where are you and your girls going?"

Kaye's daughters, ages fourteen and fifteen, already had made friends with a neighborhood teen and she'd told them that Jaycee Beach Park was where all of the cute boys their age liked to hang out. She'd offered to introduce them to her friends and Kaye's daughters had gotten their mother's permission. Kaye had also decided that spending the afternoon at Jaycee Beach with a bunch of hormone-driven teens was not for her. She wanted to relax, read her book, and enjoy some solitude.

"I'm dropping off the girls with their new friend at Jaycee Beach," she told Bonnie. "Then I'm heading to Round Island."

"That's pretty isolated," Bonnie replied. "And there are no lifeguards."

Kaye knew that. She used to go to Round Island Beach with Mike Daley when they first met at a local junior college in 1962 and began dating. Kaye, Mike, and their college pals chose the beach because it was so isolated. Tall dunes blocked the eyes of passing motorists on Highway A1A. You could light a bonfire and share a keg without worrying about sheriff's deputies showing up to check on underage drinking. Kaye and Mike had married after graduation and left Vero Beach for

California in 1968, when Mike got a good job offer there. Kaye and her daughters had returned this summer to visit Paul and Bonnie. Mike had stayed behind to play in a softball tournament.

As planned, Kaye dropped off the girls that afternoon and then drove to Round Island Beach, where she parked next to a dune and made her way to the isolated shoreline with a book in hand.

Shortly after 2 p.m., the clouds turned dark, signaling an approaching afternoon rain. Bonnie's neighbor called and said she was going to pick up the girls at Jaycee Beach because of the storm. She asked if Bonnie had heard from Kaye. She hadn't. A few minutes later, Bonnie's phone rang.

"Hello," she said.

"I'm calling to tell you about Judith Daley," a male voice said. "Her car has broken down at Wabasso Beach and she needs someone to pick up her daughters."

"Is she okay?" Bonnie asked.

Yes, the caller assured her. Daley was waiting with the car for a mechanic to arrive and fix it.

"Thank you so much for calling," Bonnie said.

She thought she had been talking to someone who was doing Kaye a favor, but as soon as she put down the receiver, Bonnie became suspicious. No one ever called Kaye by her first name, Judith, and she never told anyone her first name. Bonnie wondered if the caller had been reading her name off her driver's license. It also bothered her that the caller had said Kaye had gone to Wabasso Beach, ten miles north of Vero Beach, rather than to Round Island Beach, which was a few miles south of town.

She was about to say something to her husband about the odd telephone call when Kaye's two daughters burst inside just ahead of a thundershower. Bonnie pushed her fears aside and began chatting with them. An hour passed and then another. At that point, Paul began to wonder what had happened to his car. He needed to leave for work in a few hours. Paul decided to take Bonnie's car and drive to Wabasso Beach. But when he got there, he didn't see his car or Kaye.

Heading south, Paul drove to Round Island Beach. By now the storm had come and gone and the sun was peeking out. Paul turned off the highway as soon as he spotted his car parked near a dune. He went directly to the beach, to see if Kaye's towel and book were there. Perhaps, he feared, she had gone swimming and been swept out to sea during the storm. But the beach was empty. He decided to inspect his car. The mysterious male caller had said there was something wrong with it. Popping open the hood, Paul examined the engine and noticed that someone had fooled with the distributor cap. He lifted it. The car's rotor had been removed, making it impossible to start.

That's when Paul knew something terrible had happened to his sister-in-law. Hurrying home, he told Bonnie and they called the Indian River County Sheriff's Office. Bonnie also tried to get in touch with Mike Daley. There was no answer, so Bonnie called Mike's dad and he went to the baseball field where Mike was playing softball. Mike immediately booked a flight to Florida.

By now it was dark and the deputy sheriff who responded to their panicked call was not sure Kaye's disappearance was a case of kidnapping or foul play. Vero Beach was a low-crime area. How did Bonnie and Paul know that Kaye hadn't met someone? Maybe she was at dinner with either an old friend or even a stranger whom she'd just met. She was on vacation and sometimes women let their eyes wander. Maybe she had dismantled her own car as an excuse so she and the mysterious caller could have a liaison. Bonnie bristled: "Kaye wouldn't do that!"

The deputy did some snooping around and when a relative mentioned that Mike and Kaye were having marital problems, her disappearance seemed even less ominous. Maybe she'd just decided to take off for a while on her own to get her head together. Again, Bonnie got angry. "Kaye wouldn't leave her kids."

The deputy's theory irked Mike when he arrived at Round Island Beach on the morning after Kaye vanished. Mike pointed out that Kaye's purse was in the dismantled car. "What woman runs off without taking her purse?" he asked deputies.

Mike was a descendant of Waldo E. Sexton, a legendary Floridian who was responsible for shaping much of Vero Beach. He was one of the first to plant citrus trees in Indian River County in 1917. Later he started a cattle ranch, dairy farm, and insurance agency and developed three varieties of avocados. He was best known in the state for developing a tourist attraction called the McKee Jungle Gardens. It was a large tropical botanical garden, filled with rare plants, orchids, and lilies, as well as monkeys, alligators, and wacky buildings that Sexton had designed and furnished with odd artwork. He'd also founded the Driftwood Inn, the Ocean Grill, and the Patio restaurant, famed Vero Beach landmarks.

The Sextons were politically connected. When the patriarch of the family, Ralph W. Sexton, heard that Kaye was missing, he immediately rented a private helicopter to search the beach for her. Meanwhile, Mike and his cousin Mark Tripson rode through undeveloped acres on horseback.

But Kaye Daley had simply vanished.

Mike and his two daughters returned to California. Not long after that, Mike got a telephone call from an Indian River County sheriff's detective. David Gore had been arrested hiding in the backseat of a woman's car outside a doctor's office. He'd been charged with armed trespass. There was more. A few days before that strange incident, Gore had been stripped of his auxiliary sheriff's badge. He'd lured a teenage girl into a remote area after flashing his badge and telling her that she was a suspect in a robbery investigation.

Because of those two incidents, the detective wondered if Gore might have abducted Kaye Daley. The detective speculated that Gore might have shown Kaye his badge after he'd disabled her car. Was Mike willing to send something of Kaye's to them so they could compare it with hair that they'd found when they'd searched Gore's truck?

Mike mailed them Kaye's hairbrush. A few days later, Mike got another call from the detective. Hair from Kaye's brush matched hair that had been found inside Gore's vehicle.

There was now no doubt that Kaye had been with Gore in his truck. But Gore was not talking, and without a body, there was no evidence that Kaye had been murdered. The local prosecutor said he didn't have enough evidence to file any charges against Gore because of Kaye's disappearance.

Mike was furious. "I'd told my daughters to hope for the best, but prepare for the worst. Now we had the worst. I spent the next year pretty much drinking myself silly waiting to hear if the police had found her body."

On November 6, 1981, Gore was sentenced to three years in prison for armed trespass for hiding in the backseat of a woman's car.

In California, Mike went to a friend's house, got drunk, and called Gore's parents in Vero Beach. Gore's grandfather had worked for Waldo Sexton and Mike knew the Gore family. "I called them every name in the book and they tape-recorded my call and called the police," he recalled later in an interview. "I was told by detectives that without a body, there was nothing they could do. And that I should stop harassing the Gores."

In prison, Gore attended church and was such a model inmate that he was released after serving fifteen months. When Ralph Sexton found out, he complained to the sheriff's office. A deputy was ordered to keep an eye on Gore, but when the paroled inmate and his mother threatened to sue the department for harassment, the deputy was told to back off.

"The sheriff called us and told us they knew Gore had murdered Kaye," said Ralph Sexton's wife, Chris. "We knew a murderer was on the loose in our town and no one could do anything about it."

Within six weeks after he was paroled, Gore was hunting again.

36

Having visited where Judith Kaye Daley was abducted in 1981, Al and Tony drove north from Round Island Beach to Vero Beach. Tony took out one of Gore's letters and said, "After Gore was released and moved in with his parents, he and Fred Waterfield picked up two hitchhikers from Orlando—Angelica Lavallee and Barbara Byer." Tony began reading a letter Gore had written to him about that May 1983 kidnapping and double murder.

Dear Tony,

. . . I don't know if I ever shared with you about two of my victims. Barbara Byer and Angela? (I forget her last name.) I actually got two life sentences for their deaths. They were two that Fred and I picked up hitchhiking on I-95.

. . . Fred and I had taken this van that he had—it was one of those Econoline vans and it had a bed in the back and carpet—so we took it one night and decided to use it on one of our hunts. We had a cooler of beer and took off. We left Vero Beach around 6 p.m. and cruised and hunted our way all the way up to Daytona. We were mainly hunting for hitchhikers or a woman by herself in a car that we could get.

By 10 p.m., we had not had any luck so Fred suggested we head across to Orlando and cruise the strip for a hooker. So we did and by 11:30 we still hadn't found anything we could get so we just decided to call it a night and head home. It was about a 2½ hour drive home and we were probably half-way home, like at one a.m. in the morning, when all of the sudden we see these two chicks on the side of the road hitchhiking, and Fred and I looked at each other and we said at the exact same time, "Let's get 'em!"

I had the gun and Fred was driving so we opened the side door to the van and let them get in. They both sat on the cooler and we took off. They told us they were heading to Fort Lauderdale. I'm sitting there and can't believe our luck. Now it's dark inside the van and I'm checking my side mirror seeing if any cars are coming up behind us and as soon as I see the coast is clear, I pull my gun and reach around between the seats and point it at them and tell them to not try anything or I'll shoot. They literally froze and sort of held on to one another. I could tell they were really young— fourteen, I think. So I went to get back there with them to tie them up and as I was climbing back, Fred said to me, "Don't take their clothes off" and to let him have first dibs. So I forced them face down on the floor of the van, took the rope we had brought and tied their wrists behind their backs and told them that if they tried anything we wouldn't hesitate to shoot them.

. . . Fred pulled over and got into the back with the girls. I could hear the clothes being torn so I knew he was stripping them and every once in a while, I could hear one of them moan and whimper . . . He was back there, probably twenty minutes.

When he came back upfront where I was driving, he had this big smile on his face and he said, "NICE!"

When we got back, he told me if I wanted to take the girls to where ever and do my thing, go ahead because he was going to call it a night. I was more than happy too because I definitely wanted to spend time enjoying our catches. I told him I'd dispose of them afterwards and we could meet back later that day . . .

First let me say that the body type of Barbara and Angela was totally different. Barbara had the best little body you could imagine. She didn't weigh over a hundred pounds and the tightest and sexiest body. Here tits were perfect handfuls and her pussy was a little slit with a soft mat of hair . . . Now Angela was just chubby. She had no body shape and a little flab on her stomach and short curly dark pubic hair . . . Fred had only screwed Barbara and so I drove them into the groves and back where this forest was so we wouldn't be disturbed or seen. Remember there was a bed in the truck and Barbara was on the bed where Fred had left her and Angela was on the floor. I sat on the edge of the bed, pulled Angela up between my legs and she was whimpering and I told her I wanted her to suck me off good. I grabbed her by her hair and forced the head of my cock into her mouth and she was gagging and choking and crying and I was getting pissed and trying to force her to suck when Barbara spoke up and said "Leave her alone. She's a virgin and she don't know what to do. She's never been with anyone." So I turned to her and I said, "Oh, so you want some—do you?"

I shoved little Miss Crybaby down on the floor and I pulled Barbara down on the floor and I had her by her hair and forced her to do what her friend didn't know how to do . . . but I stopped her before I came because I wanted to screw this whore so I positioned her on her knees with her chest on the floor and I got behind her . . .

I fucked her . . . every way possible in every hole possible . . . and made her do everything that I wanted and what a fuck she was. And I said to her, now why can't your fat friend there fuck like you? And I realized I still had a virgin to deal with so I went after her next. I kept a seven inch dildo in the truck so I got it out and grabbed Angela's feet and pulled her legs apart. I made a comment like she needed her pussy fucked and I . . . shoved that dildo up to the hilt and she screamed and tried to kick and get away but I held her down while I rammed it in and out. I did it until I was tired. Of course that girl was whimpering and sobbing and the other one was trying to help her by telling me to leave her alone. She even tried to get me to untie her hands and told me she'd cooperate, but I knew she was just trying to get away and protect her friend. I worked that fat girl over really good. She wasn't the same when I finished with her.

Let me tell you, I was spent, physically and emotionally . . . I stuffed a gag in each of their mouths and took Angela out onto the ground from the van and strangled her, then got back in and did Barbara. Then I drug both bodies into the woods where I disposed of them. Oh and you can believe, I collected hair. It took a couple days to recover from that.

It was a perfect experience.

For a moment, Tony and Al were silent. And then Al said, "I can't imagine being the parents of those two girls, knowing what he did to them. He's a sick bastard."

Gore might have been emotionally and physically spent by those two killings. But not for long.

Two months later, he and Waterfield spotted two other girls with their thumbs sticking out. They were Lynn Elliott and "Melody Walker," two teens from Vero Beach. The two men offered them a ride and then drove them to Gore's parents' house on the outskirts of Vero Beach.

"Can we go there next?" Tony asked his father. "To that house?"

Al entered the address into the GPS. It took only a few minutes to reach the location, but there was no house there. Al knocked on the door of the nearest neighbor. The Gores' home had been bulldozed by a developer, the neighbor explained. The family had moved away after Gore was caught.

Tony and Al walked over to the lot where Gore and Waterfield had taken their final victims. Tony closed his eyes. He said a prayer.

37

July 26, 1983

The morning began like so many other mornings that summer. "Melody Walker" hurried from her home as soon as her mother, Carol, rounded the corner on her drive to work. The fourteen-year-old and her younger brother had moved with their mother to Vero Beach a month earlier. Recently divorced, Carol had decided it was time for a fresh start for her and her daughter. Melody had always been a great kid. An honor roll student, she'd excelled in the gifted and talented classes at her school, and played the oboe in the concert band and trumpet in the marching band. But after her parents' divorce in Fort Lauderdale, she'd turned rebellious. She'd also been caught smoking marijuana.

Carol had moved her family into a house less than three blocks from the beach. It was an hour away from the office where she recruited customers to lease retail space in shopping centers. Because she often needed to travel across Florida to meet potential clients, Carol had persuaded her nephew to spend the summer in Vero Beach with them. He was twenty-two and could keep an eye on Melody and her brother while Carol was working.

Melody had made friends effortlessly. The first day, she'd met a boy her age, Brian Elliott. He'd introduced her to his older sister, Lynn. Although Lynn was seventeen, she and Melody became instant best friends. Melody was mature for her age.

Both girls were pretty. Lynn's mother, Jeanne Elliott, liked to say her daughter was a dead ringer for a young Farrah Fawcett when the television star was in her *Charlie's Angels* prime. Lynn had long blond hair and fabulous tan, and was one of the most popular kids in Vero Beach High School. The beach was where Lynn, Melody, and their friends hung out.

Lynn had introduced Melody to Tim Mccullers. He was from a deeply rooted Vero Beach family and in the small, tight-knit beach community where everyone knew everyone, that meant something. Tim was older—in his twenties—and already had been married and divorced. He lived in a small oceanfront house that was well-known for parties. Kids gathered there to drink beer and smoke pot. Although Lynn didn't know it, Tim was planning to propose to her when the summer ended.

On this particular morning, Lynn and Brian walked with Melody to the beach to suntan and swim. Most days, Lynn had access to a car, but today her father, Carl, was having new tires put on it.

There wasn't much happening there. Tim was at work and Lynn and Melody got bored after lunch. They decided to check out another popular teen hangout, Wabasso Beach, about ten miles north. Lynn called Tim and asked if he could stop by Wabasso after he got off work that afternoon and give them a ride back to Vero Beach.

"Sure," he said, "but how you going to get there?"

Lynn said they'd find a friend to drive them. But after she hung up, she and Melody had an idea. The two teens would hitchhike along Highway A1A. Melody had done it once in Fort Lauderdale without a problem. It would be a much-needed adventure.

Brian warned his sister and Melody that it was a stupid idea. They might be picked up by a weirdo. If their parents found out, they'd get into trouble. But Lynn and Melody ignored him. As he watched, they put cover-ups over their bikinis, walked to the highway, and stuck out their thumbs, laughing as motorists sped by.

Within minutes, a pickup truck stopped. The two girls jumped in and Brian watched the truck drive north.

Court testimony would later show that Fred Waterfield was behind the wheel and David Gore was on the passenger side, effectively pinning in Lynn and Melody. At the time, Waterfield was thirty-one years old. Gore was a year younger. Waterfield did the talking. He asked if the girls wanted to smoke some pot. There was a Baggie in the glove box. They could stop when they reached a less-traveled section of the highway. A few minutes later, Waterfield turned the truck off the road and stopped behind a dune. Gore reached into the glove box, supposedly for the pot.

Instead, he pulled out a handgun. He jabbed it against Melody's temple.

"I'll kill you!" he snarled. "Unless you do exactly what you're told."

One of the men made a snide comment—something about teaching you girls a lesson about hitchhiking. You never knew who might pick up you. The other laughed.

Gore put handcuffs on Melody and tied Lynn's hands. He bound her wrists so tight that they turned red and immediately began to swell. If the girls didn't fight, they'd let them go later.

Petrified, Melody couldn't speak. But Lynn began arguing with them.

"My boyfriend is Tim Mccullers," she said.

Waterfield and Gore shot each other a knowing glance. Although Lynn wasn't aware of it, both of the kidnappers knew the Mccullers family. They'd been fishing with Tim and his uncle.

As the truck approached the Vero Beach city limits, the driver in an approaching car waved at them. It was one of Waterfield's relatives. Later, testimony would show that the woman thought Waterfield had his daughters with him in the truck. They were about the same age as his captives. The relative had not thought anything peculiar was going on.

When they reached Gore's parents' house, the girls were hustled in and separated. Each was taken into a bedroom where her feet were bound with ropes. Melody could hear Lynn arguing in the next room. Gore threatened to shoot her. Then she heard her gagging. In a statement to the police, Gore would acknowledge that he had forced Lynn to engage in oral sex and Waterfield had raped her. At some point Waterfield left, ostensibly to establish an alibi. He reportedly was worried about being seen earlier with two girls. He drove to the small garage that he operated at Oslo Road and Forty-Third Avenue. He planned to return later that afternoon after running an errand with his own daughters.

Meanwhile, Gore came into the bedroom where Melody was crying. Using a knife, he cut through her swimsuit cover-up and then her bikini. He raped her. It was the first of three sexual assaults that afternoon. He would leave the bedroom only to return moments later and attack her again. He told her during one assault that he planned to keep her and Lynn in the house for two or three days before releasing them.

While Gore was raping Melody, Lynn managed to free her feet from the ropes in the adjoining bedroom. She ran toward the front door and was trying to unlock it with her still-bound hands when Gore heard her. He picked up Melody, threw her into a bedroom closet, and told her that he'd kill her if she came out of it. Racing out of the bedroom, he got to the front door seconds after Lynn opened it and burst outside.

Although he was naked, Gore didn't hesitate. He chased after Lynn into the front yard, hitting her from behind. She fell forward into the ground, hitting it hard. Gore fired two shots into her head. He dragged her lifeless body to a car parked in the garage and threw her into the trunk.

Melody had heard the gunshots but had no idea that Lynn was dead. She could also hear chatter on a police scanner that Gore and Waterfield had been monitoring. But she couldn't make out what was being said. Gore did, however, and realized a sheriff's deputy was coming to the house.

Gore burst into the bedroom, red-faced, angry, and waving his pistol. He jerked Melody from the closet and threw her onto the bed. He screamed at her and she thought he might shoot her. Instead Gore picked her up like a sack of potatoes and carried her to an opening that led to the house's attic. He forced her up onto the joists. The summer heat made it sweltering inside and Melody gasped for breath. He climbed up next to her and grabbed her shoulders, lifting her upper torso. Melody saw the blade of a knife appear and felt its blade pressed against her throat. "Don't say a word." She knew she was about to die. She wondered where Lynn was. Her entire body began quivering.

Without warning, he released his grip on her head and went downstairs. It sounded as if he was making a phone call. Then he made another one. He returned to the attic and put his knife to her throat again.

"I'll kill you if you make a sound."

From outside, Melody could hear deputies calling Gore's name through speakers. Gore tightened his grip and pressed the knife harder against her throat. She fought back tears. Melody couldn't tell what was happening. Where was Lynn? It was so hot in the attic that she thought she was going to faint. She couldn't stop her body from shaking. She felt certain he was going to slit her throat.

Suddenly she could hear men moving underneath them in the house. It was the sheriff's deputies. In that instant, Melody thought they might forget to search the attic. Gore slid toward the attic opening to peek down through a crack.

A man's voice called out: "We know you're up there. Come down, now."

Gore didn't seem to know what to do. He was still clutching Melody. Without warning, he released her and climbed down from the attic.

The next face that Melody saw was a deputy's.

"You're going to be okay," he said, unlocking her handcuffs. Because she was naked, he pulled some clothing from a closet and gave her a pair of pants and a blouse. They belonged to Gore's mother. Melody was in shock. She still had no idea where Lynn was.

"We're taking you to the hospital," the deputy said.

"Where's Lynn?" Melody asked.

He didn't answer.

Jeanne Elliott sold real estate and was scheduled to meet prospective home buyers at one of her listings later that night, so she fixed Carl an early dinner. When Brian came in from the beach, Carl asked his son where Lynn was. Brian hesitated and then told his parents that his sister and Melody had hitchhiked to Wabasso Beach. The last time that he'd seen her was shortly after 2 p.m.

Carl was angry that his daughter would do something so dangerous. He and Jeanne were discussing how they would reprimand their daughter when someone knocked on their door. Carl recognized the sheriff's deputy.

"I'm sorry," he said. "Lynn is dead."

As promised, Tim Mccullers drove to Wabasso Beach as soon as he got off work that afternoon to pick up Lynn and Melody. But he couldn't find them. He assumed they'd caught a ride back to Vero Beach, so he drove directly to Lynn's house. They'd planned on taking a romantic walk on the beach that night. It was one of their favorite outings. When Tim got to the Elliotts' house, he was surprised at how many cars were parked outside. People stopped talking when he entered the living room. Carl rose from a couch and told him that Lynn had been murdered. Tim began to cry. He also started thinking about revenge.

Carol Walker was not a deeply religious person. But she considered herself a spiritual person and from the day that she and her children had arrived in Vero Beach, she had felt an impending sense of doom. That feeling didn't make any sense to her. She loved the little house that she had bought. Her job was going so well that she had purchased a Corvette convertible. Yet the first morning when she woke up in her Vero

Beach bedroom, Carol had had an anxiety attack. It was a premonition, she decided. But of what?

Carol had left work early on the afternoon when Melody and Lynn were abducted. She'd put the covertible top down and started the drive home along Highway A1A. On one side of her car was the Intracoastal Waterway; on the other was the Atlantic. She didn't like the music on her radio, so she switched it off, took a deep breath, and savored the warm breeze washing across her face. She suddenly burst into a song—"Mine eyes have seen the glory of the coming of the Lord." She would tell her friends later that she had no idea why the "Battle Hymn of the Republic" had popped into her mind. But she would decide that she had started singing at the exact moment when her daughter was rescued by sheriff's deputies. How could she be so certain?

Because when she finished the song, the feeling of dread that had clouded over her had gone away.

Sheriff's deputies took Melody to the hospital for an examination and to collect evidence. No one mentioned Lynn was dead. When they got to the police station, Melody was taken into an interrogation room. She assumed Lynn was in the room next door giving a statement. After Melody finished telling detectives about the attacks, the deputies took her into a room to look at a police lineup. She picked out Gore without hesitating. The deputies allowed her mother into the room. Carol had never seen her daughter so traumatized. "My daughter looked like a waif," Carol recalled years later. "She looked like she had lost ten pounds that afternoon." When they got home that night, Carol asked Melody if she wanted to talk about what had happened. Melody didn't. She just wanted to get into the shower and get out of Mrs. Gore's clothes.

Melody asked, "How is Lynn?"

Carol told her that Lynn was dead. That night both mother and daughter slept in the same bedroom with the door locked.

Tim Mccullers was one of Lynn's pallbearers. All of Vero Beach seemed to shut down for the funeral, or, at least, all locally owned businesses did. The crowd of 350 spilled outside the First Baptist Church. "Why did such a lovely young lady have to die?" asked the Reverend Jerry Ball.

By that time, everyone had heard about what Gore and Waterfield had done to the girls. The town was riddled with rumors about other missing women, including Judith Kaye Daley. The sheriff's office had received telephone calls from women who claimed Gore had raped them, too, dating back to when he was a teenager. They'd been too frightened of him and Waterfield to report the assaults.

A Vero Beach police officer came to Tim's house after the funeral and asked him about the guns that he owned. An avid outdoorsman, Tim was better than most with an AR-15 rifle. He could put a bullet where he wanted at up to three hundred yards. Tim had confided to some of his beach friends that he was going to kill Gore. He was going to shoot him when the police moved Gore into an outdoor exercise area next to the jail. The area was encircled by a chain-link fence, but Tim felt he could get a clear shot from bleachers nearby at a school. Tim had even paced off the distance. The officer confiscated all of Tim's guns.

The events of July 26, 1983, forever changed the lives of Jeanne Elliott, Carl Elliott, Brian Elliott, Carol Walker, and Tim Mccullers. "Two years before I met Lynn," Mccullers said years later in an interview for this book, "I'd gone through a divorce and Lynn was basically the first young lady I'd gotten involved with and trusted. I wanted her to be my wife. I went off the deep end for a while. I got more and more into drugs. It was a way to cope. I ended up getting busted and going to prison."

Jeanne Elliott attended Gore's trial. "There were times when I wanted to close my ears in the courtroom because I couldn't listen to what he did to my daughter. Gore just didn't shoot her in the head, you know, it was before that—the things he did to her. I couldn't bear to imagine those things. The lawyers told me that I had to be very quiet, you know, in the courtroom because they were afraid that any show of emotion might affect the outcome of the trial. I couldn't even cry. It was horrible. He is a monster."

After the coroner finished Lynn's autopsy, Carl insisted on seeing his daughter's body. "I asked my cousin to go with me and he said, 'Why, why are you going to put yourself through this?' And I said, 'I want to see her body. I want to see every mark on it, where he drug her in the driveway and all the skinned-up parts on her knees and elbows, and every damn bullet hole. I want to see every scrape and every bruise. I want to remember in case I ever get soft on this thing.' I want to remember, by

God, that's what this bastard did to my daughter.' It was awful, but I have never regretted doing it."

Carl thought about revenge. "I kept my eyes on him [Gore] the whole time in court. I watched his expressions and his smirk. I thought, 'I could easily smuggle a gun in here and shoot that bastard,' but then I'd think, 'Okay, my other kids would not have a father. I would be in jail like him and I can't do that anyway because I've always been a law-abiding person.' But I hated watching him, listening to his mother testify about how he'd been such a sweet young boy. Ha!"

The prolonged trials took a toll. Jeanne and Carl divorced. Both believe Lynn's murder played a role in the separation. Lynn's younger brother, Brian, died of a drug overdose in his father's house. "Brian felt tremendous guilt," Carl said, "because he'd not stopped Lynn and Melody from hitchhiking that day. We lost her to two cold-blooded killers and we lost him to drugs—all because of what they did that day."

Now eighty years old, Carl keeps Lynn's photograph next to his bed and another picture of her in the family room where he can see it while watching television. "I talk to her occasionally. I think of her every day. It is a scar. A terrible scar on your soul."

Carol Walker felt she was judged by townspeople because of what happened to her daughter and Lynn Elliott. "I was a single mom supporting my family the best way I could, but it's a small town and people criticized me for not being home with them that day. I went to see a psychiatrist, but Melody refused to go. The two of us had a rough time. She wouldn't talk to me about it. Then I got fired from my job because we had to go to all of these trials. I told my boss what was happening, but he didn't care. He said he needed someone who would make the job their priority. It was frustrating. I remember once we were driving home from a trial that had been moved to another county to ensure that Gore got a fair shake. The state had assigned a rape counselor to help my daughter. The counselor was from a very, very wealthy family and she was driving us back to Vero Beach. My son and daughter hadn't eaten and they asked if we could stop at McDonald's. I said, 'I'm sorry, but I don't have any money.' Now this woman knew I had lost my job and was having a tough time paying the mortgage and she just ignored them and kept on driving. They kept talking about how hungry they were so finally I said, "Look, I don't have any money, but please stop and feed my kids. I will give you a check.' She stopped and the kids had hamburgers and I wrote her a check and she cashed it the next day. It was for a lousy seven dollars. She made me feel worthless." Carol eventually moved from Florida to another state.

Of course, the person most affected was Melody Walker, the only woman known to have been abducted and sexually abused by Gore and Waterfield and then to have survived. She tried to return to her old life, but when she went back to high school, she felt alienated. "Kids talked behind my back. Lynn had a lot of friends and they blamed me because I was the new kid. They made me the bad kid from the wrong side of the tracks." Wherever she went, she heard other teens whispering about her. A few were rude. They wanted to know the details about what the two men had done to her sexually.

"I began doing drugs. Drugs are stupid, but I think it helped me cope at the time. This was the first time I fell into a pit of despair."

The trials of Gore and Waterfield dragged on for months. She missed so much school that she fell hopelessly behind and dropped out. At sixteen, the state allowed her to take the GED, exam, which she passed easily. "I just wanted to escape, to get out of Vero Beach and put all of this behind me."

Melody fled to a college in California and started over. No one there knew what she had been through and she kept quiet about it. She earned good grades, got a great job. For the first time since the attack, she felt free. "My dreams and aspirations were for the Peace Corps and then a career in international relations. I had hopes and plans. I was going to make something of my life."

And then, just before she was scheduled to graduate from college, she received a telephone call from prosecutors in Florida. Almost six years from the day when she had been abducted, an appellate court overturned Gore's death penalty conviction. The court ruled that Gore's rights to a fair trial had been denied him because his defense attorney had not introduced evidence that showed Gore was an alcoholic. Gore claimed that he had been drunk when he kidnapped, raped, and murdered Lynn Elliott. Investigators had found a half-filled bottle of vodka in Gore's parents' house, and in his appeal, he claimed that he had consumed the missing half of that bottle while attacking the two girls. If jurors had known that Gore was drunk, as he now charged, they might have considered that a mitigating circumstance and not condemned him to die.

Melody's heart sank. Job counselors were on campus interviewing pending graduates. She'd gotten an application for the Peace Corps.

She wanted to be going to graduation parties with her friends and not returning to Florida to be grilled by Gore's attorneys. She could have refused to testify, but she felt tremendous loyalty to Lynn and her parents. The state promised to pay her airfare and put her in a motel. She would receive a total of twenty-two dollars per day for all of her living expenses. Reluctantly, Melody put her schoolwork aside, agreed to postpone her graduation, and said goodbye to her friends. She returned to Florida, where, much like the first trial, Gore's new trial lasted weeks. When Melody was finally called to testify, she came under a brutal attack by Gore's defense attorneys. In the years that had passed, Melody had done her best to forget about what had happened, and whenever she couldn't remember something that she had testified to at the first trial or she said something different, the defense pounced on her statements. They were trying to intimidate her and undercut her testimony by insinuating that she was lying. The entire time that she was in the courtroom, Gore sat at the defense table beaming at her.

Gore was found guilty for a second time, and Melody returned to California, but she was an emotional wreck. Because of her long absence from college, she had missed classes and the school told her that she was three hours short of graduating with her peers. She'd also been replaced at the lucrative job that she had enjoyed, because she'd been gone for so long. All of her college friends were moving on. She wasn't.

Depressed and short of money, Melody moved to Los Angeles, rented a tiny apartment, and began searching for work. She also began smoking pot. It didn't help, so she tried harder drugs. The second trial had stirred up long-buried emotions. She had nightmares. Gore was there in her dreams, sexually assaulting her, holding a knife to her throat. She dreamed that she saw him shoot Lynn. She would wake up in a sweat and swear that she could smell him. It was the same scent that she'd smelled when he was raping her. It was repugnant. She was afraid to go out at night alone. She avoided anywhere there were not crowds. She was afraid of men.

Determined to finish college, she contacted Florida officials to see if the state would pay her three hundred dollars from a victims' compensation fund to cover her college tuition. Her request was denied, but a counselor told her that the state would pay for her to see a psychiatrist. She went and the doctor told her that she was suffering from post-traumatic stress disorder. She got angry and called her contact in Florida. "I don't need counseling, I need my college degree!"

Officials finally agreed to pay for the remainder of her college schooling. But her life was now in shambles. "I was eating macaroni and cheese
and barely surviving," she later recalled. "I was using more and more
drugs. Getting high was my only escape from him and what had happened."

One day Melody went to a public library to do research about Gore
and death row in Florida. "He was eating three meals a day, had a
television, and didn't have to work or worry about rent. He had gotten
married in prison and was having people write to him. It was costing
taxpayers $72.39 a day to keep him alive and that wasn't counting the
legal costs because of his appeals. He was costing the state $26,500
per year just in food and lodging." At this point, it had been eight
years since his arrest. In that time period, the state had spent more
than $200,000 just in prison costs. "I was the victim, yet no one was
paying my rent or making sure I got three meals a day. People were
feeling sorry for him. But what about Lynn and the others whom he
victimized? Everyone was so worried about his rights. What about
our rights? This wasn't a case of him being innocent. Everyone knew
what he had done. Yet he was sitting on death row with his every need
being cared for."

Melody became paranoid. One morning she stepped out of her
apartment to go to work and heard gunshots. She could afford only a
room in a tough neighborhood. Instantly she dropped to her knees. An
LAPD helicopter flew overhead. Melody ducked back into her apartment, slammed and locked the door, and sat on the floor with her back
against it. She had hit an emotional rock bottom. She began sobbing.
Crawling across the floor to a phone, she called her mother.

"Please come. I need you to take me home."

Today, no one would guess Melody Walker was the same woman who
placed that desperate phone call to her mother. Happily married, Melody
has children of her own and has managed to work through the post-
traumatic stress disorder that overtook her life after she was terrorized
by Gore.

"I had hit bottom because I had lost hope," she said in an interview
for this book. "When I first went to California to college, I was able to
rebuild my life. I was able to put the past behind me. I had good friends,

a good job, and dreams and aspirations. And then I had to go back to Florida for that new trial—all because of a half-filled bottle of vodka—and all of the sudden, he is taking all of these dreams and aspirations away from me again—just like he'd done the first time. I felt that no matter what I did, this man was always going to be pulling me down. I lost hope that I would ever become a productive member of society, that I could have a home and job and family. I lost hope for a future. He'd abused me the first time around only to return and take everything I had away from me a second time."

It took Melody years to finally free herself from David Gore. With each success came more confidence. Her marriage was pivotal. The birth of her children gave her a firm foundation. None of her neighbors today know about her past. She rarely talks about it. She asked that her name in this book be a pseudonym.

"I've reached the point in my life now where I realize just how extremely lucky I am. I had survived. I was alive. I was spared and I came to believe there must have been a reason that I survived. And because I had survived, I had certain obligations. One was to help the Elliotts and the families of the other victims. I have gotten closure. It is not something I think about too often. Time helps. But the Elliotts and other families—they will never have that closure. That is why I want him executed. Maybe then, they will get it."

The arrest of David Gore and Fred Waterfield solved the mystery that surrounded the disappearance of their first known victims, Ying Hua Ling and her mother, Hsiang Huang Ling. Gore also told investigators what had happened to Angelica Lavallee and Barbara Byer.

And finally, Mike Daley, his daughters, and their relatives in Vero Beach discovered the fate of Judith Kaye Daley after she disappeared from Round Island Beach.

She'd been raped repeatedly by Gore and Waterfield, tortured, murdered, and dismembered, Gore revealed in his confession.

"One of those rag newspapers, the ones that are at supermarket checkout stands, heard about the story and put Kaye's picture under the headline I RAPED HER, KILLED HER AND FED HER TO THE GATORS," Mike Daley recalled. "I went to every store in town and bought all of the copies because I didn't want my kids to see it."

Not long after Gore was caught and confessed, Mike Daley answered a knock on his door and found two Taiwanese men outside on the porch stoop. Only one could speak English and it was difficult to understand, but Daley knew who they were: the husband and son of Hsiang Huang Ling. "Because of the language barrier, it was difficult to communicate but I knew what he wanted. He just wanted to connect with someone else who was a victim, someone who had lost someone they loved. He wanted to make that connection and it helped—both of us." It was later revealed that not only had investigators found Kaye Daley's hair in Gore's truck when he first had become a suspect, but they'd also found hairs from the Lings.

After Gore confessed, the sheriff's office recovered Kaye's severed head and part of her body. Bonnie Schwey was called and oversaw the cremation. The family held a private service at Round Island Beach but Bonnie refused to go there. She refuses to go to that beach, even today. She also does not like key lime pie. It reminds her of Kaye and the day she disappeared. Kaye's remains were spread at Ralph Sexton's ranch, a place that she loved to visit.

"The state needs to execute him," said Daley's cousin Mark Tripson. "It isn't about revenge. It's about what do you do with a mad dog? You can't ever let him loose or he'll kill again."

38

Al and Tony were somber when they pulled away from the vacant Vero Beach lot where Lynn Elliott had been murdered by Gore and where Melody Walker had been rescued in an attic. Tony decided to read another letter from Gore as they continued retracing his footprints.

Dear Tony,

. . . You asked me if I ever got out of here if I would be able to keep my hands to myself. You know let be as honest as I can. I most definitely would do all within my power to keep my hands to myself. This is one reason I would get away by myself. I would never want to put myself in the position again. And I have changed so much in my thinking and my emotions. Back then I was a mess. I was so full of hate . . . I know all the books tell you a serial killer can not be rehabilitated but I disagree. I believe they can, BUT ONLY if they themselves want to bad enough and are committed to do whatever it took to change. It has to start with the person FIRST though and I believe I would be able to have that commitment . . .

. . . You asked about the town where I lived and you can imagine the horror people had when body parts started being found. Smile. You have no idea the attention I got after my arrest. What got people the most was how open I did things. I mean housewives were going missing in board daylight. It wasn't like someone was slipping around in the middle of the night doing things. One incident, I drove right through town with one—[Judith] Daley—sitting right in the front seat . . .

You know Tony, over the years in prison, I've written to women and they would tell me they always fantasized of being raped. That used to get me. Why in the world would any woman fantasize about that? And I think where in the hell were these women when I was out there? Smile. I could have fulfilled their fantasies. Smile. I honestly believe one woman got off on what I was doing but even if she'd told me, I still would have taken her life away. You'd be surprised at what they used to say to me thinking if they would go along with everything, it would be okay and I'd let them live . . . Of course, I never did.

By now Al and Tony were driving west again away from Vero Beach on the same road they had come into town on the night before, the same road where they had been directed by Gore to begin their hunt for his hidden stash.

"We've got to be doing something wrong," Al said. "There aren't that many roads leading into this town. Jones Road has to be around here somewhere according to his map. Once we find it, we can find his stash."

Tony said, "So is this the same highway Gore used when he kid-napped Kaye Daley in his truck?"

"Yes," Al said. "We're on the same road."

Tony was quiet, thinking. "What did she feel like when she was hand-cuffed and riding with him? Do you think she knew in her gut he was going to rape and murder her—that she'd never see her kids again?"

"I'm sure she was terrified."

When they reached the same dirt road where they had turned the night before and ended up stuck at dead ends, Al parked the SUV on the side of the blacktop. Once again he consulted Gore's hand-drawn map and instructions.

As he studied it, he suddenly realized that he'd made a critical mis-take. Gore had drawn the map on a sheet of notebook paper and marked the directions with the traditional N, S, E, W, indicating north, south, east, and west.

But Gore had put S at the top of the paper and N at the bottom, which is the opposite of how professional maps are drawn. Simply put, Al had turned north onto the dirt road that led into the orange grove last night, when he should have turned south, which is where Gore had indicated on the map that they should drive.

"We went the wrong direction!" he exclaimed.

There was a fruit stand across the road, so Tony and Al stopped there to ask its owner if he'd ever heard of Jones Road.

"You're on it," the man said.

Al pointed to a dirt road that ran south from the blacktop.

"That's it?"

"Yep, that's what old-timers call it."

From the fruit stand, they turned right onto Jones Road and began clocking the distance as directed. Gore had told them they would reach a narrow one-lane bridge during their route.

The SUV soon came to a slight rise that took them onto a one-lane bridge over an irrigation canal. From the center of the bridge, they could see miles of orange groves spread out before them—a forest of orange-speckled trees.

"It's just like he described!" Tony exclaimed. "This is the bridge Gore drove over with his victim handcuffed in his truck. We're seeing what they saw on that afternoon, what she saw during the final day of her life."

Al kept his eye on the SUV's odometer and at exactly the mileage point that Gore had given them, a clearing next to Jones Road appeared in a grove.

"There's the storage barn—the place where he told us they parked vehicles and stored chemicals!" Tony yelled.

The building was exactly as Gore had said it would be. They parked and hurried out of the SUV.

A trailer was near the building's most southern end.

"Do you think this is where Gore raped and tormented his victims?" Tony asked.

They rushed over to inspect it, taking turns pressing their faces against a grimy window. The trailer was filled with spraying equipment and looked small inside.

How much room did someone need to rape and torture a kidnap victim?

Both of them did a quick survey of the surrounding groves. A field worker was driving a tractor about three hundred yards away, spraying some sort of chemical onto tree branches. He was heading in the oppo-site direction and didn't appear to have noticed them.

Gore had chosen this location well. It could not be seen from the highway or from any houses. He would have been completely alone with his victims, and their cries for help would never have been heard.

Al checked Gore's map. The murderer had written that he'd buried his stash near the shed. He'd marked an X on the map, but the map was not drawn to scale and there was no way to determine how many feet they needed to pace from the shed before they began digging.

Al and Tony slowly walked to where they thought Gore had marked his X.

The area was overgrown with weeds. Tony kicked the brush aside and jabbed the shovel into the loose topsoil. He furiously began scooping up dirt. The afternoon sun was hot and soon he was sweating and winded. He hit a piece of plastic two feet down from the surface. Falling to his knees, he gently began removing it from the ground. It came up in pieces. Each worn plastic scrap was a few inches long.

"Is this it?" he asked, nervously.

Al examined the plastic and realized that he had no idea what something buried for nearly thirty years would look like if it had been exposed to water. Were these shreds all that remained of Gore's prized stash? Or were they simply discarded remnants from the lining of a bag of fertilizer or chemical spray? He wasn't sure.

Tony stopped digging.

"You want me to take a turn?" Al asked, figuring his son was tired. He reached for the shovel.

"No," Tony said. "I'm just not sure we should be doing this."

"What?" Al asked, clearly surprised.

They had been discussing Gore's stash ever since the murderer had mentioned it. They'd come to Florida to meet with him face-to-face, to get more details and then drive to Vero Beach to find his trophies. Unearthing them would be a huge coup. Tony would be a hero when he handed them over to local authorities. Al felt sure of it. This was Tony's moment to shine. The payoff. Why would he want to stop searching now?

"That woman—Daley," Tony said. "I can't get her out of my head. I can't get those two hitchhikers out of my head, either. Or that mother and daughter."

When he'd been exchanging letters with Gore, Tony had not paid attention to the victims. They'd been a series of written names without faces. Words in letters. The victims had been at the wrong spot at the wrong time and had met the wrong man.

It had been easy to dehumanize them.

But all of that changed when he and his father began retracing the murderer's bloody trail. Judith Kaye Daly seemed more real now. Paul and Bonnie Schwey, Daley's sister-in-law and husband, lived not far from the grove. Ralph Sexton's historic family was here, too, along with Lynn

Elliott's grieving parents. And so was Lynn's boyfriend, Tim Mccullers, still wanting revenge. Vero Beach was alive with memories of Gore's victims.

When Tony had received Gore's letter about how he had abducted, raped, and murdered Angelica Lavallee and Barbara Byer, he'd been spellbound. The graphic, violent description that Gore had written hadn't bothered him. But reading the letter to his father as they were searching for the orange grove had caused Tony to see the murders with fresh eyes. All of the horror had become much more real.

There was more at play than simple sadness for Gore's victims.

If the Polaroids existed, they would be evidence. There could be photos of cold-case victims—still unsolved disappearances. The stash might be the only clue left about their fates—the only evidence that could ever link Gore to the murders. Would Tony and Al be tampering with and possibly destroying evidence if they kept digging?

"I don't feel so well," Tony said.

"It's probably the heat," his dad said.

Al looked at Gore's map and then let his eyes rise up and again appraise their surroundings. An inch to the right, an inch to the left, and they would miss their mark. Now that the two of them were actually standing here, Al realized that uncovering Gore's stash without more precise instructions was going to require a miracle. They could dig for days and still miss it. They had 99 percent of the puzzle, but not the vital last percent that would solve it.

Had Gore known this all along?

"I don't think we're going to find it today," Al said, his voice filled with disappointment. "I think you're going to have to get Gore to send us more information. We know he's been telling you the truth so far. He led us right here. Everything he wrote was just like he said it would be. But we need more details."

"Are we going to give the map to the cops?"

They discussed it for five minutes and then discussed it more. They decided against it. Neither of them was ready to hand it over.

"I think you can get Gore to talk to you again," said Al. "We need to at least try. The stash has been here nearly thirty years. A few more months won't matter."

"If he doesn't tell me, we can tell the cops then and they can find it."

Al agreed. The police would have the manpower to stake off the area, much like an archaeologist, and patiently dig through the sand until they found it—if it still was here.

It made sense. Still, Tony was let down.

Al noticed that the field worker had reached the end of a row of orange trees in the adjoining grove and was turning the tractor around. He would now be working his way back toward them. They were trespassing. Tony was holding a shovel.

"We gotta go," Al said.

They climbed back into the SUV and drove onto Jones Road, heading north.

"I really believe it's buried back there," Al said.

"Me, too," Tony said.

"We'll come back the minute he tells us where to dig," Al promised.

When they reached Highway 60, Al turned left, heading west. They were bound for Orlando International Airport to catch a flight home.

Although they had done their best to convince themselves that they'd made the right decision, both felt bummed out.

Al said: "Tony, I'm proud of you."

"Why?"

"Because you didn't get upset when we didn't find it." Tony had thought about the victims. He'd considered the consequences of their actions. There was a time when Tony was not capable of that. He couldn't pack a suitcase for an overnight trip. He couldn't control his emotions because of his brain injury.

Because of the number of American soldiers coming back from fighting in the Middle East with traumatic brain injuries, scientists were spending more time studying TBIs. Doctors were now claiming that the brain, in some cases, could rewire itself. They called it neuroplasticity. Was it possible that Tony's brain was slowly finding tiny ways to repair some of the damage that it had suffered? Al hoped so.

The flight to Las Vegas departed as scheduled and Tony slept for most of it. He was awakened by the pilot's voice announcing they were a half hour away from landing.

"Thanks for doing this," he told his father.

"It was a good trip," Al replied.

Tony said, "The experts say serial killers are incapable of caring about other people and that is what you and Nick Ponzo told me—that I can't really be their best friend."

"That's right," Al said.

"Well, I think they're wrong."

Al braced himself. After everything that they'd seen, Al had hoped that Tony would realize that he had to make friends with people who were not serial killers. He'd hoped the trips to visit Shawcross, Metheny, and Gore would have shown his son how all three serial killers cared only about themselves. Their own wants, their own needs were paramount. It was likely that Shawcross had reinvented the past in his confessions. He lived in a world of his own fantasies. Metheny clearly enjoyed manipulating the police and others. He yearned for a spotlight, attention. Gore and serial killer Rogers had panicked when they'd realized that Tony and Al were hunting for their cold-case victims. When it came to putting themselves into jeopardy, suddenly Tony was no longer their friend.

What Al wanted Tony to understand from their trip was that none of the serial killers whom they'd visited had a moral center. They cared only about themselves. They lived in a world where there was no right or wrong, no morality or immorality. It was a world of moral weightlessness. There was only what each of them wanted, their own selfish needs, whatever those might be at the moment. Everyone else was a pawn, a prop, a puppet on a stage to satisfy whatever sick desires they felt at any given moment. They were predators. The rest of mankind were rabbits to be eaten.

"I used to think I was lucky because I got them to write to me," Tony said. "I used to think they were doing me a favor. I was proud to call them *my best friend*. But now I realize they are lucky because I am writing to them. I don't mean to sound stuck-up. It's just that, well, even the worst, most cold-blooded bastard doesn't want to be alone. He doesn't want to believe his life doesn't matter to someone—that no one cares whether he is dead or alive. Even if he is narcissistic and cold-blooded, he still needs another human being—because he is narcissistic and cold-blooded. He needs someone. Otherwise, he doesn't matter. What I mean is that I don't need them to be *my* best friends. I can have other friends. But they do need *me* to be *their* best friend because without me, they don't have an audience. Without me, they don't matter. I listen."

Al knew that his son's traumatic brain injury had damaged Tony's ability to do many things. But Al had never doubted his son's intelligence. Listening to him now, Al felt a sense of relief. Their trips had been well worth it.

It was late when they landed at McCarran International Airport. Tony went straight to bed. The next morning, he wrote to David Gore. He mailed the letter that same morning.

Now that they were back from Vero Beach, there was something else that needed to be done. A phone call had to be made.

39

Cancer had ravaged Sarah Twotrees for six months. That was a month longer than her oncologist had expected her to live after a hospital X-ray revealed a mass in her left lung. She was seventy-two and opted for only palliative care.

Keenly aware of her approaching death, Sarah lay in bed coughing and thinking about her life. She tried to focus on only the happy times and not her regrets. But there were more of them. The one that tore most at her heart was the disappearance of her only child, Rose.

From the moment Rose had entered the world screaming, mother and daughter had seemed at odds. The first sign was when Rose broke out in a rash from drinking Sarah's breast milk. Sarah's mother told her that Rose had bad blood. To many whites, an Indian was an Indian. But there were more than five hundred different tribes in the United States, and Sarah had married into a tribe that had been a historic enemy of her own. Cats and dogs.

The union had been cut short. Sarah's husband died when Rose was three. The child had no memory of him. The doctors told Sarah the last time that her husband was in the hospital that it was cirrhosis of the liver killing him. She was not surprised. She'd watched his eyes sink into his skull, his once muscular arms reduced to flab over bones.

As a toddler, Rose had always seemed in a rush to go somewhere else. Anywhere away. If Sarah turned her back, Rose ran. She'd throw tantrums. Bite and spit. Despite her mother's warnings about the dangers of alcohol, Rose began drinking at age eight. By her teens, Rose was getting drunk every weekend with friends. Sex came quickly. Shy and overweight, Rose suffered from low self-esteem, according to her public school teachers.

At home, Rose and Sarah constantly argued. When Rose was fifteen, her mother slapped her. Rose punched her mother in the face, giving her a black eye. Rose dropped out after ninth grade. She went to work cleaning motel rooms. The drinking grew worse. A couple of six-packs per night. It helped her sleep. Rose had a miscarriage, and that led to a truce between mother and daughter, but it didn't last.

When she turned eighteen, Rose moved in with a biker, ten years her senior. They rode on his Harley-Davidson to South Dakota for the Sturgis motorcycle rally. He was white and dealing drugs. A year after Rose met him, he got busted and went to prison. Rose moved back home. The bickering picked up where it had stopped. The next five years formed a vicious circle. Mother and daughter would argue. Sometimes they would get physical. Rose would leave, only to return out of necessity. Sarah would welcome her back and begin nagging her, mostly about her drinking. They would fight. Rose would leave. Boyfriends came and went. Rose spent nights in bars, drinking herself into a stupor.

When a childhood friend invited Rose to visit her in Washington, D.C., Sarah bought her daughter a bus ticket. Rose's friend had joined the military and was stationed at the Walter Reed Army Medical Center. Rose told her mother that if the visit went well, she might cut back on the booze. She might sign up for military service. Then she could go back to school. Maybe she could live in Washington, D.C.

But the visit had not gone well. Her friend was married, came home tired from work, and became short-tempered when Rose wanted to party every night.

After a few days, Rose decided to move on. Another girlfriend—Jessie Swimmer—lived in Fort Lauderdale. Rose called and invited herself for a visit. When she telephoned her mother and explained her plan, Sarah asked how Rose was going to afford the trip.

"I'll hitchhike," Rose said.

Her mother sent her a hundred dollars through Western Union and Rose promised to buy a bus ticket. She also promised to telephone when she got to Jessie's apartment. A week went by. Sarah waited, but there was no call. Finally, after ten days, Rose called from a pay phone. She was in Daytona Beach. Instead of buying a bus ticket, Rose had caught a ride with a trucker to Daytona and had checked into a cheap hotel to hang out at the beach for a few days. Getting rides was easy, Rose said. All a woman had to do was hang out at a truck stop and ask a driver where he was headed. Drivers were always eager for company, she explained.

Sarah got mad. She didn't think truckers gave women rides without getting something in return. She and Rose began arguing. Rose hung up. It was April 15, 1981. Tax day to most Americans. For Sarah the date would have a different meaning.

Sarah got a call five days after she heard from Rose. It was Jessie Swimmer in Fort Lauderdale. She wondered if Sarah knew where Rose was. Jessie said Rose had called her from Daytona Beach on the same night that Sarah had spoken to her. Rose had mentioned how she and her mother had argued. Rose said she planned to hitch a ride to Fort Lauderdale and would be there in a day or two. Now Jessie was worried.

Sarah didn't know what to do. She'd never traveled outside Minnesota. She didn't have much money. She called the Daytona Beach police department but when she explained that her daughter was in her twenties and mentioned their contentious relationship, the officer on the end of the phone line brushed her off without taking a report.

Sarah began calling Jessie each morning to see if Rose had arrived in Florida. She hadn't.

The National Crime Information Center (NCIC) hot files—reports of wanted persons; missing persons; and stolen vehicles, articles, guns, license plates, securities, and boats—were being reported at a rate of 300,000 per day in April 1981. That was nearly 10 million monthly. The number of missing persons that year exceeded 50,000. Nearly 140 per day. It was easy for Rose to be overlooked in those numbers. But not by her mother.

Each time Sarah's phone rang, she thought it might be Rose. Each time she heard a car drive by late at night, she wondered if it was her daughter coming home. She refused to give up hope. Some nights, she would imagine Rose living in Florida. Maybe she'd met a nice man. Maybe she'd stopped drinking. Maybe Rose had simply wanted to start over. Maybe she was a mother, too, now.

But deep down, Sarah didn't believe her maybes.

In January 1984, Sarah received a letter from Jessie. She had gotten married and moved to Miami. Inside the short note was a December 31, 1983, newspaper article that Jessie had clipped from the *Miami Herald*. It described how a serial killer had been attacking women hitchhiking along Interstate 95 near Vero Beach. That was two hours south of Daytona Beach along the route that Rose would have been taking to reach Fort Lauderdale. The article noted that authorities knew of at least six dead women, but thought there were more. The serial killer had admitted killing a mother and her daughter in February 1981 and had abducted another woman in July 1981. Rose had vanished in April 1981 and had been in the same vicinity as the serial killer. Was it possible that he had picked her up hitchhiking? That would explain why she hadn't called. It would explain what had happened to her.

Sarah read the serial killer's name in the newspaper article that Jessie mailed. David Gore. She would later recall that her fingers had started to shake when she first read it. "I felt something," she remembered. "Evil."

Sarah tucked the newspaper story into her Bible for safekeeping.

The years passed. Ten. Eventually twenty. Nothing from Rose. "The first couple of years, I cried at night. There was no peace in my life. I told myself I should have done something, stopped my daughter from going."

Over and over, Sarah replayed her last conversation with Rose. She begged God to forgive her for arguing so much with her only daughter.

In his letter to Tony, David Gore described how an Indian woman had ridden into town with a trucker but had stayed behind at a truck stop and had started frequenting a bar across the street. He'd targeted her because she was a drifter. Gore figured she would never be missed. The Indian woman and Gore had gotten drunk together and then he'd suggested they go to a different bar for a change of scenery. She'd passed out in his truck, so he'd cut off her clothes and raped her, and then when she began to stir, he'd sat on her chest and choked her to death. He'd scalped her and disposed of her body.

Despite all of the years that had passed, Sarah Twotrees recognized the name David Gore when she received a telephone call about the letter that the serial killer had sent to Tony. She listened closely while Gore's letter was read to her. Then she removed the yellowed *Miami Herald* newspaper story that Jessie Swimmer had mailed her in 1984. She took it from her Bible and examined it to make sure it was the same man.

"This Gore, did he ever mention Rose by name in his letters?" she asked.

"No, not by name. He just described how he had picked up an Indian girl in a bar near a truck stop after she'd been dropped off there by a trucker and then he killed her."

"He said she was small?"

"No, he said she was chubby. They got drunk together on the night he murdered her."

"When I first read that man's name, I think I knew then that he'd killed my Rose but I didn't want to believe it. That letter, it tells me it's true. I know she's dead."

Because her daughter's body was still missing, it was impossible to determine for certain if Rose was the Indian woman whom Gore had described in his letter. Gore had not mentioned a name. Most likely, he'd never bothered to learn it.

Everything about Gore meeting Rose that night was entirely circumstantial. For Sarah Twotrees, however, there was no coincidence.

"He did it," she said sadly.

"You can't be sure."

"I'm her mother. I feel it."

For the first time since Rose disappeared in 1981, Sarah said she felt a sense of calm. "When you read that letter—my daughter was telling me it was her. I think she sent me that message in that letter because she wanted me to know before I died."

Perhaps it was simply the final wishes of a cancer-stricken woman racked from years of guilt about her troubled relationship with her daughter. Perhaps it was an old woman's desperate desire for closure. Regardless, Sarah said: "I know now."

Sarah began to cry while still on the telephone, and within seconds, she was coughing.

"Thank you," she said, her voice coming between gasps for air. "Thank you for telling me what happened to my Rose."

Without waiting for a reply, Sarah continued, "Rose is in heaven. I'm going to be with Jesus and her soon. I can tell her I'm sorry. We will not argue now."

Four days later, Sarah Twotrees died in her sleep. A friend found Sarah's Bible next to her bed, but the *Miami Herald* article was no longer tucked inside it. Sarah had gotten her answer and thrown the article away.

PART FOUR

a new pen pal

The dead cannot cry out for justice. It is the duty of the living to do so for them.

—Lois McMaster Bujold, American novelist

40

June 13, 1984
Anchorage, Alaska

It was an uneventful night on the tenderloin strip in downtown Anchorage. Cindy Paulson, a nineteen-year-old prostitute, was frustrated. She'd moved north from Seattle after hearing stories about how much money topless dancers and hookers earned because of a scarcity of women here—at least, women willing to spread their legs for cash.

She'd not had a single john approach her all evening.

Around midnight, a car eased to the curb.

"Wanna date?" she asked the driver.

They settled on two hundred dollars for a blow job in his car.

"Pull into that parking lot," Paulson told him after they'd driven a few blocks. It was a safe area she often used. He parked and lowered the driver's seat and she went to work. Just as she was about to finish, he ran his fingers through her hair. She didn't think anything of it until he grabbed a handful and jerked her head back. At exactly the same moment, he pointed a .357 Magnum handgun at her face.

"You'll do exactly what I say," he said. "I know what I'm doing . . . I've done this before . . ." She noticed he was stuttering.

Releasing his grip, he expertly shackled her wrists with handcuffs and drove north toward Muldoon, an upper-class neighborhood. "We're going to my house," he announced. As they passed Merrill Field, an airport favored by locals, he added, "I'm a pilot, you know." It was as if he was trying to impress her.

Paulson spotted a rack of caribou antlers above the double garage doors when her kidnapper pulled into a driveway. Forced inside at gunpoint, she was led into the house's den. Animal heads jutted from the walls. A towering, stuffed grizzly bear stood upright in a corner. Her kidnapper attached a leather collar to her neck and chained it to a hook on a ceiling beam. He removed her pants and raped her. Several minutes later, he raped her anally. After he was done, he walked over to a nearby sofa, leaving her still standing and chained.

"I need to pee," she said.

He let out a loud groan, clearly annoyed, and then fetched her a towel. Throwing it at her feet, he said, "Pee in that" and returned to the sofa for a power nap.

When he woke up, he told her that he had brought other women to his den for sex—at least seven others. He'd kept some as long as a week. He'd flown the really good ones to a cabin that he owned in the mountains. Taking them there was like a sex vacation for him—and for them, if they relaxed and enjoyed it. The cabin was in a remote area. He'd built it himself and he didn't mind taking off the women's handcuffs there. The area was so remote that there was nowhere to escape.

The man freed the chain from Paulson's neck and led her to a trophy case. He told her to look at the awards that he'd won for shooting wild animals. He was especially proud of the big-game trophy that he'd been awarded for bagging a horned Dall sheep. It was a world record, he boasted. No one had shot a bigger sheep. No one in the entire world.

She saw his name engraved on the trophy and realized that he didn't seem worried that she would later be able to identify him. After all, he'd brought her to his house. That frightened her. "He's going to kill me," she thought.

"Time for a trip," he declared. She'd passed his sex test. He was taking her to his remote hunting cabin in his private airplane.

Without removing her handcuffs, he led her to his car, forced her into the backseat, and tossed a blanket over her. "Stay down," he ordered.

A few minutes later, he parked the car and said, "I'm going to load my airplane. If you try anything, I'll kill you!"

As soon as she heard him walking away on the gravel, she peeked out from under the blanket. They were at Merrill Field. Crawling over the front seat, she spotted him loading supplies into a nearby airplane. She shoved open the driver's-side door and hit the ground running.

"Stop, bitch!" he yelled. "Stop or I'll kill you!"

Paulson ran as fast as she could go.

"Help me!" she screamed.

Robert Yount was driving to work when he saw Paulson running barefoot from the airfield. He pulled over and she leaped into the front seat of his truck.

"Go! Go!" she yelled. "He's chasing me!"

Yount drove to a nearby motel, where they called the police. Paulson was still handcuffed when Anchorage Police Officer Gregg Baker arrived at the Big Timber Motel. Amid sobs, she told him about the kidnapping and rape.

A security guard at the airport had seen Paulson fleeing and had written down the license number of her attacker's car when he'd sped away, according to *Fair Game*, a book written by Bernard DuClos. The car's license plate and registration numbers painted on an airplane at Merrill Field—a plane that Paulson later pointed out—both were registered to Robert C. Hansen, a local bakery shop owner and married father of two.

Forty-four-year-old Robert Hansen seemed an unlikely suspect. He was a churchgoer, a devoted father, and well respected by employees at the bakery. He was admired in Alaskan hunting circles for his shooting skills.

When police confronted him that night at his house, Hansen offered them an ironclad alibi. The small-framed man, who had adult acne, said he'd been out drinking with two friends. His wife and children were on a family vacation in Europe, which is why he'd been partying with his buddies. When contacted, both friends backed up his story.

It was their word against the accusations of a known prostitute.

"You can't rape a prostitute, can you?" Hansen jokingly asked detectives.

A few days later, Paulson and her boyfriend left town. The case was shelved without Hansen's being charged.

Police did, however, forward a copy of Paulson's complaint to a special Alaska State Troopers task force that was investigating the disappearance of five Anchorage women. All of them had worked in the tenderloin as topless dancers or prostitutes. Two of the women had been found shot to death with a high-powered rifle favored by sportsmen. They had been buried in shallow graves in the rugged Knik River valley, a vast hunting region.

The task force didn't pay much attention to Paulson's complaint until FBI forensic profiler John Douglas joined the investigation. By that time, two more women's bodies had been discovered in the Knik River valley and Alaskan officials suspected they were dealing with a serial killer.

Douglas didn't look at the state troopers' list of potential suspects.

Instead he studied the evidence. On that basis, he told investigators to look for a white male in his forties, who owned his own business, was married, probably had children, and more than likely had a stutter. He also predicted that the killer would have collected "trophies" to remind him of the pleasure he'd received by murdering his victims.

Douglas's forensic profile described Hansen perfectly—down to his stutter—and when investigators began taking a closer look into Hansen's past, they found a series of disturbing incidents almost identical to the Paulson abduction and rape. Records showed that several prostitutes had accused Hansen of sexual assault but no formal charges had ever been filed. Either the women were scared and had failed to follow through with the police or they'd not been taken seriously because they were hookers.

Almost entirely on the basis of Douglas's profile, the task force persuaded a judge to issue search warrants for Hansen's bakery, house, airplane, and car. It was the first time in history that search warrants had been issued because of similarities between a suspect and an FBI forensic profile.

The state troopers took another piece of advice from profiler Douglas. Before they brought Hansen in for questioning, they staged the interrogation room with large photographs of the four murder victims and maps that showed where their bodies had been found. They wanted Hansen to believe they had overwhelming evidence against him.

But Hansen didn't fall for it.

He proved unflappable during questioning. Meanwhile, the searches at his home and bakery weren't turning up anything incriminating. It seemed as if Hansen was going to walk away free.

And then investigators caught a break.

A state trooper climbed into the attic at Hansen's house and noticed that some of the insulation strips were off-kilter. Someone had moved them. Lifting up one of the paper-backed strips, he found several rifles. One was a .223-caliber Ruger Mini-14 rifle, the same type the murderer had used to shoot his victims.

When the trooper looked under another strip, he discovered a black garbage bag. Inside he found women's jewelry and driver's licenses. Several of the items had been taken from the four women whose bodies had been discovered buried in the Knik River valley. Also in the bottom of the bag were newspaper clippings about the unsolved murders and missing women.

The trooper had found Robert Hansen's "trophies."

Investigators knew Hansen was their serial killer.

In addition to the rifles and garbage bag, they found an aerial map hidden behind the headboard of his bed. It had been taped there for easy access. Someone had marked the map with twenty-one X's that pinpointed exact locations in the Knik River valley. Initially, the investigators assumed the X's were spots where Hansen had shot some of the wild animals whose heads were proudly on display in his den.

But when they compared the X's on the map with the four locations where they had found murdered women, they matched. The X's were not big-game trophies. They were where he'd shot and buried his victims.

Faced with overwhelming evidence, Hansen's attorney negotiated a plea deal for his client. In return for Hansen's cooperation, prosecutors agreed not to charge him with any additional murders and to recommend that he receive the equivalent of a life sentence—461 years in prison without the possibly of parole.

As soon as the deal was signed, Hansen gleefully admitted that he had spent more than a decade abducting women in the tenderloin and murdering them because they were transients. Although he wouldn't admit it directly, he hinted that he had flown his victims in his private airplane into isolated areas of the Knik River valley. He'd given them a head start and then hunted them as human prey.

Because it was winter, the ground in the valley was frozen and covered with four feet of snow, making it impossible to recover the bodies. Just the same, troopers flew Hansen in a state helicopter to each of the X's on his map.

Hansen became visibly excited each time the chopper landed at a grave site. He shuffled over the deep snow on snowshoes and fell to his knees, digging through the powder with his hands. His behavior was so disturbing that troopers decided never to take him on future searches because the trips appeared to sexually arouse him.

When the ground thawed that spring, troopers were able to recover eleven more bodies. They were added to the four already found. Investigators speculated that the final six X's on his map marked the burial sites of women whose corpses either had been eaten by animals or were buried near where Hansen had taken investigators but not exactly in the spot that he'd pinpointed.

Despite repeated attempts by reporters and authors, Hansen refused to discuss his killing spree. Because he had never been put on trial, the public had never heard directly from him about what motivated him to hunt women and kill them.

This is why Tony had put Hansen on a short list of infamous serial killers to whom he wanted to write. He'd sent the killer several letters, but had not gotten a response.

And then one day when Tony drove to his private mailbox, he found a letter with an Alaskan postmark. Tony didn't recognize the prison inmate's name written in the return address spot.

He hurried home and opened the note with his parents.

Dear Anthony,

I'm Robert Hansen's roommate. He doesn't write many people, just family. He mostly rips up all the pen pal letters he gets or gives them to me. . . . He did read your letter but he thinks you might be the press or undercover FBI, which he distrusts. To be honest with you, I don't blame him. The press has hurt him and me. We have no way of knowing who is who from in here . . . I've been his roommate for seven years . . . I'm fifty years old and I can write to you if you want . . . We can be pen pals.
Sincerely, "Bryan Tompkins"

41

Tony read everything he could about "Bryan Tompkins." Although the Alaskan convict was not a serial killer, he was serving a ninety-nine-year prison sentence for murder. He'd fatally shot a homeowner during a burglary. Tompkins had a long criminal record and had run with outlaw motorcycle gangs.

Enthused, Tony replied:

> Dear Bryan,
> . . . I will be the best pen pal you have ever dreamed of having. I'm smart, funny and have the best stories to share with you about my time being a high roller in the city that never sleeps . . .

Tompkins answered quickly.

> *Dear Tony,*
> *Robert has a cold . . . He sleeps all the time. He's not in good health . . . As I lie here in my cell, I wonder why you would want to write to him or anyone in prison? You see, 95 percent of the prisoners here are losers. They brag, they lie, and they're not interested in changing . . . I live with these assholes, eat with them, walk in the yard with them, so I always wonder why someone outside would bother to contact them.*

As Tony had done in his previous pen pal relationships, he described his WaveRunner accident, his traumatic brain injury, and his near-death experience. He wrote about how he sometimes erupted into uncontrollable rages. He talked about his medications and how he was trying to find a useful purpose in life.

Tompkins seemed genuinely touched. In his letters, he shared his own troubled history, often decorating the pages with cleverly drawn cartoons.

Tompkins had grown up in a remote area of New York state along the Canadian border. His family lived in a "tar paper shack" without electricity or running water. His father received a monthly subsistence check because he was a Native American. That payment and whatever the family could catch fishing or hunting kept them afloat. His father was a mean drunk who suspected Tompkins was not really his son. "My mother had cheated on him," Tompkins wrote, "and he made me pay for that." Beatings were frequent. Once while drunk, his father fired at his son's feet to make him dance, just like in old western movies.

> *I tried to take my life when I was eight years old. I took a bottle of pills. My father and mother took me to a hospital and they pumped my stomach. When the doctor got into it with my father, my father hit him and broke his nose. Five state troopers came to our house to arrest him. They knew he had guns so they called into the house. All of us kids had to come outside with our hands up. I wanted to tell them where he was hiding, but I didn't say a word.*

His father committed suicide when Tompkins was ten. "No loss to me," he wrote. One of his brothers murdered their grandmother. Another brother was arrested for child molestation. A third was diagnosed with a severe mental illness. Meanwhile, Tompkins replaced his father as the family drunk.

> *At age ten, I could drink a full bottle of whiskey—any make— and not pass out. At age 15, I ran away and began hanging out with some hippies and then some bikers and getting into trouble with drugs, robberies and burglaries . . . Society told me I was a worthless piece of shit and I proved society right.*

Tompkins moved into an apartment with an older woman who sold drugs. He spent his afternoons breaking into houses and his nights getting high. A friend stole a cache of guns, so Tompkins accompanied him to New York City to sell them. They were arrested and Tompkins was jailed for the first time. When he got out, he bummed around the country, often burglarizing houses. He began running with a motorcycle gang and one night watched eight men gang-rape a teenage girl. "When they passed out, I cut that girl loose. She went to the cops and told them about everyone but me." Afraid of retaliation from the gang, Tompkins fled to Alaska, where he continued burglarizing houses and getting drunk and high.

Tompkins was committing a burglary when the homeowner walked in on him. The two men exchanged gunfire. Tompkins wasn't wounded but the owner was fatally shot. Tompkins fled but was caught and sent to prison a short time later.

Tompkins had done fifteen years in prison when he began corresponding with Tony. He'd spent the last seven sharing a cell with Hansen in the Spring Creek Correctional Center, a five-hundred-inmate maximum security prison in Seward, Alaska.

Tompkins said that he hadn't trusted Hansen when they first became cellmates. And the serial killer had not trusted him.

> *In here, he's a celebrity. People write to him all the time. They try to get close to him. But you can't trust anyone in our position, not even outsiders. Once a prisoner friend of ours got a pen pal request from this woman. They start writing and pouring out their hearts to each other and this prisoner falls in love and a year later, he proposes and this woman comes to visit him so they can be married. That's when he found out the girl was a he/she— really a guy. People don't think of us prisoners getting fucked over a lot in here by outsiders, but we do.*

Over time, the two cellmates let down their guard. They became close—or as close as a murderer and serial killer can become in prison.

> *Hansen really liked hearing stories about rape. I told him about this 18 year old chick, a hard body from hell. She was an old lady in the Hells Angels and she dressed up like a nurse and told me that she wanted me to come through the window in her apartment and rape her. She said it was the only way that she could get off. I said, "Sure, why the hell not?" I was supposed to come through the window and hide behind a door, then she would come in and turn on the lights and I would grab her from the back, pull her hair, rip her dress off and rape her. Fuck, I*

wanted to do her, but it took three tries. The first try, I couldn't stop laughing. I was all coked up on drugs and it was fucking funny. That pissed her off. The second time, the window came down and hit me on the head when I was going through it. She got mad because I didn't pull her hair and I couldn't get her dress to rip. The third time, I was so pissed, I just went in and fucked her. Now, I hear later that this was all a scam being run by the Angels. They had a video camera in there and they would get it all on tape. The FBI raided the place and found the tapes. The Angels either used them to blackmail some dumb ass or sold them as sex tapes. . . . When I told Robert that story, he really liked it.

Tompkins and Tony exchanged weekly letters for six months. By that time, Tony had mentioned how he thought at one time that he might be a serial killer because of his traumatic brain injury.

Tompkins replied with a confession of his own.

Dear Tony,

I'm going to tell you something, I've never told anyone. I wanted to kill my father from about age six. I did try once when he was drunk and passed out, but failed. I remember thinking I might be a serial killer, capable of doing it. But I kept my serial killing urge in check, but it was always there in the back of my hairy brain. After I killed that man in that burglary, I almost lost it. I felt that urge to kill come up from the darkness and become even stronger. The cops caught me, of course, before I acted again on it. But I felt it. I truly did. I think when you murder someone; you reach a point where you decide—should I stop, or should I do it again and then maybe again. Once you do it, it becomes easier.

After being roommates for about a year, I told Hansen about that killing urge and I believe he took a liking to me because he could feel I had this in me, just like he had it in him. But what he didn't know was I kept mine in check. I refused to fall in love with killing. He told me that he didn't keep his in check. After that first time, he had to keep doing it. It became a ritual to him—the hunt, the abduction, the rape, and then he let them women go and got to hunt them down and kill them. It was that tremendous feeling of power, control. The more we talked about it, the more I was glad that I had never done what he did. Take that step, Tony, and you have a tough time coming back. But I never let on to him about how I kept my urges under control because I felt it was a bond between us.

42

Had Robert Hansen ever talked about unsolved murders?

Tony wanted to know.

In his reply, Tompkins wrote that he'd never been a "rat." In prison, snitches got themselves killed. He added that Hansen, in particular, was not someone to trifle with—even in prison.

Hansen did try to cut me once. I'm not sure if he was joking . . . I had dumped water on him as a joke. He got mad and grabbed me around the neck and he had a pen in his other hand and he tried to stick it in my ear, but I broke away from him. He had this odd look on his face and then he said, "I was just fooling" but I could see that he wasn't. After that, I never joked with him.

Tony let the matter drop. Instead, he and Tompkins chitchatted in their letters about other subjects. As with his other prison pen pals, Tony asked Tompkins about his crimes.

Dear Tony,

. . . I learned not to cry at an early age and I learned to not have feelings or show them. Most of all, I learned to not trust anyone. Ever. Now at age 50, I'm just starting to get some kindness in my heart, some feelings for others. I lived a fast, hard life—guns, drugs, fast women, you name it. I was in-and-out of jails and prisons. But in these past years, I've come to realize that if I ever want to be free again, I have to change. Not just say that I am changing but to really change. I believe a person can change if he wants to change. It's all in one's hand. I never had a plan in my life and then I killed a man. I was in the wrong. But I can't go back and change that. All I can change is who I am today. I am getting my shit together, Tony. I swear it. And you have helped

me believe that I can actually change. You are dealing with a brain injury. And you have a good life. I never had anyone like you encourage me. I have never had anyone call me a friend or trust me like you have. You have helped me think of myself as someone who matters. I now realize I am an artist. I have a gift. I'm not a fucking, hard ass biker anymore. I'm not a drug dealer anymore. I am not a burglar anymore. I'm not a worthless piece of shit like I was told I was. I can be someone more. I am someone more. I've changed so much since I've been in here and met you that I don't like dealing with my old friends anymore. I'm not the same person I was. Life is important to me now. Before I lived on the edge, without any goals or plans or caring about anyone else. But not anymore . . . Thank you for believing in me!

Not long after that, Tony received a letter from Tompkins with a surprising revelation. Tompkins had been thinking about Tony's interest in cold-case murders and how Tony wanted to help the families of victims. He'd also been thinking about Robert Hansen.

"I've decided to talk to the Big Indians," Tompkins wrote. Tony knew from previous letters that "the Big Indians" was the term Tompkins used to refer to the FBI.

Dear Tony,

    . . . As I told you, Hansen is very private and it took me hours and hours of talking to get him to trust me. He only opened up after I told him about how I wanted to kill cops, blacks, and others. He only opened up after I told him about how I had the same urges as him. I would make-up shit, and he would slowly open up and talk too. He would tell me stories. One thing I noticed over the years is that his stories never changed. Most prisoners' stories change. That's because they are lying. They want to be somebody so they make up shit. After a time, they start believing their own lies, but Hansen's stories always stay the same and that makes me believe they are true and very scary.

    Tony, I have been in that deep dark place that Hansen lives in . . . and it's a fearful place. It is as real as any hell. Matter of fact, Hansen makes Hell look good. I'm damn well ready to never be his roommate ever again. But I need to hold out a little more . . . I need a bit more information from Hansen before I talk to the Big Indians. . . .

Tompkins asked Tony for help.

I need information about a place up in Prince William Sound. A place called Icy Bay. I'm not sure if you can pull up anything on Icy Bay on your computer, but it is off the Chenega Glacier. I'm only interested in Icy Bay because my cellmate has told me some interesting things about what he did there.

. . . I don't blame you for not wanting to get mixed up in this, but if you can send me geological information, I'd appreciate it. I'm trying to find an exact location that Hansen mentioned to me once. Thank you my friend.

Tony found Chenega Bay in Prince William Sound when he checked maps on the Internet. Chenega Bay was a Native village with a population of only seventy. Icy Bay was near it and it looked completely isolated. It was one of those Alaskan areas best reached by airplane. A pilot could fly into the area, land on the snow-packed ground or a frozen lake, and do whatever he wished without being seen—including hunting women. Was this where Robert Hansen had taken victims who were still unknown to the police today?

Tony printed copies of the maps that Tompkins had requested and mailed them to him.

"I think he's going to tell the FBI where Hansen hid some cold-case bodies," an excited Tony told Al.

Tony could hardly wait for his next letter. When it arrived, it contained troubling news.

43

Bryan Tompkins was in serious trouble.

He had been removed from the cell that he'd shared with Robert Hansen. Tompkins was now locked in a one-man cell inside the "prison inside the prison"—a segregated cell block cut off from the general prisoner population. It was where inmates who were being punished were kept. It also was where sexual perverts and snitches were housed away from other prisoners who wanted them dead. It was not a good place to be.

But Tompkins had asked prison officials to put him there. If they hadn't, he felt sure he would have been the serial killer's next victim.

In his letter, Tompkins wrote that his troubles had started shortly after he asked prison officials to contact the FBI. He planned to tell federal agents about two murders that Hansen had committed in the 1970s. He planned to tell the FBI where the serial killer had disposed of the women's bodies. "But I blew it," Tompkins wrote.

Instead of being straightforward, Tompkins had tried to cut a deal. He'd demanded that the FBI get his ninety-nine-year prison sentence reduced in exchange for what he knew.

> *I wanted a time cut. Whenever you do something for selfish reasons, it can come back and kick you in the ass and I have been kicked. Lesson learned . . . The bottom line is FBI agent didn't believe me . . . It was my fault because I held back information. I didn't tell him what I really had because I wanted to make that deal first. Now it is too late . . .*

After the FBI agent left the prison, rumors began to swirl.

> *Word spread I was talking—I was a snitching to the FBI. Someone leaked it. A friend who watches TV in the cellblock with Hansen took me aside. He warned me that Hansen was being*

told I was a snitch. Hansen had told me if I ever talked to anyone about him or what he told me, he would kill me . . .

I could feel something was wrong. Robert also was acting odd in our cell . . . I didn't want to take that chance . . . So I asked them to lock me up. Of course, as soon as I did, everyone knew I was a snitch. Going into segregation means you're a snitch.

Tompkins wrote that Hansen had saved more than eight thousand dollars over the years from cutting hair inside the prison. That was more than enough to pay for a "hit" in the segregation unit. Hansen could pay another prisoner to demand that he, too, be put into segregation. Once inside, that inmate could find a way to murder Tompkins. "It happens in these places. No one is really ever safe."

Tompkins needed Tony's help. He asked if Tony could help him locate the families of two women whom Hansen had slaughtered nearly forty years ago.

Now I realize this information that I got from him shouldn't have been about me. It should be about those dead girls. I want to help their families now. I blew it with the FBI. But those dead girls shouldn't be punished because of my dumb move. What I did was wrong, but I just hate being here. I am truly a changed person and I spent seven years listening to that sick son-of-a-bitch talking. I thought I deserved something in return and my ego got involved. I should have just told the Big Indians what I knew.

In his answer, Tony wrote that Tompkins would have to tell him more about the Alaskan serial killer's unsolved murders if he was going to help.

Dear Tony,

From now on, only refer to Hansen as "the worm" so people will not know who we are discussing. I don't trust prison officials here. I think they leaked the information about my meeting with the FBI.

I've always had this uncanny way of getting along with other criminals . . . but getting into the worm's dark side was difficult. The worm is the most twisted person I've ever gotten close too.

Let me tell you a little about how I got the worm to trust me.

He was real suspicious at first and left booby traps in our cell . . . One day he was feeling sick and went to medical clinic, I put a piece of paper over the window on the cell door. You can do that if you're using the toilet. I went to check Hansen's locker. I noticed he left pieces of paper on the top. He'd arranged the paper so it would fall if the locker door was opened. I carefully removed the paper, remembering exactly where it was, and how it was put there, and then I opened the locker and saw that he had another booby-trap. There were little pieces of cookie crumbs on this folder. I used a short piece of paper to remove three crumbs, re-membering where they were and how they laid on the folder and then I checked his papers. I put it all back and the worm comes back in about a half hour. I pretended I was sleeping and even snored a little bit to fool him. He watches me for a time to make sure I am really asleep. Sometimes, he even made fast movement in the air—like he was going to hit me—to see if I'm really sleep-ing. I never blinked and then he looked at the locker, checks the paper by opening the door and watching the paper fall. Then he looks at the crumbs . . . anyway I wanted you to know it wasn't easy doing what I did. It was a pain in the ass. . . . Tony, I want to help these girls' families. I believe what the worm told me is true . . . I used to keep a small piece of paper inside my Alcohol-ics Anonymous notebook and I would hide the pen under my leg when I was lying in my bunk and I would sneak out the pen and write notes about what he told me when we talked.

. . . It was interesting watching him when I got him to finally discuss his crimes. The first thing I noticed was his tongue dart-ing in-and-out of his mouth. His eyes would get glazed over when he talked. Most times, he would catch himself and snap out of it, but other times you could tell he was off some other place, reliv-ing it. A place you didn't want to be in. But he had this charm about him . . .

Continuing, Tompkins wrote:

. . . It's important that you know what I have learned in case something happens to me. As far as what Robert Hansen told me, well, we talked a lot about his crimes. He told me that he

abducted two girls both from Seward. They never came back and
their bodies have never been found . . . The girls were [Megan]
Emerick, age seventeen, who disappeared on July 7, 1973 and
Mary K. Thill, age 23, who disappeared in 1975 . . .

Tony searched the Internet for information about both girls. He
found plenty.

Megan Emerick moved from Delta Junction, Alaska, population nine
hundred, to Seward after she'd completed high school. She'd enrolled
in a two-year trade school there and was living on the campus of the
Seward Skills Center when she'd disappeared. Megan had done her
laundry in the girls' dormitory that morning and then started walking
downtown for lunch. That was the last time anyone saw her.

Mary Kay Thill was married and known in Seward for her wavy red
hair and pink-framed eyeglasses. She'd disappeared after several of her
friends had dropped her off in the same vicinity of Seward where Emerick had gone missing two years earlier.

The Seward police had questioned both girls' families and friends.
They'd given polygraph exams to potential suspects. But no one had a
clue about what might have happened to the girls until Robert Hansen
was caught in 1983.

The Alaska State Troopers had long suspected that Hansen had abducted, raped, and murdered more women than the ones he'd admitted.
They suspected that he'd started his killing spree in the early 1970s and
had killed women who were not prostitutes. Hansen had denied it.

"He tried to make us think that he had some kind of moral code,"
Glenn Flothe, the Alaska state trooper who oversaw the Hansen investigation, told a newspaper reporter. "He wanted us to believe he only
raped and killed prostitutes."

But Flothe thought otherwise—and with good reason.

Several women had come forward after Hansen was arrested and accused him of rape. None of these women were prostitutes. The women
had given several reasons for not reporting the attacks earlier. Some said
they had been afraid of Hansen. Others had been married when they'd
gone out on dates with him. Detectives theorized that Hansen had first
started raping women possibly as early as the 1960s. At some point, he'd
started committing murder, too.

But when?

Detectives knew he'd started killing prostitutes in the mid-1970s. That was when workers began building the Alaska Pipeline and women seeking easy money had poured into the state. But how many women had Hansen murdered before he'd set his sights exclusively on street-walkers?

Neither of the women who disappeared in Seward was a prostitute, and investigators believed that Emerick had been one of Hansen's first victims. He was a suspect in both the Emerick and Thill cases because detectives knew that he had been in Seward when the women vanished. The serial killer kept his fishing boat, a thirty-six-foot Chris-Craft, called the *Christy M.*, moored at the Seward dock. It was about a two-and-a-half-hour drive from Hansen's home in Anchorage. Hansen had been in Seward taking part in Independence Day festivities on July 7, 1973, when Emerick disappeared and on July 5, 1975, when Thill went missing.

Investigators also had learned that Hansen had targeted women when he'd visited Seward. In 1980, Hansen was working on his boat at the Seward dock when Joanne Messina walked by. He'd chased after her and invited her to dinner. They'd been having a nice meal together, Hansen later confessed, until she'd mentioned that she'd recently lost her job at a canning factory and was broke. Hansen told investigators that he'd gotten angry. He'd felt that she'd accepted his dinner invitation only because she planned to ask him later that night for money in return for sex. He considered her a prostitute. When they left the restaurant, Hansen drove her to the outskirts of town and fatally shot her, dumping her body beside the highway.

Clearly, Hansen had no qualms about targeting women in Seward.

In his letter to Tony, Tompkins explained that he'd asked Tony in an earlier letter for information about Icy Bay because that is where Hansen had taken Emerick and Thill after he'd abducted them.

> *I got the worm to tell me about this cabin he built. . . . Now Tony, we're talking about a cabin that is isolated. There is no way to find this cabin unless you know exactly where it is . . . Anyway; I believe I can find it being all the details I have gotten from the worm. I even have a list of firearms hidden in that cabin and stuff he collected over the years . . . Can you help me find these girls'*

relatives or get someone else, besides the FBI, to investigate their
cases? Please Tony, help me!

Tony had to do something. He looked up the telephone number of
the Seward, Alaska, Police Department on the Internet, picked up his
bedroom phone, and called.

Sheila Squires, the department's dispatch supervisor, answered.

44

"I have information about two girls from Seward who Robert Hansen raped and murdered," Tony announced. "Their names are Megan Emerick and Mary Thill, and I know someone who can tell you where they're buried."

"Who are you?" Sheila Squires asked suspiciously.

Tony told her about his correspondence with Bryan Tompkins.

"He's in the Seward prison and he's afraid Hansen is going to pay someone to kill him," Tony said. "He wants to talk to someone who's in law enforcement."

Like most other longtime Alaskans, Squires knew about the serial killer. She'd also heard about Megan Emerick and Mary Thill. In Seward, population three thousand, young women who disappeared under mysterious circumstances were not easily forgotten—especially by the police.

At first, Squires thought Tony was a prankster, until he mentioned that Hansen had a secret cabin hidden in the wilderness. That was new information. She wrote down Tony's contact information and went to see her boss, Police Chief Tom Clemons.

Clemons was a retired Alaska state trooper, with thirty-one years' experience, when he decided to go back to work as Seward's chief in 2003. He had ten uniformed patrol officers and another dozen nonuniformed employees under his command. The nonuniformed officers worked as dispatchers for the police, fire, and emergency services, and ran the town jail.

Despite its small size, Seward's police force kept busy. The town had been founded on Resurrection Bay as a military port because the bay was one of the few in Alaska that remained ice-free year-round. Over the years, Seward had become the final seaport for northbound cruise ships and the starting point for the Alaska Railroad. The Seward Highway took travelers north 125 miles to Anchorage. Each year, thousands of tourists, whom the locals called "outsiders," arrived in the picturesque town. It wasn't unusual during the summer for five or six cruise ships to be docked there. On Fourth of July weekends, hundreds of runners piled into Seward to compete in the Mount Marathon Race. Competitors ran up a 3,022-foot peak.

Although Squires was not a uniformed officer who could issue summonses or make arrests, she'd served a stint in the British Army as a military police investigator before arriving in Seward with her husband in 1981. More important, she had a soft spot for missing children. She'd taken a course taught by the National Center for Missing and Exploited Children (NCMEC) in Arlington, Virginia, and been shocked to learn how vulnerable teenagers, especially young, naive girls, are to predators.

"I'd like to check into what this guy in Las Vegas is saying," Squires told Chief Clemons. "He sounded very serious."

"Go for it," Clemons said, "but I'm not going to assign anybody officially to this because you're working on speculation."

Squires would have to pursue the cold case on her own time.

Although Megan Emerick and Mary Thill had both vanished in Seward, the two cases had been handled by two different agencies. The Seward police had taken charge of the Emerick case. The Alaska State Troopers were in charge of the Thill investigation.

From an old file box, Squires pulled the department's 1973 incident report about Emerick. It was a scant two pages long and contained few details. Emerick's roommate at the trade school had waited three days before reporting her missing. She'd mistakenly thought Emerick had gone home to visit her parents during the Fourth of July holiday.

After reading the officer's missing persons report, Squires telephoned the Spring Creek Correctional Center, located four miles outside Seward, and told officials there that she wanted to speak to inmate Bryan Tompkins. They agreed to bring him to a telephone. They chatted for about fifteen minutes. Squires thought Tompkins was respectful, eager to help, and, most important, believable. She also wrote in her notes that he had not asked for anything in return for his help.

Squires called Tony in Las Vegas and asked if he would send her copies of letters that Tompkins had written to him about the two missing girls and Hansen. She told him that she had talked on the phone with Tompkins and he had been okay with it. When a thick envelope of letters arrived a few days later, Squires read through them and knocked on Chief Clemons's door once again.

"I think what he is saying about Hansen seems credible," Squires reported.

Whether Tompkins could actually lead them to the two dead girls' bones was impossible to know. But Squires felt strongly that the prisoner's claims about the serial killer needed further investigation.

"If someone I loved was missing, I wouldn't care how long ago she had disappeared. I'd still want her case investigated," she said. "We owe the family that much. We owe Megan Emerick that much."

Chief Clemons agreed, but he didn't have any patrol officers to spare, especially to investigate a cold case that was now nearly forty years old. He wasn't even sure if any of Emerick's relatives were still alive. While she'd been a student at the Seward trade school, no one in town had really known her.

"I have an idea," Squires said. While she'd been undergoing her training at the NCMEC, she'd learned about a program called Project ALERT. That acronym stood for America's Law Enforcement Retiree Team. It was a squad of more than 170 retired federal, state, and local law enforcement officers who volunteered their time without charge to police departments, such as Seward's. The retired officers were not allowed to make arrests, but they were veteran detectives chosen specifically because of their skill at searching for missing persons. Because Megan Emerick was seventeen when she'd vanished, Squires thought Emerick might meet Project ALERT's missing persons criteria.

Clemons gave Squires the go-ahead to contact Project ALERT. She also called the prison and told officers there that the Seward police had decided to take another look at the Emerick case based on what Tompkins had told her.

Prison officials decided to move Tompkins out of Alaska for his own protection. They arranged for him to be transferred to a prison in the lower forty-eight states where he would not be readily identified as a prison snitch.

A short time later, Squires received word from NCMEC that two Project ALERT detectives were being dispatched to Seward.

Tony's interest in cold cases and his letter exchanges with Tompkins had started the ball rolling. After nearly forty years, the Emerick case was getting a fresh pair of eyes. The two detectives being sent to Seward had never worked together. They would prove to be a colorful pair.

45

It had taken Janet Franson twenty-two years to track down the killer who'd murdered "the Cookie Lady" in Lakeland, Florida, but the self-deprecating detective had always believed she'd catch him. It had been her investigative work on that cold case that had impressed the gatekeepers at Project ALERT when they plucked her application from the hundreds they received each year from retirees who were not quite ready to stop being gumshoes.

Franson had been a patrol officer in one of Lakeland's tougher neighborhoods when a 911 call came in on May 7, 1984, about a homicide. Anna Houston, who baked cookies for neighborhood children and her Nazarene Church congregation, had been stabbed to death inside her apartment in a low-income housing project. The murder weapon, which detectives speculated was a knife snatched up from Houston's own kitchen, was nowhere to be found. But Anna had fought with her attacker and he'd apparently cut himself while repeatedly stabbing her, leaving a sample of his blood behind.

Despite that crucial piece of evidence, detectives were unable to identify a suspect and the murder case got stuck on a storage shelf where it seemed to have been forgotten—by everyone except Franson. She didn't like that a murderer had gotten away with stabbing a seventy-nine-year-old woman to death in her own apartment.

The first thing Franson did when she became a homicide detective in 1990 was ask her boss if she could take a look at the then six-year-old Cookie Lady case.

"As long as you do it on your own time," he told her.

Franson recruited fellow detective Brian Shinn and together they began canvassing people in the victim's old neighborhood. They also got Rick Rousos, a reporter at the *Lakeland Ledger*, to write a story about the cold case. By chance, two tipsters, both of them people who normally did not read the newspaper, happened to see the article. Both telephoned Franson, and both offered up the same suspect—Robert

Austin, Jr. He'd apparently bragged about killing the Cookie Lady when he was fifteen years old and lived in the same housing project.

Finding Austin proved easy. He was in prison on drug dealing charges. He denied knowing anything about the Cookie Lady murder. But Franson remembered that the killer had left his blood behind and she got a judge to order Austin to provide a blood sample for comparison. A DNA check showed there was a 1 in 7.25 quadrillion chance that it might be anyone but Austin. He was put on trial and sentenced to life in prison for the murder.

"Brian and I didn't solve that homicide," Franson told reporters. "It was the good Lord. He don't like people killing kids and little old ladies."

When Franson got her call from Project ALERT, she'd just come into the house from working with horses on a ranch southwest of Roundup, Montana, where she'd retired with her husband. The caller told Franson that she'd be paired in Alaska with Gary Murphy, a thirty-three-year veteran from the San Diego Police Department.

Living in northwestern Washington state, Murphy spent his retirement days playing golf. He'd spent most of his career as a detective investigating juvenile sex crimes and homicides. He'd also been on duty on July 18, 1984, when James Huberty strolled into a McDonald's restaurant armed with an Uzi semiautomatic rifle, a shotgun, and a pistol and started shooting. The melee continued for seventy-seven minutes until a police sniper shot Huberty in the heart. By that time, Huberty had murdered twenty-one people and wounded nineteen others, earning a spot in record books as a mass murderer.

Once a cop saw carnage like that, it either drove him out of law enforcement or made him even more committed. Murphy was in the latter category.

Franson called Murphy to see how he wanted to handle the Megan Emerick case in Seward.

"You taking a laptop to Alaska?" she asked.

"They didn't have 'em in 1973 when that girl vanished," Murphy replied. "I don't think I'll need one now."

"You're my kind of detective," Franson said.

The two of them met for the first time at the Seattle airport, where they were catching a flight to Anchorage. Franson walked up to a big Irishman who was standing back against a wall watching other passengers. "You look like a cop," she said.

"You don't," he replied.

Franson laughed. At one point in her career, a television producer had asked if she would be interested in being in a reality show. "You got the wrong gal," Franson had quipped. "I'm too old, too short, too fat, and too blunt for prime time."

When the detectives arrived in Seward, Sheila Squires showed them the information that she'd compiled about Megan Emerick, including the letters that Tompkins had written to Tony.

The veteran detectives decided to start at the beginning—as if they had just learned about a murder and were starting fresh. They told Squires that they wanted to read every incident police report that had been filed between 1971 and 1976. It didn't matter if it was about a lost cat, theft of a bicycle, or vandalism. They wanted to see if there was anything in the police records that might help them solve the Emerick case.

The Seward department wasn't computerized in the early 1970s. Murphy and Franson found themselves shuffling through badly yellowed typed reports retrieved from an old cardboard box that had been in storage. It took them two days to read through hundreds of reports. There was one in particular that caught their eyes.

A 1973 police report noted that a boat motor and depth finder with the serial numbers filed off had been found on Robert Hansen's boat. Both items had been reported stolen. The police suspected that Hansen was the thief but he claimed that he'd bought them from another boat owner. He just couldn't remember the seller's name. An officer had given Hansen a lie detector test but it had turned out inconclusive. No charges had been filed.

Could it be that Hansen had managed to beat the lie detector because—unbeknownst to the police at the time—he was a serial killer? Serial killers were supposed to be convincing liars.

If nothing else, the 1973 report was additional evidence that Hansen had been frequenting Seward at the same time Emerick had been reported missing.

Murphy and Franson had been given enough money to stay in Alaska for eight days. They spent the rest of their time interviewing Emerick's relatives and friends. Her parents had died and most of her acquaintances had left the area. As in many cold-case investigations, those well-covered trails led to dead ends. The detectives approached Hansen, but he refused to speak to them. It was his right. They were no longer sworn officers.

Despite their dogged footwork, the detectives didn't discover any-thing new or startling in Seward that would help them solve Emerick's disappearance. It was the telephone call from Tony and Tompkins's let-ters that had prompted the police to reopen the probe and it was those same letters that now gave the two detectives a reason to keep pursuing the investigation.

From Alaska, Murphy and Franson traveled to the prison in the lower forty-eight states where Tompkins was now being housed. He wel-comed them, didn't ask for anything in return for his cooperation, and talked openly about what he'd written in his letters to Tony and what he'd discovered during the seven years when he was Hansen's cellmate.

This is what he told them. Hansen had noticed Emerick when she was leaving the trade school on her way to lunch. He'd lured her into his vehicle and pulled a gun. He had taken her to an isolated area outside Seward, where he'd raped her. He'd then flown her in his airplane to the remote hunting cabin that he'd built. After Hansen had grown weary of sexually assaulting the teen, he had stripped her naked, unlocked her handcuffs, and nonchalantly told her that he was giving her a short head start before he came after her with his rifle.

The teenager had been so numb from being repeatedly raped that she apparently had not understood. So Hansen had pointed his rifle at her and told her to start running or he'd shoot her where she was stand-ing. Hansen had never told Tompkins how much time he'd waited before he'd gone after her. But it hadn't taken him long to track and shoot the disoriented teen.

If Tompkins's account was accurate, then there was a good chance that Megan Emerick would have been one of Hansen's first human hunt-ing targets.

"Robert could have lied to me," Tompkins warned Franson and Mur-phy. "But I don't think he did."

After the detectives finished interviewing Tompkins, they flew to Las Vegas to speak with Tony. They already had read copies of Tomp-kins's letters, but they had not seen what Tony had written to Tompkins. They wanted to read Tony's letters to see if he had gleaned details from public records and sent them to Tompkins so that the murderer could sound convincing when he described Emerick's disappearance. They wanted to make sure Tony and Tompkins were not colluding in some sick scam.

"Whenever the bad guys reach out of prison to people on the outside and talk to them," Franson explained later in an interview for this book, "it's usually because the bad guys are working a con. And when someone reaches out to a person in prison and befriends them, it's usually because they're doing the same thing. So we wondered, quite frankly, why this convict was talking to Tony Ciaglia and why Tony Ciaglia was talking to him. What were they trying to pull together?"

It wasn't until she and Murphy were sitting at the dining room table inside the Ciaglias' house with Tony and his family that Franson lowered her guard. She was impressed with the family and couldn't figure out why any of them would be lying about Tony's motives.

"I felt Tony was telling us the truth about everything he'd done and he'd learned," Franson said later. "As far as Gary and I were concerned, when we were talking to Tony, we absolutely believed him."

After they finished questioning Tony, they asked if he'd show them the letters that he'd written to Tompkins. He disappeared into his bedroom and returned with a huge stack of correspondence. He offered to let them drive to a local store and copy the letters. Clearly, he wasn't nervous about having them plow through them.

Tony then asked if they would like to see copies of letters that he had exchanged with other killers, including the likes of the Hillside Stranglers, Harvey the Hammer, the Sunset Strip Killers, the Scorecard Killer, the Night Stalker, and the Casanova Killer. The list went on and on.

"You have copies of all the letters you've written them and copies of their letters back to you?" Franson asked, clearly surprised.

Tony nodded and explained his procedure. As soon as he received a letter from one of the serial killers, he slipped it and the envelope that it came in into a clear plastic sheet to protect it. With his dad's help, he then recorded the date when the letter was written and a short synopsis of its contents in a computerized index that he kept. Each letter was then put into a binder. There was a binder for Arthur Shawcross, another for Kenneth Bianchi. Tony also had collected hundreds of newspaper articles, books, and court records about individual serial killers. The result was a de facto library of letters and information written by and about serial killers.

Franson and Murphy exchanged glances. Neither of them had ever met anyone outside law enforcement who had such extensive information about serial killers. They'd planned to spend only a few hours interviewing Tony about the Emerick case. But they found themselves spending the day talking to him—not only about Hansen, but about other notorious murderers, too.

"I've never seen anything like what we just saw," Franson told Murphy when they were finally on their way to McCarran International Airport.

Murphy agreed.

Continuing, Franson said, "I'm not a trained therapist, but I think the prisoners write to him because of his demeanor—he's almost like a child. That brain injury made him so damn nonjudgmental that he can stomach these pieces of shit. They can write to him or call him and talk to him about whatever it is they want whether it's crimes or whatever and he just listens to them."

Not long after their trip to Las Vegas, the two detectives asked Tony if he could squeeze more information out of Tompkins. Because of his close relationship with the convict, the detectives thought Tony might be able to learn details from him that he was holding back from them. They were especially interested in learning more about where Robert Hansen's remote cabin was located in Alaska.

Tony asked Al if they could visit Tompkins face-to-face now that he was in a prison in the lower forty-eight. Al agreed and bought two airplane tickets. Once again, father and son were jetting off to a prison to speak with another killer.

46

The prison where Bryan Tompkins had been transferred for his own protection was run by a private company, Corrections Corporation of America, the first such business to cash in on a boom in prison growth during the 1980s. Driven by the Reagan administration's tough stance against drug dealers and the president's fondness for contracting private companies to perform services traditionally done by federal agencies, CCA was rapidly becoming a favorite with investors on the New York Stock Exchange. It ran prisons for the Federal Bureau of Prisons, U.S. Immigration and Customs Enforcement, the U.S. Marshals Service, nearly half of all states, and a dozen counties.

Tony and Al had timed their visit to coincide with a "potluck picnic" at the prison. It was a special day when relatives and friends were allowed to eat in the prison yard with inmates who had earned that reward for being on their good behavior.

In a letter to Tony, Tompkins mentioned that he was worried about seeing them. "I've not had a visitor in fifteen years," he noted. "I'm not sure we'll have much to talk about."

Minutes after they met in the prison yard, Tony, Al, and Tompkins were chatting as if they were lifelong friends.

The prison was serving food buffet style on long tables in the prison yard. It was a warm day. Guests and convicts ate off paper plates. They sat on grassy spots or in metal bleachers at a baseball diamond. Tompkins went through the serving line three times and ate eye-popping portions of chicken, fish, and roast beef.

"We never get real food like this," he told them. "They're doing this to impress you and the others. Most stuff we get is processed shit."

Al was wearing a Hublot Genève wristwatch and he noticed Tompkins staring at it.

"Why are you looking at my watch?" Al finally asked him.

Tompkins grinned. "Force of habit." He could have easily fenced it in Alaska for a thousand bucks.

Tompkins loved motorcycles and Al mentioned that his father-in-law had been an avid rider. Tompkins questioned Al about the different bikes that Chris's father had owned. He said, "Riding was where I did my thinking. Nothing was better than an open highway, a clear day, a good bike, and tunes such as 'Ride Like the Wind.'"

Tompkins talked freely about his criminal past. During one Alaska burglary, he stole twenty thousand dollars in cash and several gold nuggets. He put one of the nuggets in a stream where tourists panned for gold. He was high on drugs when he hid it. "Someone found that nugget and there were five hundred people there the next day panning for gold. I laughed my ass off."

During a New Year's Eve celebration in a tough biker bar, Tompkins climbed on a table and stripped naked. "I got a good beating that night and ended up dumped outside in three feet of snow in twenty-below weather, then off to jail with a broken nose, two broken ribs, and frozen toes. But it was a damn good party."

"You're lucky to be alive," Tony said, admiringly.

"I'm the luckiest person on earth. I've been shot, cut up, dumped out of a speeding car, beaten to an inch of my life and I'm still here, have all my teeth except for two, make that three. I do need glasses and wear a hearing aid that I need because of a shoot-out I had inside a car and I walk funny because I got shot in the knee, but otherwise, I'm in damn fine shape."

Everyone laughed.

Tompkins said: "You know the worm reads a lot and he watches sports on TV constantly. I can't stand sports. I mean, you got these guys running up and down a field, going after a pointed ball, running into one another and they call it football when I can't see how the foot has much to do with it."

Tompkins asked Tony to tell him about the Las Vegas Strip. "I'm so isolated here," Tompkins explained. "You know, I just found out this week what an iPod was."

After about an hour, their talk turned to the "worm" and retired detectives Franson and Murphy. Tompkins liked Murphy, but he'd been uncomfortable about Franson. He'd preferred talking to a man.

Tony said, "They think you might be holding back. Not telling them everything you know."

Tompkins bristled. "They brought me these maps that weren't worth a damn and they wanted me to point out where the worm had taken girls to the cabin that he'd built. I couldn't show them exactly because we're talking about forty or fifty miles of coastline here. I told them that I had drawn a map after the worm told me where the cabin was. I memorized it and then flushed that map down the toilet. But them maps they brought me looked different from what I had drawn."

Tompkins was clearly irritated the two detectives were suspicious of him. "Only two people know where that cabin is," he said. "Only two people have been there and survived."

"Who's that?" Tony asked.

"Well, there's the worm, of course. He knows where to find it. But he also told me that his old lady—she knows about it. She's been there."

"Do you know what happened to her?" Al asked.

"They divorced. But I know where she lives and I know where his kids live, too. The worm used to get a card from his old lady on his birthday and on Christmas Day. His old lady is Christian hard-core. She's my ace in the hole, really. I asked the worm once about her and he said his old lady helped him build that cabin. I asked him if she still used it and he remarks, 'She couldn't never find it without me.' When I asked him if his old lady ever told the cops about that cabin, the worm tells me that she didn't tell no one, never. He said if she had told the cops, then they would have found a lot more evidence against him. He says, 'I would have been arrested for what's out there.' That's when he started telling me about them girls."

Tony said, "If the FBI or the detectives think you're lying about that cabin, they can contact the worm's ex-wife. She can tell them it is real."

"That's right," he said. "But she doesn't know how to find it. I know where it is, but I need better maps."

Tompkins said he would mail them the name, address, and phone number of the "worm's ex-wife," adding, "I memorized it. You tell Detective Murphy that if he wants to verify that cabin is real, all he has to do is talk to her."

Tony and Al were having so much fun talking to Tompkins that they didn't realize visiting hours were over.

Two days after they flew back to Las Vegas, Tony got a letter from Tompkins.

Dear Tony,

It's odd. The murder investigation of 1973 in Alaska . . . I wasn't even in the state, but I now hold some cards that may bring peace to that dead girl's family. I've lived around so many underground people. I've lived in the dark spots most of my life. Who would have thought that we would meet? Who would have thought that you would help bring me back into the light? Who would have thought that together, we might be able to reunite that dead girl with her family?

Tony notified detectives Murphy and Franson and they returned to Las Vegas to debrief him about his prison visit with Tompkins, who had included information about Hansen's former wife in his most recent letter.

About a month later, Al telephoned Murphy. He was curious and Tony was growing impatient. They wanted to know if Tony's information had been helpful.

"I can't really tell you anything about the status of this case," Murphy said, "because we're working for the Seward police. It's their case. They've got to be the ones who make any official announcement."

"C'mon," Al replied, "all I want to know is if what Tony has given you guys has been helpful. You owe us that much, don't you?"

The phone was silent for a moment and then Murphy said, "Yes, I guess we do. What Tony has done is crucial. I can tell you this. I believe at this point, if I am able to get one more piece of information, I may very possibly be able to determine the location of the missing girl."

That's all Al needed to hear. He hurried to tell Tony the news.

Not long after that, Tony got a phone call from Tompkins. Hansen's ex-wife had confirmed his story. She had told investigators about the cabin.

After nearly forty years, there was no way to know what kind of condition the bones of Megan Emerick might be in—if they were found. The cabin might not be standing any longer, Tompkins said. "But, at least, they know I was telling the truth about that cabin," he declared. "I've given them a general location to look in. When the snow melts, it will be up to them to decide if it's worth searching for that little girl. But we've done good, Tony. We've solved that cold case for them."

Tony beamed.

The next morning, Tony came into the kitchen while Al and Chris were eating breakfast. He said that he had something important to tell them. He'd barely slept all night thinking about it. He was excited.

Recognizing how serious their son was, both listened closely.

"I think I know why God allowed me to come back to earth. I know what my special purpose is and why he let me live after the accident."

"What is it?" Chris asked.

"I am supposed to use my traumatic brain injury to help others," Tony said proudly.

God had sent him back to be an example.

"Even a brain injury can be used to do good."

Tony was convinced that his brain injury had been specially tailored by God for him—so that he would be able to feel many of the same feelings as a serial killer and think many of the same thoughts without actually becoming such a killer. This is why the murderers responded to him. And this is what his special purpose was—getting those killers to share their innermost thoughts and secrets.

To someone who didn't know his story or the family, it might have seemed like a huge leap. But Al and Chris didn't need convincing. Every day the murder phone in Tony's bedroom rang nonstop. The post office delivered a thick wad of letters. The number of serial killers writing just kept growing. It had been Tony who had gotten the Seward police to reopen the Emerick case. He had gotten Shawcross, Joe Metheny, and David Gore to write openly about what made them kill.

Still in a pensive mood, Tony said, "That day—July 23, 1992—it changed everything." He was referring to the date of the WaveRunner accident. "I believe it was a blessing when God sent me to you and Mom the first time. But it was an even greater one the second time around when he gave me a choice and let me come back to earth to be with you guys and Joey. I know there were many times when you guys were at the breaking point. I know you could have quit on me because of my brain injury and the things it caused me to do. You could have taken the easy way out and put me in an institution somewhere and just left me."

"Stop it, Tony," Al said. "We were never going to give up on you. We're your parents. We love you. We're a family."

"But you could have."

Tony had read how Tompkins's family had treated him. Arthur Shawcross's, too. Many of the serial killers had come from horrible homes.

"I want to thank you," Tony said. "I always knew God was challenging me. He was challenging me to do something important. Now I understand, it wasn't just me. He was challenging you guys, too. My challenge was to search for my special purpose in life. I had to do something useful with my life. But until now I didn't understand that God was challenging you, too. *I was your challenge.*"

Tony wasn't finished. He said, "You know, if I could go back in time and change everything that has happened to me, go back and somehow stop that WaveRunner from hitting me in the head, I wouldn't do it."

"Really?" Al asked, clearly astounded, given all that his family had endured because of Tony's TBI.

"I wouldn't want to be a teenager again and go through all that. I'm not going to lie. None of this has been a walk in the park and I think I was much stronger than any of my friends were or ever will be because of what happened. Okay, they just wouldn't have survived the trauma I've faced and overcome. But I did survive and I did overcome it and I did get my answer from Him. It's just taken me a long time to understand it."

The "starburst effect" was what nurses had called what happened inside Tony's brain. Like a baseball hitting a windshield, splinters from the impact had sent ripples out in thousands of unknown directions.

The Ciaglias now understood that the WaveRunner had caused a starburst effect in their family, too. The fates of a son and those who loved him had been dramatically altered and they had gone in directions that none of them could have imagined.

Epilogue

Even though David Gore had refused to meet with Tony and Al when they visited Florida, Tony continued sending him letters. When it was Gore's birthday, Tony mailed him a card. He sent Gore newsy updates about Las Vegas and what was happening in the Ciaglia house. He acted as if there were nothing amiss between them.

Gore didn't respond. A month went by. And then another. And another. Finally, four months after zero contact, a letter from Gore appeared in Tony's murder mailbox.

The serial killer apologized for his decision not to visit with them. "I was going through a bad period," he wrote. Gore had learned that his final legal appeal had been denied. All that stood between him and execution by lethal injection was Florida's governor. In many other states, the timing of an execution was decided by the courts. But Florida left picking an actual execution date entirely up to the governor and no one had ever been able to figure out why he picked a specific date for a condemned man to meet his maker. The entire process was arbitrary when it reached this stage.

Florida had more than four hundred inmates on its death row, more than any state besides California. Now that Gore was standing in line to be put to death, he'd decided it was best for him to keep his head down. Telling Tony about cold-case murders would put him back in the news. He also didn't think having Tony and Al dig up hundreds of gruesome photographs of women being tortured, along with their scalps, was going to help him stay out of the governor's sights.

Tony responded, and the two men were soon exchanging letters just as they had been. Tony told Gore about Megan Emerick and how he had helped two retired detectives investigate her disappearance. Gore replied with an offer. The serial killer wrote that he still hoped his stash could be found. He also had been thinking about women whom he had abducted, raped, tortured, and murdered, but whose fate was still a mystery. He was willing to tell Tony about more of his victims.

Gore wrote that mail written by inmates was opened and read by prison officials. But inmates were allowed to send letters to lawyers without their letters being read. Gore was willing to send details about cold-case murders to an attorney if that could be arranged. He'd also pinpoint in his letters to the lawyer where he buried his trophies. Of course, he would prefer for Tony to wait until after he was executed to investigate the unsolved cases and find the stash.

In his reply letter, Tony also asked Gore a question.

> Dear David,
> . . . To be honest, I don't think most people really care about getting to know you as a person. That makes me wonder about how you feel about yourself and your self worth. What do you think is in store for you when you pass on?

Gore's answer came a few days later.

> *Dear Tony,*
> *. . . You know that is a hard thing to answer. I mean people are going to only remember me as a killer. They always remember the bad part . . . I'd like to be remembered as someone who always wanted to be a good person and especially a good husband and good father. But unfortunately, I failed. It didn't matter how much I wanted to, I wasn't able to.*
> *I guess most people want to do good, me included . . . I think there is a place inside all of us that is drawn to a dark side. It's just that most people can resist it and take control. While some of us give into it.*
> *I think that was one of the reasons I used to love to enter women's homes when they weren't there. I found true pleasure in seeing things that they didn't want people to see . . . I used to find so many photos of women nude, and dildos and sex toys . . . You see, they had a secret side just like me.*
> *You asked me what I thought was in store for me in the afterlife. I was raised to believe in God. And all through my life, I knew there was a God—although I didn't really get serious with this until I came to prison. But yeah, actually, I think I'll go to heaven when they finally kill me.*

Tony continued writing to Joe Metheny, too. The killer replied with short letters decorated by his trademark ball-headed baby armed with a butcher knife and innocent smile. If Tony still wanted to know where, as Metheny put it, "my dead bitches" were buried, then he would have to pay for the information. "I'm fat ass broke and need money."

Tony didn't send money. But he did mail him a birthday card and enclosed a poem that he'd written. Tony explained that the wife of a family friend had died. Tony had been deeply touched by the man's grief. The first stanza read:

Close your eyes, give me your hand, a tear blurs my vision as I reach out to grasp your palm but you're not there. The softness of your flesh helped ease my pain like the beauty of a rainbow when sun shines through the rain.

Metheny's response came a few days later.

Hey Anthony,

My friend pull your finger out of your ass and don't write me no more soft ass, fuckin letters like that ever again. I'm going to tear this letter up after I get done jerking off on it, we will pretend this never happened. So man up and act like one. Or stop writing me.

It was signed with Metheny's bloody thumbprint.

In the same batch of mail that arrived with Metheny's letter, Tony found a letter from yet another serial killer whom he'd been corresponding with for several months.

Tommy Lynn Sells was suspected of murdering as many as seventy people, including several children, between 1980 and 1999 while he wandered aimlessly across the country, often hitching rides, hopping onto trains, and supporting himself by doing menial labor. He'd murdered for the first time when he was sixteen. The victims were Ena Cordt, a twenty-nine-year-old single mother in Missouri, and her four-year-old son. He'd met them at a small-time traveling carnival.

Sells's rampage ended in Del Rio, Texas, when he broke into the bedroom of a sleeping thirteen-year-old named Kaylene "Katy" Harris. He was about to rape her in her bunk bed when she woke up and cried out for help. Her scream woke up her ten-year-old friend Krystal Surles, who was sleeping in the top bunk. Sells stabbed Harris sixteen times and then slit Surles's throat, leaving her to die.

But the brave little girl did not die. She survived and testified against him in a Texas court, where jurors could see an ugly red scar across her tiny neck. Sells was sentenced to death for Katy's murder.

It had taken Tony months to gain Sells's trust, but the serial killer had begun opening up. In one of his most recent letters, he'd asked if Tony would attend his execution when it was scheduled.

> *Dear Tony,*
> *. . . I just don't want to die alone and without someone I can trust and I've not figured out what I am going to do with my body yet. I don't want to be put on peckerwood hill—that's the name of the boot hill for those of us who don't have no place to go. Can I count on you to see that I end up someplace nice after they kill my ass?*

Tony promised he would make arrangements for Sells's body. He also asked Sells about cold cases. In 2002, author Diane Fanning had corresponded with Sells and gotten him to confess to the 1997 murder of Joel Kirkpatrick, a ten-year-old boy. The child's mother, Julie Rea-Harper, had been found guilty of killing her son, even though her family had told police that Sells had broken into the house and killed Joel. Armed with Sells's confession, author Fanning had helped Rea-Harper win a new trial. A jury later acquitted her. Fanning wrote a book, *Through the Window*, that described the case and Sells's cross-country murder rampage.

Had Sells committed other murders that either were still unsolved or had led to innocent people being falsely imprisoned? Tony asked in a letter.

"Yes," Sells replied. "Both."

The only problem was that he had killed so many victims that he couldn't remember all of them. Sells offered to tell Tony about those he could remember—if he and Al were interested in pursuing them.

Tony talked to his dad. They quickly agreed.

Tony had found his next project.

Note on Sources

All of the quoted material from serial killers in this book comes from correspondence or telephone calls provided to me by Tony. While the letters quoted here were edited for length, great care was taken to ensure that the writers' words remained in context. Additional information about the murderers and their crimes was gleaned from court records, previously published accounts, and interviews. The names Bryan Tompkins, Carol Walker, and Melody Walker are pseudonyms but information about the individuals is factual. I have also altered the directions that David Gore gave to Al and Tony when he sent them a map. I've done this because the Ciaglias continue to hope that they can find Gore's gruesome "trophies."

One purpose of this book was to give readers an unguarded glimpse into the minds of serial killers. Sadly, this could not be done without printing their versions of the horrific crimes that they committed. Whenever possible, I have attempted to point out obvious rationalizations and self-justifications. I've also tried to talk to families of victims. Still, reading a killer's account of the suffering that he caused and enjoyed causing is difficult. I apologize for any additional distress this book might have caused. Rest assured that no one was paid for his or her cooperation in this book. Nor will any criminals profit from the sale of this book.

Conversations and scenes that I did not personally observe were reconstructed. They were based on the recollections of the participants. In nearly all of these instances, the text was shown or read to them to ensure accuracy. In cases where memories differed, I have chosen the version that in my judgment seemed most likely to be accurate. I was with the Ciaglias when they were traveling in Maryland and Florida.

Acknowledgments

This book could not have been written without the cooperation of the Ciaglia family, including Al, Chris, Joey, and, Tony. They spent countless hours speaking to me. I also traveled with Al and Tony when they made their trips to New York, Maryland, and Florida so that I could observe their efforts to help solve cold cases. From the start, the Ciaglias were adamant about fully disclosing how Tony's traumatic brain disorder had impacted the family. They answered every question, including deeply personal ones. They also signed release forms that permitted me to interview Tony's medical doctors, psychiatrists, and therapists. The family's candor in this book has been both extraordinary and courageous.

I especially want to thank Tony for talking so openly about the self-described "demons" that have haunted him since his traumatic brain injury. In interviews and in his writings, he was brutally frank.

When I finished this book, Tony asked me if he could write a personal note to readers. Here is what he wrote:

> Since the beginning, all I have wanted to do is touch the world with my story and show people that miracles do happen. Always have hope and let your faith lead you through the darkness. No matter how long the tunnel; there is always light on the other side.
>
> Back in 1992, when I was injured, there was little known about traumatic brain injury. My loving and supportive family got me through the toughest times, when I could have easily given up. No matter how hard times were, or how difficult the road became, my family was always there to guide me and pick me up when I fell. I cannot express how important love and support of family can be for a survivor of brain injury.
>
> I want to stress the fact that I do not condone nor glorify what these men have done. When I find myself getting too close to the horror and madness I think of the victims. I look at their faces

pondering over the pain that these cowardly men have caused
their families that can never be healed.

In dealing with these men it was sometimes hard to put my
feelings aside considering the atrocities that they have commit-
ted. I had to call upon my strong spiritual faith and realize it
wasn't my place to judge them. They all will face a higher power
than I or any court could render upon them come judgment day.
God Bless,
Anthony Ciaglia

In addition to the Ciaglia family, I wish to thank the following persons for speaking to me for this book: Mike Benedetti, Leonard Borriello, Jake Brown, Andrew W. Bulino, Carol Bulthuis, Tom Clemons, Grant Cooper, George Cravens, Mike Daley, Sean Duffy, Carl Elliott, Jeanne Elliott, Casey Emerson, Janet Franson, Rick Hersch, Gene Kilroy, Russ Lemmon, Tony Maraco, Tim Mccullers, Tia McElvany, Gary Murphy, William "Buddy" O'Connell, Christian Papas, Lou Papas, Rita Papas, Peter Papas, Nick Ponzo, Molly Ray, Bobby Roe, Ralph Schwartz, Bonnie Schwey, Chris Sexton, Ralph W. Sexton, Charlene Sher, Darren Sher, Dr. Geoffery Sher, Karen Shoemaker, Nancy Smith, Sheila Squires, Robert Stone, Erik Per Sullivan, Fred Sullivan, Bonnie Sweitzer, Jessie Swimmer, Crystal Torres, Mark Tripson, Sarah Twotrees, Carol Walker, Melody Walker, and Jennifer Yoder.

I also wish to thank my literary agent, David Vigliano, for finding a home for this manuscript, and my good friend and fellow author, Mike Sager, for reading an early draft and giving me his editorial comments. Thanks also to Daniel M. Rosenberg of InVenture Entertainment for tipping me off about the Ciaglias and their incredible story. I wish to acknowledge my editor, Sulay Hernandez, for recognizing a good story and for her editorial insights. Thanks also to Alessandra Preziosi for additional editing and to Tom Pitoniak for copyediting this manuscript.

As always, I am grateful to my wife, Patti, and my children, Steve, Kevin, Tony, Kathy, Kyle, Evan, Traci, and granddaughter Maribella. Other family members whom I'd like to acknowledge include my parents, Elmer and Jean Earley; Gloria Brown, James Brown, LeRue and Ellen Brown; Phillip Corn; Donnie and Marcie Davis; Matthew Davis, George and Linda Earley; Michelle Holland; William and Rosemary Luzi; Charlie and Donna Stackhouse; and Jay and Elsie Strine. Close friends who have supported me include Nelson DeMille, William Donnell, Walt and Keran Harrington, Marie Heffelfinger, Dr. Allen Howe, Don and Susan Infeld, Kelly McGraw, Dan Morton, Richard and Joan Miles, Jay and Barbara Myerson, Jessica Phung, Tracey Skale, Lynn and LouAnn Smith, and Kendall Starkweather.

I invite readers to post comments about this book and my other books on my website, www.peteearley.com. While I may not be able to respond to every message, I do read them all.